TAKE CONTROL

of

YOUR

LIFE

ESCAPE *the* GRIP *of* CODEPENDENCY

TAKE
CONTROL
of
YOUR
LIFE

ESCAPE *the* GRIP
of CODEPENDENCY

DR. JAMES B. RICHARDS

rill &
associates

Take Control of Your Life: Escape the Grip of Codependency

ISBN: 978-0-9832536-5-5

Printed in the United States of America.

© 2012 by Dr. James B. Richards

Contents derived and adapted from *Escape from Codependent Christianity*, by Dr. James B. Richards, copyright 1996, 2005.

Rill and Associates
P.O. Box 119
Orrstown, PA 17244
303.503.7257; Fax: 717.477.2261

12 13 14 15 16 17 18 / 7 6 5 4 3 2 1

TABLE OF CONTENTS

READ THIS FIRST!

To be dependent on someone else means I am not depending on me. If I am not depending on me, I have no true control. After all, the only thing I can actually control is me! Therefore, depending on you means I am out of control! There are few things that make an individual feel as helpless, defenseless, afraid, frustrated, stressed and angry as feeling out of control!

Through centuries of systematic programming, the masses of the world have been made to feel powerless. By creating dependence on outside sources we have succumbed to the illusion of no control! Corrupt governments leave the individual feeling his or her voice and vote cannot really change anything. In the recent banking scandal that ripped over a trillion dollars from the individual taxpayer, the logic was "they are too big to allow them to fail," thus creating the illusion that we had no choice; that somehow the needs of the corporations were greater than the needs of the individuals. Good parents lose custody of their children by the decision of judges—taking away any sense of rights or control by those parents. This ideology of disempowerment even permeated religion— making the individual believer feel he or she has no voice with God!

It seems that government, business and controlling individuals deceive us into giving them our power. The momentary false sense of security we received in exchange is soon swallowed up in a vague, nebulous, yet all-consuming sense of having no control. We all find ways to manage this desperate feeling. Some just give up and give in to the controller in the situation. Others become angry and lash out. Because they have been so conditioned to control, they didn't think rationally enough to identify the true culprit. Paradoxically, they tend to allow the controllers to tell them with whom they should be angry. Some come together and picket the "straw man" created by the lies of their controllers. Some riot in the streets, burning buildings and attacking people. In a marriage some commit adultery, while others attack their spouse. All of this acting out is a vain attempt to create the feeling of having some control. Contrary to the emotional impetus driving this illogical behavior, it actually causes the problems to grow worse, not better.

It is such an irony. As some people lose self-control, they tend to want to take more control of others. The most insecure people, with the strongest propensity toward narcissism, need to control others to feel safe. They proclaim themselves to be leaders. The syndrome only grows more diabolical as others who feel out of control give away more of their personal choices and freedoms to someone who offers to "fix things." How did we get here? Why do the majority tend to consistently make the wrong choices? How did the world get so out of control and what can we do about it?

> THROUGH INTIMIDATION AND SEDUCTION OUR SPIRITUAL VALUES HAVE BEEN MINIMIZED WHILE SECULAR IDEAS HAVE BEEN EXALTED AS THE ULTIMATE SOLUTION TO THE WORLD'S PROBLEMS.

It All Started in the Garden

The more "normal" is defined by the secular world, the less normal we experience in the world. Through intimidation and seduction our spiritual values have been minimized while secular ideas have been exalted as the ultimate solution to the world's problems. It all started in the garden of Eden when the very first temptation was embedded in the idea, "You are not who God says you are and you don't have what God says is yours." Humanism[1] was born in the garden and was expressed in the first murder. Cain decided that his way of sacrificing to God was more appropriate than what God said to do. The way he solved the problem was by killing the evidence of God's disapproval: Abel!

The next quantum leap in the logic of disempowerment took place at the tower of Babel with the birth of socialism. Instead of following God's inspirational directive to fill the earth and become who you want to be, Nimrod, the first dictator, deceived and ultimately forced people to give up their choices and follow him. Through fear and intimidation Nimrod presented the idea that we could throw away God's wisdom, band together and have a better life. We can all be like bricks…we'll all be equal!

Although there have always been oppressive ideologies and religions, there also have always been those who have advanced this lie in significant ways. The birth of communism, socialism and then progressivism are the ideas that have grown to fill the earth. They take away individual freedom of choice. They thrive on disempowering the masses. Oddly enough, they do so under the banner of power to the people. Capitalism, on the other hand, when taken to extremes, becomes the straightforward oppression of the rich over the poor. But at least it doesn't seek to rob you of opportunity and choice. Then there is the church that may package it in any of various ways—i.e., the sovereignty of God or the elevation of the priests over the people—but in the end it still leaves the people powerless.

Where Is the War?

If you seek help through almost any of the commonly known channels, you will lose even more of your power to choose. Modern godless, humanistic thought, while sounding compassionate and loving, destroys those who seek help by the very treatment it gives. The educational system, many substance abuse programs, government agencies and even many churches blame society for our problems. Society no doubt contributed to our problems, but if society is the problem, then that is too big to solve. So in the end we are still left feeling powerless and out of control.

There is a war eternal. The war is not between God and the devil in the sense that we have understood. That war was won when Jesus was raised from the dead. But there is a war, according to the New Testament, that takes place in the mind, heart and beliefs of mankind. Our enemy is the devil. Yes, he is defeated and virtually powerless. But he is still an incredible liar. In fact, he is the father of all lies. His names *devil* and *Satan* mean slanderer and accuser. A slanderer puts people down, makes them feel insignificant. An accuser points out their faults and shows them what they have done wrong. Regardless of what you believe about the devil, you must believe that he wants you to be aware of your faults and that he wants you to feel less than God says you are.

There is an interesting word in the Greek New Testament. If it was translated literally it would probably be *demonized!* To be demonized seems to indicate being influenced. The Apostle Paul said that all people who walked in opposition to God's wisdom were under the influence of the prince of the power of the air. In other words, they are demonized! Any person, doctrine, philosophy or policy that attempts to make you feel less than what God says about you is seeking to take your power away from you. Once you surrender the sense of who you are in relation to God, you lose your sense of dignity and worth. You start looking to destructive sources to make you feel as you should. You go out of control!

> ANY PERSON, DOCTRINE, PHILOSOPHY OR POLICY THAT ATTEMPTS TO MAKE YOU FEEL LESS THAN WHAT GOD SAYS ABOUT YOU IS SEEKING TO TAKE YOUR POWER AWAY FROM YOU.

The feeling of having no control manifests itself through what is called codependency. The ultimate codependency is the attempt to meet a need through an external source that can only be met in your heart with God! Everything in the world's system is designed to take away your control and make you codependent. The world is out of control and codependent!

Change *Can* Happen!

Is there any hope for a world so far out of control? Yes! But the solution may not be what you think. The world is out of control because people are out of control. Once a person loses consciousness of and confidence in the fact that he or she is created in the likeness and image of God, that person loses his or her sense of dignity and worth. God crowned mankind with dignity and worth and gave him dominion over planet Earth. That dominion, which should produce a world of peace and order, degenerates when man loses his sense of identity with his Creator and surrenders his power of choice. When individuals believe the lie that they are not created in the likeness and image of God, they have no sense of control.

If we attempt to fix the world, the problem immediately becomes too overwhelming to consider. However, if we seek to solve our personal problems, then nothing is too big or beyond immediate solutions. In fact, it will only be when each individual says "I will take control of my own life" that we will actually see solutions. This book is about regaining the control of your life by identifying and overcoming all tendencies toward codependency. As you shed the layers of emotional addiction you will find a freedom you have never before known. You will become the light in a dark world.

People change one at a time. The world changes when people change. When people change, they discover a new realm called the Kingdom of God, a place where righteousness, peace and joy reign. This realm is in your heart. As you free yourself from looking out there, you can look "in there" and discover the world you've always desired.

Endnote

1. A system of thought that is based on the values, characteristics and behavior that are believed to be best in human beings, rather than on any supernatural authority, per Microsoft's *Encarta Dictionary*.

DEFINING THE PROBLEM

1

CODEPENDENCY: WHAT IS IT?

It seems that as every year goes by, new diseases of the mind and body emerge. Medical science is working day and night trying to develop cures for new viruses that threaten the very existence of humanity. Likewise, those professionals who address emotional pain and conflict continually seek new answers to the problems that plague the emotional lives of the human race.

There seems to be a million different kinds of emotional problems out there. Some sectors of society try to deny their existence, but the effects of emotional dysfunction abound despite whether or not we can define them. There are experts in the medical, social and religious fields who try to explain away problems as if society had willfully conjured them up for some selfish reason. Such denials reflect a lack of realism, concern and understanding. In fact, such attitudes reflect a part of the problem.

There are others, however, who recognize the legitimacy of the seemingly new flood of complex emotional conflicts. However, because they do not understand the concept of "fruit and root," or behavior and beliefs, they are seeking a thousand different answers for the thousand different problems that exist. The attempt to find this multitude of individual answers is quite overwhelming for both the patient and the practitioner. It puts the ability to solve the problem out of the reach of those in need. It causes them to place their hope in the *expert* who sometimes becomes an extension of the problem.

A Multitude of Problems…a Handful of Answers

Although there are hundreds, if not thousands, of different emotional disorders, there are only a few solutions. A healthy emotional life functions around some very basic and somewhat simple realities. Thus the principle of the fruit and root! One tree can grow an unlimited amount of fruit. Regardless of how often we pick the fruit, it grows back. Why? *The source of its growth is in the root.* Thus we must solve the problem at the root. By dealing with root or core issues, we can often eliminate many problems that seem unrelated!

> THE ROOT IS A BELIEF THAT EMPOWERS THE SYMPTOM.

Identifying and understanding the root issues will facilitate the freedom that is never found by picking through fruit. Root is the cause; fruit is a symptom. Fruit is what we see. It is the dysfunctional behavior. It is what we present to the world around us. The root is a belief that empowers the symptom. The root feeds the symptom just like it feeds the fruit on a tree. Without the root, the fruit dies by itself!

Regardless of a person's particular beliefs, society itself bears witness that there are certain immutable truths that will cause one to experience peace of mind, a sense of well-being and healthy relationships. When these truths are violated, just the opposite occurs. When beliefs that promote destructive behavior are embraced, everyone suffers—the individual as well as all the people in relationship with him or her. People around that individual are affected and society as a whole suffers. Violence, domestic instability, substance abuse and many physical sicknesses are the result of people abandoning these immutable, unchangeable truths.

The medical profession is very quick to admit that a large percentage of physical illness is stress-related. Some sources believe that all sickness—unless genetic or structural—are the product of stress! Stress is a non-measurable phenomenon created from a non-physical source that manifests in both behavior and physical health. In other words, stress is the product of our emotional life. It is created from thoughts, beliefs and opinions. It is negative emotional energy that can ultimately manifest in the physical body.

Stress in the body can turn into a destructive energy that causes high blood pressure, migraines, cancer and all manner of immunosuppressant diseases. Stress, because it is an energy, will always be expressed somewhere. In the emotions, stress can be expressed as anger, hatred, worry or fear. These emotions can turn into violence and other acts of aggression that destroy relationships between husbands and wives, parents and children, friends and neighbors.

> BEHAVIOR IS A SYMPTOM. A CHANGE IN BEHAVIOR NEVER RESOLVES THE INNER STRUGGLE OF TORMENTING EMOTIONS.

Stress is a subjective, individualized reaction to stimuli. It is the way we react to any given circumstance based on our beliefs and perceptions. That which stresses one person can stimulate another. It is the individual beliefs of people that form the *root* of their reaction to the world around them. Therefore, emotional conflicts can never be resolved by dealing with behavior. Behavior is a symptom, a fruit. A change in behavior may benefit society, but a change in behavior never resolves the inner struggle of tormenting emotions.

It is time the human race begins to observe the truth that has been proven for thousands of years in every culture. We must manage our life and emotions in a different way if we expect to see different results. If we are in emotional pain, we cannot continue to think and believe the way we always have and expect anything to change. Psychiatric drugs will numb the pain, but they will not solve the problem. Learning to cope will cause us to shut our eyes while the problem grows. Trying to change others will create a pressure cooker that will explode into more problems. We must face the only sure source of peace and relief. We must deal with the root, our own beliefs!

Codependency: The New Catch Phrase

In the 1980s a terminology began to emerge describing what seemed to be a new emotional problem: codependency. At first this terminology was used to describe people who were dependent upon someone else who was dependent upon some destructive substance like alcohol or drugs. Even though the codependent was not a substance abuser, he (or she)[1] was dependent upon someone who was. Therefore, he was "codependent." It was as if he joined in and participated in the addiction through a relationship with the person who was addicted. Over the years, the concept of codependency has developed and expanded. It now takes several pages to describe the tendencies that have been labeled as codependency.

A simple root definition of codependency would be this: "to look to someone or something outside of ourselves to meet a need that can only be met in ourselves." In relation to people, the codependent tends to depend on others for something he has no right to expect. For example, the codependent often seeks the approval of others as a substitute for self-worth. He may depend on others to make his decisions. He may expect others to make him happy. Whatever the need, the key is he looks to others for something that they cannot truly give.

Melody Beattie does a great job of identifying codependent tendencies in her book, *Codependent No More*.[2] As you peruse her list, you will certainly find some codependent tendency of your own. No one is free from every codependent tendency. Any time our behavior is driven by insecurity or the feeling of lack, that behavior is a codependent expression. Sadly, codependency is actually encouraged and nurtured in many relationships. Codependent behavior calls for codependent responses. These codependent responses often become the false security around which a relationship is built.

For example, a controlling person may need others to agree and submit as a way to boost his struggling self-worth. He will instinctively seek out a relationship with someone whose insecurities drive her to give in to his control. They are both driven by insecurity. Their individual behavior calls for a codependent response from the other. He wants to control someone to boost his ego. She wants to be controlled to avoid responsibility. They may both complain and criticize one another. But, the truth is, they both deeply need the codependent responses that are inspired by their own behavior.

Codependency is not a new thing. Only the name is new. This is a 1980s and '90s terminology for an age-old problem. Actually, it is one of the oldest problems found in the Bible. It is at the root of every inter-relational conflict. It is the underlying and often unseen force that works behind every addiction. It is the cause of aggressive behavior. It can lead one person into total aggression and another into total passivity. It is deceitful; it changes form so as not to be easily detected. In some circles it is rewarded because it can disguise itself as commitment, dedication and loyalty. It can appear as love, and it is rarely identified even as its toxicity erodes a marriage. It can make a man faithful to one woman, even though he hates her. It can make another man unfaithful to his wife, even though he loves her.

> CODEPENDENCY IS ONE OF THE OLDEST PROBLEMS FOUND IN THE BIBLE.

Codependency can work its way into every good thing and destroy it. It can become the leaven that permeates and spoils the entire loaf. It can become the strange quirk that causes a good business to fail. It can be the unpredictable factor that eventually makes a good relationship go bad. It can be the unseen "demon" that seems to follow you through life to destroy every good thing that happens. It is the root of why you lose control in certain settings. When the beliefs that empower codependent behavior are present, it will grow as fruit in every area of your life. Yet, because its form changes from situation to situation, you and I are deceived into picking the fruit but never identifying the one root that connects all the various manifestations! In other words, we may deal with some of our behavior, but we very seldom identify and address the true root issue.

Whether you are a classic codependent or not, you will find that it is when you give in to codependent tendencies that destruction and pain come into your life. By identifying the root and establishing new beliefs, the fruit will fall from the tree and you will find a new quality of life filled with peace, joy and meaningful relationships!

Endnotes

1. In order to simplify this writing, I am going to primarily use "he" rather than the politically correct "he or she." Of course, this in no way limits codependency to the male species! Every human being is susceptible, regardless of gender.
2. Meolody Beattie, *Codependent No More*, 2nd edition (Hazelden Publishing, 1986).

PERPETUATING THE CYCLE

For years I have observed codependent tendencies in the lives of the people who came to me for counsel. But in the early days I had no name for it. I recognized the symptoms and pattern, but I couldn't tie the pieces together around the root issue. It took many years before I was able to catalog the similarity of actions. It took even longer to come up with a compassionate understanding of the problem. But, in time, it was obvious that these seemingly complex patterns of dysfunctional behavior all grew from one root. Dealing with the root issue brought sweeping changes to numerous areas of life.

For years I noticed that the majority of people, including myself, repeated the same destructive patterns over and over. As such, I knew it had to be related to core beliefs. Core beliefs are those beliefs so connected to our sense of identity that they affect everything we do!

Another interesting, yet disturbing, anomaly presented itself with this pattern that ultimately came to be identified as codependency: whatever problems people had before they surrendered their life to the Lord were basically the same *types* of problems they had after coming to the Lord. Although these problems would not usually be acted out in the same way as before, people's current chaos would be motivated by the same beliefs and feelings.

I noticed that women who dated abusive men would reach such a place of pain that they would break up with the current abuser, only to date another person with a similar problem. In the end, they would usually marry another abusive person. The odd thing, however, was that the person they married may never show one tendency toward violence until after the wedding. Then the mask would come off and the unsuspecting woman would be trapped in the very scenario she had attempted to escape!

CORE BELIEFS ARE THOSE BELIEFS SO CONNECTED TO OUR SENSE OF IDENTITY THAT THEY AFFECT EVERYTHING WE DO!

I often wondered how one person could end up in so many abusive relationships. How could people repeat the same mistakes over and over again? It's like the young man who has been in a little trouble at school. It's not too serious yet. He doesn't really want to be a bad kid, but he is drawn like a magnet to other young boys who will lead him astray.

I've seen it across the counseling desk a hundred times. A man is sitting there, heartbroken. He is crying and sobbing, "Are all women sluts? Why is it that every woman I love is unfaithful? This is the same thing that happened in my last marriage. I will never trust a woman again!" I'm sitting there wondering to myself, "How do you find such bad wives?"

It's like the person who gets married only to discover his or her mate is a closet alcoholic. Or the woman who finds this is the third man in a row who has been a sexual deviant. Or the man who finds that this woman, just like the last four, is a clinging vine. Or the woman who finds that her husband is just like her controlling, dominating father. Or a struggling alcoholic who walks into a room of 300 people and the person he ends up talking to is also a struggling alcoholic with whom he ends up binging and falling off the wagon…again!

What is happening in these bizarre repetition of events? Did God decide He would torment them by continually putting these other people in their path? Is there an invisible demonic force that is planning their life? Is there a sign on their back that says, "I have a weakness for abusive women [or men]"? Why do they keep ending up in the same situation over and over again?

It All Goes Back to One Root

Unfortunately, our experiences forge our perceptions and our perceptions guide our decisions. If our perceptions were formed from incorrect evaluations of data, then all of our decisions will be equally incorrect. Because of the way we interpret the world around us, we create a perception (belief system) that ensures we will perpetuate the cycle, no matter how painful.

I have actually known men who decided that all women are bad. I have known women who reached the conclusion that all men will hurt you. I've known people who decide that love will always end badly. I've seen too many people, based on the perpetuation of the cycle, assume that God must be bad and mean. Once that corrupt extrapolation process begins, people deduce that they must have done something terribly wrong for God (or life) to be treating them so cruelly. Millions of people have decided they will never be happy and some even believe they should not be happy.

> CODEPENDENCY'S COMMON DENOMINATOR OF BELIEF IS THIS: "THE PROBLEM IS OUTSIDE OF ME; I AM NOT RESPONSIBLE."

All of these wrong conclusions are derived from incorrect perceptions. The incorrect perception is based on an interpretation of events that repeat themselves over and over. Even though the events are a product of our own core beliefs and are in fact our own making, they reinforce the faulty beliefs that spawned the cycle. The evidence produced by destructive beliefs always becomes the perpetuation of the deception that the belief must be true! Regardless of how it all plays out, when codependent concepts are at the root, there is one common denominator of belief: "The problem is outside of me. I am not responsible. I have no control over these events. This is someone else's fault." Yet, the one and only constant factor in every person's problem is him or herself. I have been present in every one of my problems. Like the country song says, "Wherever you go, there you are."[1] No matter where I go or what I do, I am always there, I am the constant; therefore, I must look into my own heart to discover the problem.

I am the constant factor in all my problems. If I move to a different city, get a different job, find a new set of friends, and the same thing happens there that happened before, it is time that I view it differently. I must admit that I am somehow involved in this. I must do what is nearly impossible for the codependent to do. I must recognize that the problem is in me. But I should do it in a healthy, constructive way.

The codependent person has no capacity to assume responsibility without personal blame. It is this very issue that forms the root that grows the fruit that falls from the tree to fertilize the root. If how I feel about me causes me to look outside of myself for solutions, then I have no control over the problem. But even worse, I feel too badly about myself to accept responsibility without contributing to the growth of the problem through self-hatred or self-criticism.

THE ROOT OF EVERY NEGATIVE THOUGHT, FEELING AND BEHAVIOR IS FEAR.

As I dealt with these tendencies in people, I came to realize that we all have certain beliefs and opinions; we all have certain needs and we all display certain characteristics that always attract the same kind of people into our lives. It has become second nature for us to pick up on the way people walk and talk. We have become able, on a subconscious level, to read the verbal and nonverbal behavior of people and identify that which is familiar.

An interesting phenomenon of the mind is that it always seeks that which is familiar. The root of every negative thought, feeling and behavior is fear. It is wired in us as human beings to inherently resist anything that causes fear. The unknown is treated as a threat; therefore, it creates fear. On a very subconscious level we repel that which would deliver us from the cycle and are drawn to that which will perpetuate the cycle simply because it is familiar. Since we feel safe with what is familiar, we tend to not notice the negative familiar factors and focus solely on the familiar factors that make us feel safe! And, we are repeatedly drawn to a particular behavior without realizing why.

Me and My Ego

In my own life, I realized that I was always in relationships with women whom I came to despise. At some point in every relationship I would always come to realize that I had chosen another "clinging vine." I could not understand how it could happen...again! If there was anything that repulsed me, it was a clinging, smothering person. Yet, at some point in my every relationship, the blinders would come off and I would realize that I was snuggled up to a clinging vine who had her tentacles wrapped around me and desperately needed for me to be the source of her existence!

No matter how angry I felt toward that person, I had to admit that *I* was the one who had gotten me into this. But why didn't I see it at the beginning? Why didn't I see the signs? Were all these women so incredibly deceptive or was I so foolishly blind? Looking back, I realized that these were not mean, vicious, deceptive women. Rather, there was something that attracted me to this kind of person, and this kind of person to me. What was it?

As painful as it was, I realized that the needs of these women appealed to my ego. When I first met them, they thought I was everything (that should have revealed something to me!). I liked that! I was the hero! These women thought could do anything. Oh man, did that make me feel good about me! Everything about the relationship met a need that I wasn't getting met in my own heart through a relationship with the Lord. This very issue, and the abiding emptiness I sought to fill through these unhealthy relationships, actually became a major factor in my search for God!

After I blindly rushed into one of these relationships, it wasn't long before the other person wanted me to make decisions she should make for herself. At first that was all right; it revealed how smart I was. Then she wanted to see me every day. That was all right, too; after all, I was such a desirable person. This sick progression moved right to the stage of "I need you." Then it usually took the quantum leap to "I'll kill myself if you leave me."

In reality, I didn't believe I was that smart. I didn't think I was all that attractive, and neither did I think I was a good catch. But when someone else expressed those things to me, it met a need in my life. I actually began to depend on that person to meet a need that should have been met somewhere else. I was as codependent as she was. I just didn't express my codependency through helplessness. I expressed my dysfunction through control. My problem was just as real and I was the constant factor in every romantic scenario. I made the choices that perpetuated everything I despised in a relationship and a person.

Blinded by Need and Greed

Our needs blind us to reality. Every con artist in the world knows this. If he (or she) has what you need and if he can get you acting in greed, you will close your eyes to all rationality. You will ignore the warning signs along the way. You will walk into the snare with eyes wide open. He won't even have to deceive you. Our need and our greed to have someone else meet that need blinds us to what we could easily identify if we were not expecting that person to meet our need!

In every counseling session with a person who had been in a codependent situation, he or she was able to look back and say, "All the warning signs were there. I should have seen them." However, our need and greed blind us. Greed is that factor of selfishness that is so concerned with getting our need met that we enter into what I call willful confusion.

James 3:16 says, *"For where envying and strife is, there is confusion and every evil work"* (KJV). The word *envy* is from the Greek word *zeal.* Zeal is when a person is ambitious. The New International Version of the Bible translates it as *selfish ambition.* When there is selfish ambition, there will be confusion. I can't see things as they are as long as I am moving in greed, i.e., selfish ambition. If I think you can give me what I need, it is essential that I enter into confusion about the warning signs. Otherwise, I would have to apply wisdom and self-control and run the risk of not getting my need met. The only choice, therefore, in the mind of those seeking to meet their need, is confusion about the facts. "I don't understand" is the mantra of people who willfully close their eyes!

My needs do not have to move me to greed. There is nothing wrong with having a need. The problem emerges, however, when I depend on someone else to meet that need for me. I can never look outside myself to discover what should be found in my own heart. The codependent has developed a pattern of looking to others to meet the needs that can only be met in his (or her) own heart. Because certain needs cannot be met by others, the codependent is blinded through desperation. He or she chooses to perpetuate the cycle in the vain hope of a different outcome. And as we all know, "doing the same thing over and over again and expecting different results" is insanity.[2]

Endnotes

1. Clint Black, vocal performance of "Wherever You Go," by Tom Weir, Larry Weir, and Michael Parnell, on *One Emotion*, RCA Records, 1994..
2. Albert Einstein, www.brainyquote.com (accessed July 11, 2011).

3

FINDING MY SOURCE

Codependency has grown in the world because the world has lost touch with its source. Secular humanism, socialism and progressivism, which have permeated every aspect of the world's thinking, seeks to alienate man from his Creator. Although the church uses the proper vocabulary, it has little knowledge of dealing with the heart. To the church, the knowledge of God as our source is more academic than experiential.

Colossians 2:10 makes one of the most profound and unbelieved claims of the entire Bible: *"You are complete in Him."* The church has drifted away from the cornerstone of faith-righteousness. By His death, burial and resurrection, Jesus obtained righteousness for all who would believe. But the church clings to the Old Covenant idea of each person earning righteousness by his performance, fundamentally neutralizing the cross of Christ. New Covenant faith is defined by our belief in the resurrection of the Lord Jesus and the free gift of righteousness. Nearly every epistle in the New Testament was written to bring mankind back to righteousness as a gift. Through the rejection of this cornerstone truth, coming to Jesus is not really seen as making you complete. It is seen as the first step toward completeness. Much like the Galatian church, we have some concept of Jesus forgiving our sins, but believe that it is by our performance we finally attain righteousness, i.e., completeness. This insidious deviation from the New

Covenant drives people into deep insecurity. Insecurity propels dead religious works as a means to righteousness, which never give us the sense of peace, wholeness or security we so desperately need. As a result, since we cannot find what we need in Christ, we look to other sources.

We attest to our lack of believing and experiencing this truth every time we depend on someone to meet a need for us that can only be met "in Him." The world has mastered the use of codependency. It is the philosophical root of propaganda and advertising. However, since the world has no concept of what God can do in the heart of a believer, it does not know how to meet the need. The world is like a doctor who can identify the symptoms and give them a name, but not cure the disease! Because society does not consider the love of God as a viable factor, it can never find the real solutions. In fact, leaving God out of the psychological equation was the cause of codependency to start with. Leaving Him out of the healing equation is like putting a Band-Aid® on a cancer and hoping it will heal!

A Degree of Relief

Without God, people can experience a degree of relief, but they can never experience wholeness. An alcoholic, for example, can get clean, but he (or she) cannot get free without the righteousness of God as a free gift. He will simply fill the void with meetings, therapy or some other substitute. That substitute enables him to stay off of alcohol, but for the rest of his life he must remind himself that he is merely an alcoholic in recovery.

Please understand, I am in no way condemning a program that gets people clean. I have great respect and admiration for those who develop and participate in programs that help people in this way. They have often done more for the needs of society than the church. They are bringing a degree of relief and peace to the individual who has lived his or her life trapped in addiction.

Some of the most codependent people I have ever seen, however, are people who are in recovery. They become dependent on the recovery process and never really get free. They have simply transferred their dependency from something totally unacceptable to something that is a little more socially acceptable. But the truth remains: This is not freedom; it is only relief.

Every arena has its own version of self-righteousness and hypocrisy. Just like Christians who point out the faults of others, the codependent in recovery is able to quickly identify and point out the codependent tendencies in others. And as if that was not enough, he also insists that everyone should participate in his group or receive his type of therapy because, after all, it is doing him so much good. Being able to identify the faults of others is no substitute for dealing with our own faults. Yet, it is acceptable and sometimes rewarded within any given culture or group.

It is not the intention of support programs to nurture this kind of attitude any more than it is the church's intention to create hypocrites. It is a reflection of the heart of the person. This is merely the extension of the codependent's beliefs projected into his (or her) current environment. The root has not been eradicated. The fruit is still growing. It just looks different in a different environment. All that has changed is the expression of codependence. This is called *transference*. Every new environment has something that facilitates the transference of our addiction onto something more acceptable. We cannot blame the program for the weaknesses of the people any more than we can blame God for the weaknesses of Christians.

> OUR OWN LIFESTYLE IS THE EVIDENCE THE WORLD USES TO REJECT AND DENOUNCE OUR CLAIMS CONCERNING GOD.

Codependents who become Christians do the same thing. They try to shove God "down the throat" of the world. Yet, our own lifestyle is the evidence the world uses to reject and denounce our claims concerning God. This has been a problem with believers since the beginning. *"For the name of God is blasphemed… because of you"* (Romans 2:24 NIV).

The problem is not necessarily the system; it is the people in the system. The Old Testament law had all the information a person would ever need to maintain great friendships, enjoy wonderful marriages, raise emotionally healthy children, succeed at business and experience an all-around good life. But it had a weakness: *the people!* The law *"was weak through the flesh"* (Romans 8:3).

Even the law, which was perfect in content, had a weakness—the people who used it! It would be more than arrogant for us to think that we could devise a system that was better than God's. It would be delusional to assume that our system could perfect people when God's system of information could not perfect people. The law itself never perfected anyone. *"For the law, having a shadow of the good things to come, and not the very image of the things, can never with these same sacrifices, which they offer continually year by year, make those who approach perfect"* (Hebrews 10:1).

COPING IS NOT CONQUERING!

The sinner, who continually attended all the right meetings and said and did all the right things, was still a sinner. No matter what his (or her) accomplishments, he stood before God and man only to continually remind himself, "I'm a recovering sinner." He may be a sinner who is doing better; he may be a sinner who doesn't sin like he used to; he may be a sinner in a way that you cannot see with your eyes; but in his heart, he is still a sinner.

Likewise, the alcoholic, drug addict, sex addict or codependent will always be just that, until he (or she) is set free. He may be in recovery. He may have been clean for ten years. He may be living a clean life, but he is still an alcoholic, drug addict or codependent at heart. Coping is not conquering! In order to avoid slipping, it is essential that he remind himself that he is just that; an alcoholic. The day that he forgets he is an alcoholic, sex addict or codependent will be the day he allows himself to run risks he cannot handle. It will be the first step toward falling!

Freedom Comes From Connecting to Our Creator

Don't condemn the person who can only stay clean by reminding himself. Even the Christian who is clean, but not free, had better remind himself of his problem or he will fall. Denial is not victory! False confessions and affirmations are not power! Being a Christian and experiencing the power of God in a specific area of life are two entirely different things. The Christian knows in his heart whether he is merely clean or if he is indeed free.

A person will not be free until he or she experiences the power of *completeness in Christ!* The theology of that verse will only make one knowledgeable. But knowledge only acts as guideposts on the path to wholeness. Knowledge doesn't change you. Knowledge is what puffs you up and makes you think more of your system than you should! Knowledge gives a false sense of security that is little more than the ego of feeling good about knowing something new. *"The kingdom of God is not in word but in power"* (1 Corinthians 4:20). Until we have experienced the power of the truth we know, we are simply reading the signposts on the path toward freedom. That information may motivate us to get clean, but only the power can make us free.

Christians are just as bad as any other group about transferring our addictions. We look to our programs or even to our leaders to meet the needs in our life. We look to people and methods because we do not really trust God or experience the wholeness He promises. We may trust those who represent Him, but we do not trust Him. We trust in our doctrines and creeds as a substitute for trusting in the character and faithfulness of God. We form groups (denominations) around our doctrines as if the power of numbers will prove us right and being right will somehow make us whole! The problem is not belonging to a group. We are wired to function better in groups. The problem is when we use the group as a substitute for an intimate connection with God.

The codependent, from his (or her) distorted perception, misunderstands the nature of his need. From this misunderstanding he incorrectly diagnoses the problem. From the improper diagnosis he prescribes the wrong therapy. The wrong therapy feeds the problem. We use the same corrupt logic to solve the problem that created the problem and are surprised when the problem gets worse.

But what is the problem? The problem is a disconnect from our Source...our Creator! The current philosophies of the world and the unscriptural concepts of God embraced by the church make it nearly impossible for a Christian to experience the love of God in any meaningful way! Acceptance of the most current doctrinal dogma will give at best a limited experience of conditional love.

In reality, codependency is when we depend on anyone to do for us what only God Himself can do. People around us can contribute to our freedom, but they cannot be the source of our freedom. A method or a system can facilitate the journey to freedom, but it cannot be the power that brings freedom. Freedom comes when something happens in my heart with God because I have truly made Him my source.

I must experience the liberating power of God or I am not free; rather, I am simply clean. But I cannot experience that power unless I trust God. He must be my source. He must be my all in all. I must find my completeness in Him, not in the method, not in the messenger—in Him!

The Chinese have a saying, "If you think you can learn from a book, don't buy the book. If you think you can learn from a teacher, don't get a teacher." Books, teachers and programs are not the way. Jesus is the way. Our books, teachers and programs should point us to the way. If they do not point us to God as our source, they become part of the problem.

> FREEDOM COMES WHEN SOMETHING HAPPENS IN MY HEART WITH GOD BECAUSE I HAVE TRULY MADE HIM MY SOURCE.

Books, teachers, preachers, church and, yes, even the Bible, can become a substitute for God. Instead of being a path that leads us to Him, each can become a wall that separates us from Him. Experiencing the love, acceptance and peace of God in our own heart is the fruit of wholeness. Wholeness is experienced "in Him," not as a position but as a vital connection!

Books, teachers, preachers, church and the Bible can be powerful tools that help us as long as we keep them in proper perspective. That perspective starts by determining that everything you read, hear or see will bring you to one qualifying question: How will I use this to know God in a more meaningful way? When you read your Bible, ask God to show you what you need today. When you attend church, ask yourself, "How will I apply this sermon to my life in a way that helps me trust God more?" Jesus said, *"This is eternal life, that they may know You, the only true God, and Jesus Christ whom You have sent"* (John 17:3). Only those things I am using to know and experience God lead me down a path of life. Everything else leads me to a deeper codependent deception.

4

Knowing God

"*Because he has set his love upon Me, therefore I will deliver him; I will set him on high, because he has known My name*" (Psalm 91:14). There is one basic reason people do not love God: they do not know Him! There is only one factor that causes people not to trust God: they do not know Him! There is one reason people do not look to God as their source: they do not know Him! There is one reason the world is in a mess: *they do not know God!*

Understand, I am not saying that millions of people have not *met* Him. I am saying they do not know Him...as He is! Religion has distorted the image of God. Through its codependent logic, the leaders of God's people throughout the ages have used a false image of God to control the masses! Fear has been the major component for control. Undermining man's sense of dignity and worth through the perversion of works-righteousness and condemnation has been the propaganda used to mold the mind for control. From Israel to the church, the leaders have unwittingly had the opposite effect on the world that they intended. As the prophet Isaiah pointed out, God's "*name is blasphemed continually every day*" (Isaiah 52:5). He clearly points out that this is the result of the leaders.

Jesus said, "*Take my yoke upon you, and learn of me*" (Matthew 11:29 KJV). The born-again experience is the beginning of our relationship with God, not the climax. At the new birth we have the opportunity to become involved with God in a very personal way. Righteousness is given to us as a free gift, to prevent fear and rejection from being a factor in coming to know God. Through the safety of a loving relationship we have no need to lie, hide or avoid responsibility for our destructive tendencies. In Christ, we can face God with no fear and find the help we need to live the life we desire.

> TO KNOW HIM PERSONALLY IS THE SOURCE OF LIFE.

Only through knowing God, as He is, can we experience Him as our source of liberating power. Paul said he wanted to *"know Him and the power of His resurrection"* (Philippians 3:10). If the message does not point me to a safe, personal relationship with God, it will point me away from Him. If the method does not move me toward security through personal intimacy, it will move me toward fear and religious performance. All of the churches, preachers, prayers and programs should encourage us in the pursuit of a personal, intimate, trusting, loving relationship with a loving, merciful God. Neither the church and the preacher nor their prayers and programs should ever be a substitute.

Knowing God Is the Source of Life

In John 10:10 Jesus said, *"I have come that they might have life...more abundantly."* He then went on to explain the source of that abundant life: *"And this is eternal life, that they may know You, the only true God, and Jesus Christ whom You have sent"* (John 17:3). To know Him personally is the source of life. This is not referring to life in a simply natural sense. The Greek word for life comes from a word that reflects quality. In fact, some references say it is speaking of the quality of life possessed by the Giver, i.e., the quality of life that He has. Quality of life addresses every spiritual, physical and emotional aspect of life. Among the many things never included in the quality of life God offers is the feeling of fear, lack and condemnation!

All negative emotions emerge from fear. When fear is woven into the fabric of knowing God, trust cannot emerge. According to the Apostle Paul, faith, i.e., immovable trust, works by love (Galatians 5:6). If the image of God I embrace does not allow me to see Him as He is, I will default to a negative, religious, superstitious concept that robs me of all He offers! We will not become intimate with a God we fear. We may serve Him, we may sacrifice for Him, but we will never love, trust or know Him intimately!

I am not saying that people do not know certain aspects of God. But as a whole, we have rejected the picture of God that Jesus modeled. We have instead opted for a religious, legalistic concept of an angry God searching relentlessly for our faults. Jesus showed us God in a way that we could understand and relate to. Hebrews 1:3 in the New International Version says He was *"the exact representation of God."* It is only the image of God modeled by the life of the Lord Jesus that I can accept as accurate and legitimate.

If the theology that I "twist" out of the Scriptures does not confirm what Jesus showed me, my theology is obviously wrong. If what I believe about God makes Him hard to trust or hard to love, I am most certainly confused. This is not the picture that Jesus came to portray. Most of the messages preached Sunday after Sunday are totally incompatible with the portrait Jesus presented of God. The result of this mass departure from reality is that people have a hard time trusting and depending on God. We are nurturing the very problem that Jesus came to solve. Religion makes it impossible to trust God as our source.

> RELIGION MAKES IT IMPOSSIBLE TO TRUST GOD AS OUR SOURCE.

God Is Our Source for Love

God created us in His likeness and image. We are social, emotional, relationship-oriented beings. There is something inherent in our psychological makeup that causes us to look outside of ourselves for certain needs. For example, we need love from another being. The word love basically has to do with value. Therefore, we will to a great degree determine our self worth by the value others place on us. The desire for validation outside of ourselves was God-given. It is present in every human being. It can work for us or against us, based on who we look to as our source.

I believe God factored this in so we would look to Him to meet those needs. Love was meant to be our bond to God. He is our only reliable consistent source of love. He is the only one who will ever love us unconditionally with a perfect love. It is the realization of His great love and value for us that should give us our sense of self-worth. All of this should work to bring us into a healthy, trusting relationship with God. He should be the source of meeting all of our deepest needs.

Because God is love and because He never changes, we have the opportunity to experience constant, positive internal input. But if we do not trust Him, if we do not know that He is loving and merciful, if we do not recognize the value He has for us as demonstrated at the cross, we will look somewhere else to have our deep needs met. We then become willingly controlled by whatever source we choose as our source of worth.

LOVE WAS MEANT TO BE OUR BOND TO GOD.

There is no one who can love us perfectly or constantly but God. Because the love that others have for us fluctuates, our sense of worth and confidence fluctuates. We are up and down with the inconsistencies of those upon whom we depend. Our inconsistencies then become justified by the inconsistencies of others. I am no longer responsible for what happens in my life. I do not have an anger problem; the problem is other people do things to make me angry. I do not have a depression problem; other people do things that cause me to be depressed. My life becomes an outward focus of cause, effect and justification.

This codependent scenario is even more complicated by our attempts to earn the love and acceptance of others. This is a great source of bitterness and anger. As a social, emotional, relationship-oriented being who has certain needs that can only be met from an outside source, I decide to look to you to meet those needs. You may even have committed to meet those needs. But I soon realize that if I don't act right, according to your definition of right, you will no longer have value for me. My needs will not be met!

If you are my source, I must either please you or manipulate you. You can't show me love when I offend you. So I work hard to do all the right things. But, since you are human, you too have occasional "bad days." On those days, you don't meet my needs. Now I not only fail to feel loved, but I also have done what I think should have earned me something and you won't give it to me. You are now the justifiable focus of my frustration and anger. You are the one who is causing my pain. You are my problem!

The codependent is always looking to an imperfect source to give perfect love. He or she is always depending on people for something that only God can do. As people fail us, we become more afraid to trust. By the time we are presented with the concept of God, our hearts have been so hurt by trusting others that we are afraid to trust God. Our painful experiences, coupled with all the preaching about an angry God, make Him the last being in the universe whom we would look to for love and acceptance.

God Made the Way

God has made peace with man through the Lord Jesus (Colossians 1:20). He has taken the law that was against us and nailed it to the cross (Colossians 2:14). By the finished work of Jesus, we now stand before God holy and blameless (Colossians 1:22). He demonstrated His great love for us in the fact that Jesus paid the full price for our sin (1 John 4:9-10). He has freely given us His love so that we would have no fear of Him at all (1 John 4:18). All of this makes it possible for us to come boldly before the throne of grace (Hebrews 4:16). This is the gospel that should be preached and believed. The Apostle Paul called it the gospel of peace (Romans 10:15).

There is no reason we should not trust God and draw near to Him. He has made the way open. But because we do not see Him *as He is,* and we only know our unscriptural opinions, we are afraid to trust Him. We have judged God to be untrustworthy. We have believed a lie about God and we are reaping the fruit of hearts afraid to trust the only true and reliable source. As a result, our only option is to look to others and bear the weight of continual disappointment.

The law said, *"You shall not make for yourself a carved image—any likeness of anything that is in heaven above, or that is in the earth beneath, or that is in the water under the earth"* (Exodus 20:4). Among the plethora of reasons we should not make any graven image is because that image reduces and perverts the concept of who God really is! It is man's idea of God rather than God's revelation of Himself!

In the Old Testament, people would cut down a tree and fashion it into what they thought the image of God was like. Then they would bow down to the image and say, "You are my god." Our problem today is not that we cut down a tree and fashion an idol. No, we are far too intelligent for that! Instead, we pervert the image of God that Jesus presented and replace it with a concept that has been imposed upon us by religion, an image that is more to our liking. Then we say, "This is what God is really like." In the end, we have no capacity to trust the image of God we have created.

> ONE WAY TO IDENTIFY THE SOURCE OF ANY EMOTION IS TO DETERMINE WHO CAN TAKE IT AWAY.

We are like the man with one talent in the parable of the talents. His opinion of God created an obstacle to abundant life. The man assumed his master to be hard and mean. That false image made it impossible for the servant to trust his master. He became paralyzed with fear. Based on his faulty logic, he developed his own plan. Not only did his plan fail to meet the objective, but it also brought about the very thing he feared. Likewise, we create unscriptural opinions about God that make it impossible for us to trust Him. We don't know Him as He is; we only know the image of Him that we have created or accepted.

Our Source of Feelings

God is the great *I Am*. He is all I need. He is omnipotent and omniscient. He is for me and not against me. He is the source of my life. He is the spring from which flows all the rivers of life. He is my source of joy, peace, confidence and self-worth. Others can participate in these feelings; they can contribute to them, but no one else is the source of those feelings. They can affect these feelings, but they cannot take them away. In fact, one way to identify the source of any emotion is to determine who can take it away. Whoever can take away our positive inner emotions in any area of life is who we have made our source!

One way God reveals Himself to us is by His name. In fact, one of His names is, "the One who reveals Himself by His name." Through His names God progressively showed His natures. Each name revealed an aspect of His being! There was a time I read and pondered the names of God and realized that all of His names were good. He didn't have any bad name. He did not have a name that reflected anger or rejection. All of His names reflected peace, love, healing, victory and dozens of other life-giving attributes. These names found their ultimate fulfillment in the eternal covenant in Jesus.

In Jesus all the names of God take on new value. They reveal aspects of what Jesus has now made available through the New Covenant. If I want to know who God is, I must know His name; I should look to the life modeled by the Lord Jesus; and I must look to what was accomplished by His death, burial and resurrection. Too many times we embrace some doctrinal position that is incongruent with the names of God and in direct opposition to the finished work of Jesus. This is usually a concept of God that provokes fear instead of inspiring love. When the names of God and the finished work of Jesus become my basis for knowing God, I always see a God I can trust and draw near to in love and intimacy. When I look at the life Jesus modeled, I experience the reality of what He said in John 14:9 (NLT): *"Anyone who has seen me has seen the Father!"*

When I realized that though others could contribute to many aspects of my life, *God* is my source, I found a freedom from depending on people that changed every relationship. I couldn't be controlled and I had no need to control. I appreciated people's approval, but I didn't need their approval. I felt good when people expressed love for me, but I was not depressed when they didn't. I had a new constant in my life: the love and acceptance of the unchanging God.

Only when we release people from being our source can we discover how to give and receive genuine love. We no longer demand from others what they cannot give. We no longer attempt to take what they do not have. Conflict in relationships all but disappears. Moreover, when I do not need others to make me feel loved, I am free to contribute to the relationship. Instead of being a constant taker, I can be a constant giver! But I am only free to *give* true love when God is my source! I can only *know* true love when God is my source! I can only know God as love when I see Him as presented through His name, the life of the Lord Jesus and the finished work of the cross!

5

CONTROL IS THE GOAL

Control is a major dynamic in almost any codependent relationship. Control manifests on many different fronts for many different reasons. For instance, there is the person who needs to be in control, and there is the person who wants to be controlled. Based on the individual's self-worth and core beliefs, either end of the control continuum can make him or her feel safe. It could be an expression of superiority or submissiveness. It may make you feel right. Even your allowing me to control you can be an expression of love, albeit a twisted expression.

Internal definitions, which are linked to core beliefs, determine what control means to an individual. If you are the source of my happiness, I must control you so you will make me happy. If I don't control you, you may do something that will constitute the loss of my happiness, security or self-worth. I can't run the risk of that kind of pain. Or, I could give you control of my life because I had a dominating parent who taught me to associate submission with love. Regardless of the complexity of the reason, the understanding is simple: I'm either taking control or giving up control to meet a need that only God Himself can meet in my heart!

The codependent can never have a truly meaningful relationship with anyone. Parenting, friendship, marriage and work are all tainted with desperate expectations and warped paradigms of fulfillment. Every relationship is entered with the expectation of what the other person can do to "meet my needs." Every person (victim) becomes a possible source for happiness.

This mentality produces a deep self-centeredness. The self-centeredness is always masked in corrupt logic of some kind. "I only do this because I love you so much!" "Isn't this what friends do?" Others are of value only to the degree they can meet the codependent's needs. This is why the codependent finds himself (or herself) in bad relationships over and over again. He is so consumed with getting his own needs met that he is all but oblivious to the needs of the other party. Then when trouble begins, he never notices the blaring warning signs.

> THE CODEPENDENT CAN NEVER HAVE A TRULY MEANINGFUL RELATIONSHIP WITH ANYONE.

Reality vs. Fantasy

Because codependents see something they think will meet their need, they fantasize what the relationship will be. They don't see the other person; they see the imaginary person. They see how this person can meet their need. They never really get to know the person, nor does the person ever get to know them. They have a fantasy in their mind that they must make come to pass.

Numerous times, I have seen this delusional fantasizing in premarital counseling. When the bride-to-be would describe her potential mate, I would be thinking, "Are we talking about the same guy? Because I've never seen that side of him." As they would continue to describe their relationship, I would realize they were describing their fantasy. Most people do what I call "painting the picture." They paint the picture of what they want in life and simply insert the other person into the already completed picture. The person is but an afterthought to the entire picture.

The codependent has a fantasy of marriage. When codependent people find someone, they simply paint that person's face on the picture in the fantasy. All too soon, they find that it is not the person they love, but the fantasy. When that person turns out to be different from the fantasy, codependents either quickly move on or attempt to take control and create their fantasy. Seldom do they actually build a relationship. A relationship could, after all, demand change in both parties! The codependent does not feel obligated to change. Whether driven by insecurity or arrogance, the outcome is the same. The other person is pressured, belittled or manipulated to feel the need to change!

Although we all have standards of what we want and expect in marriage, there should be some room for variation. When we meet someone, we should become friends, develop a relationship and see how it will unfold. We should see if we like what it becomes without our control. Only then can we actually know the other person and the potential for the relationship.

Because codependents seek a fantasy, they don't know for sure if their idea of a relationship will actually make them happy. They never experience different things with different people. They do not expand their social experience. They simply try to force everyone into the fulfillment of their fantasy, thereby cheating themselves of opportunities to know others. They ensure that they will never grow beyond their current limited capacity for love and friendship.

As long as we control others, we can never know them. We only know the image we have created. Usually we don't do that well on our creations; we never seem to get it right. We must continually recreate them. Ironically, no matter how much we mold them, we never find the happiness we expected. So we continually remake them.

> AS LONG AS WE CONTROL OTHERS, WE CAN NEVER KNOW THEM.

The dominant person has a need he (or she) seldom recognizes. He must be able to respect his partner. When the dominant person can't respect you, he has little value for you. Sadly, most dominators do not understand this about themselves. After a dominator molds you into the person he wants you to be, he doesn't respect you. After all, if you were any kind of person, you would not allow someone to control you. Once there is a loss of respect, the dominant controller will reject you!

The passive person, on the other hand, gives in to your every demand. This is another form of control. By giving in, he (or she) makes you responsible. Everything is your fault! He can play the victim and avoid one of the greatest fears of his life: responsibility! But, after a time of giving in, thereby creating a self-centered monster for a mate, the passive person feels used and angry. He has no life of his own. He despises the aggressive control. Typical for the codependent, he never says, "I gave control of my life to another." He always says, "That person took control of my life."

Different Types of Controllers

This is a good time to point out that every behavior pattern has a slightly different way of controlling. When we talk about controllers, every subtle controller looks at the strong personality and says, "He's the controller, not me." But everyone has a way in which he (or she) attempts to control. Some are just more obvious than others.

When the dominant person controls, it is obvious and open. Such people seldom try to hide it. They openly attempt control by sheer force of character.[1] Because of this, they are usually the ones blamed for controlling while the other controllers continue in the shadows undetected. In some ways, the dominant person is the easiest to control and certainly the easiest to blame. He can't deny being a controller, but he does have ways of justifying it. "I do it for your own good. I do it because I love you. I do it because you won't."

The analytical, critical thinker controls by creating standards that make him appear to be right. In his own mind, he is right. He is the "quality control" person. Since he never tries to control openly or by force of character, it is easy for him to deny being a controller. He would be appalled at being accused of controlling. He's only doing what is right. It is very easy for him to shift blame. He can easily provoke the other behavioral types into extreme reactionary behavior, which make *them* appear to be the only ones emotionally out of control. This person is diplomatic and subtle, but calculating and cold as ice when it comes to getting things done the "right" way.

Then there is the sincere, steady person. This person is loyal and personable. He has many wonderful traits, but when he decides to control, he will dig his heels in and become immovable. This person can easily function in toxic relationships. He uses his "servant's attitude" to enlist specific responses. Failure to respond properly to his efforts can produce extreme anger.

Although this person puts great emphasis on loyalty, his true loyalty is to his own goals and not yours. However, he is doing what he does for you. You should appreciate it. When you fail to agree with what or how he is doing his tasks, he not only feels unappreciated, but he also feels betrayed! In conflict this person feels very justified in soliciting others to his side. He operates in the "strength by numbers" mentality. In other words, he seeks to control by the force of the group. After all, he feels victimized. He has sacrificed so much for you and you have given so little in return.

> PEOPLE WHO ARE LOOKING TO OTHER PEOPLE TO MEET NEEDS THAT ONLY GOD CAN MEET CANNOT RESIST THE TEMPTATION TO CONTROL.

Last of all, there is the inspirational, people-oriented, "I want you to like me" person. This type is a very friendly, outgoing individual who wants to be liked. This person will go ten extra miles to make you like him, which becomes the whole problem. Regardless of the situation, in his mind it is always about him. Much of his agreeing, kindness and verbal influence is all for the response that you will give. He is not as concerned about the task as he is your liking him when he completes the task. He seeks to control by friendly influence. He'll flirt, he'll "suck up," he'll be your buddy. When you like him, he will get what he wants!

All of these people can be wonderful individuals and have admirable traits. I am not saying that they always do these things. This is simply the motivation and the method they employ when they attempt to control. People who are looking to other people to meet needs that only God can meet cannot resist the temptation to control. It is their only hope of getting some of their deep-rooted, God-given needs met.

What Is Your Motivation?

This entire scenario is the antithesis of true love. Biblical love is self-sacrificial. Biblical love does not lose value for self; it is just not self-motivated. In fact, biblical love is rooted in a strong sense of self-worth inspired by the realization and experience of God's great love. Because I have a deep realization of being loved, I am able to give for a motive other than response. I can actually look to the other person's need. I do not need for the other person to respond in a certain manner. I am not working a secret agenda.

> CONTROL IS WHEN WE INVADE A PERSON'S LIFE IN A WAY THAT GOD HIMSELF WILL NOT DO.

Rather than entering every relationship with needs that must be met, the emotionally whole person can allow each relationship to exist on its own merit. The relationship can become whatever it becomes. For this person, every friendship is an adventure. Every friendship is different. Unlike the codependent, the person walking in love does not require that every friend fit into a self-satisfying role designed to meet his (or her) personal needs. Neither does he continue to destroy relationships through his need to control them.

Every person who controls convinces himself that he has a good motive. The controller can even make the motive seem noble, but know this: *control is when we invade a person's life in a way that God Himself will not do.* We must allow people the freedom to succeed and fail on their own. We can advise them in areas they ask for advice. We can ask them if they want our input, but we can never control.

Personal growth is an impossibility for the person being controlled as well as for the person who is controlling. If I am having difficulty relating to you, I can either control you or I can grow. I can turn to God and get the grace to accept you. I can even develop new personal skills. I can learn more about you as a person. I can do a thousand positive, constructive things, or I can do one negative, destructive thing…I can attempt to control you.

No matter how noble it seems, when we control, we do it for us, not for the other person. Instead of asking why people won't listen to us, maybe we need to ask why we are not listening to them. Instead of demanding that other people understand our needs, if we are walking in love we will first seek to understand their needs. The person who trusts the power of love realizes that unconditional love has the potential to draw the very best out of a person. If love fails to draw out of a person that which will make us compatible, it will certainly never be found through control. Control will only produce disingenuous, insincere behavior that never resonates with the healthy needs of my heart for a meaningful relationship!

Endnote

1. The models of behavior are based on the *DISC Behavioral Profile*; Inscape Publishing, Inc., formerly Carlson Learning Company, Mount Prospect, Illinois.

6

GOD OF MY WORLD

The first act of codependency came in the garden of Eden. It establishes the pattern for all temptation. It clearly reveals codependency as one of the most basic elements of temptation. Our current concepts of temptation and its process are not only unscriptural, but they also encourage the codependent victim's mentality. We have the unscriptural idea that the devil attacks us and throws some temptation upon us, which then becomes a battle we must fight to prove our spirituality and win our Lord's approval. The entire concept of "testing" is codependent, unscriptural and enabling.

Adam's temptation, like ours, did not start with the devil. The entire concept of the devil having that scope of power or authority leads to all manner of codependent spiritual warfare, which does little more than shift the blame onto a true enemy that we have inflated to bigger-than-life status. Neither does temptation come from God as a test. This is another way for us to make ourselves to be the victims while blaming God for our own dysfunction. James warned these early believers, *"Let no one say when he is tempted, 'I am tempted by God'"* (James 1:13a). God does not tempt, test, try or scrutinize anyone![1]

Temptations Are Not the Devil's Attack

If temptation isn't an attack of the devil and it isn't a test from God, then what is its source? Where does it originate? Temptation always starts with our own desires. In the Book of James we are taught plainly that temptation begins with us, not the devil. *"Temptation comes from our own desires"* (James 1:14a). Since temptation originates within my own heart and mind, it stands to reason that the problem must be dealt with in my own heart and mind. But the codependent's tendency for identifying problems as well as finding solutions is to look outside of him or herself and focus on some external source.

> THE ENTIRE CONCEPT OF "TESTING" IS CODEPENDENT, UNSCRIPTURAL AND ENABLING.

The codependent ignores the entire issue of responsibility. Responsibility feels like blame. To admit that our desires are corrupt is more than our theology or our self-worth can bear! But when we get a more scriptural understanding of the process, we can accept responsibility without blame. You see, no desire is actually evil within itself! Desires only become evil in an unbelieving heart. *"Unto the pure all things are pure: but unto them that are defiled and unbelieving is nothing pure; but even their mind and conscience is defiled"* (Titus 1:15 KJV).

Desire in an untrusting heart always leads a person away from God. This heart does not know God's goodness and does not trust Him to fulfill its desires. The believing heart, on the other hand, takes its desires before the Lord. This person looks for the biblical way to gratify those desires. The believing heart depends on God as his source for fulfillment. As the trusting heart follows God into the fulfillment of personal desires, it results in thanksgiving, praise, worship and a greater love. As the scripture says, *"A longing fulfilled is a tree of life"* (Proverbs 13:12b NIV). The untrusting heart, however, is always destroyed by his or her desires. As the other half of that same verse reads in the Message Bible, *"Unrelenting disappointment leaves you heartsick."*

Every desire a man has originates from a God-given need inherent in the fabric of mankind's being. The problem is never the desire. The problem is the process whereby we seek to gratify the desire. However twisted and perverted it may become in the way we seek to fulfill it, all desires could be fulfilled in a biblical manner. However, when we do not trust God, when we do not believe there is a biblical way we can fulfill those desires, then we look to other sources. This leads to sin. *"But each one is tempted when he is drawn away by his own desires and enticed. Then, when desire has conceived, it gives birth to sin; and sin, when it is full-grown, brings forth death"* (James 1:14-15).

It Started in Eden

God gave Adam dominion over planet Earth; he ruled as a god in this world. Adam's desire to rule planet Earth came from his God-given nature. Like all root desires, the desire to rule is the fulfillment of who we are created to be. At the same time, Adam, like us, had to look to God to determine what was good and evil. God would show him the proper expression of his authority.

Adam had authority in planet Earth, but he was dependent on God for the wisdom to use that authority properly. Satan came along and offered him the opportunity to rule apart from trusting and depending on the Father. *"You will be like God, knowing good and evil"* (Genesis 3:5b). Adam's fall started by internally questioning the wisdom of God. At some point he chose not to trust and depend on God. Ironically, he wasn't even choosing to trust Satan! He was choosing to trust himself, thereby becoming his own god. Thus, we have the fall of man. As we look closer at this scenario, we may find some hints of what was working behind the scenes.

TEMPTATION ALWAYS STARTS WITH OUR OWN DESIRES.

For Adam to rule with God, he had to trust God. God still owned planet Earth; man was the steward. He was to rule under the wisdom of God. To trust God, he must maintain a relationship. If he took Satan's offer, there would be no need for a relationship and there would be no basis for trust. At the heart of this temptation, we find man pursuing a life apart from a trusting relationship with God. At the heart of every human difficulty, we find this same dynamic: people who do not trust God.

James said we are tempted when we are drawn away by our own desire. Desire should have the opposite effect. It should not draw us away from God; it should draw us near to God. When desire arises in a heart filled with trust, that person will draw close to God to discover the path to the fulfillment of the desire. It is not the devil that draws us away; it is the beliefs of the heart, the need to be right, the need to have our way. After all, we trust ourselves more than we trust God! The desire that will draw one person to God will cause another to run away from God!

EVERY DESIRE A MAN HAS ORIGINATES FROM A GOD-GIVEN NEED.

James went on to say that we are then enticed. The word *enticed* has to do with being entrapped and beguiled. If our desires draw us away from God, we will always enter into a self-induced state of confusion, which James refers to in James 3:16: *"For where you have…selfish ambition, there you find disorder [confusion] and every evil practice"* (NIV). The state of confusion that allows me to justify my perverted path to fulfillment is the trap that brings death and pain into my life. Neither God nor the devil can be blamed for this end result. It was merely the path I trusted to best fulfill my desire!

The reasons for not trusting God may vary, but the end result is the same. Some people think they have to get enough faith to compel God to do good things. Some seek the promises as if they were by works. Still others just believe we are destined to suffer. Regardless of the particulars, the root is the same: they do not believe what Christ has (past tense) accomplished at the cross. Notwithstanding the reason, unbelief is unbelief, and it always leads one to depend on someone or something other than God!

From the garden to this very day Satan has nothing to offer. What he offered Adam was precisely what Adam already had. Adam had absolute authority in planet Earth. God had given him dominion. He already was like God! He was created in God's likeness and image. The one capacity that Adam did not have was the ability to determine good and evil for himself. When we doubt who we are in relationship to God or what we have in Him, we feel a self-generated sense of lack. Lack becomes the emotional platform from which we launch into every manner of codependent behavior.

From an underlying feeling of lack the codependent falls for the oldest temptation in the world: "You are not who God says you are; you do not have what God says you have; therefore, you must look to an outside source to meet your needs." Then the codependent makes the critical error. He, acting as god of his own world, chooses his own process for meeting the need, totally abandoning the most critical aspect of being a New Covenant believer: Christ in you!

> LACK BECOMES THE EMOTIONAL PLATFORM FROM WHICH WE LAUNCH INTO EVERY MANNER OF CODEPENDENT BEHAVIOR.

Endnote

1. *Biblesoft's New Exhaustive Strong's Numbers and Concordance with Expanded Greek-Hebrew Dictionary* (Biblesoft, Inc. and International Bible Translators, Inc., 1994, 2003, 2006), NT:3985; test (objectively), i.e. endeavor, scrutinize.

7

FEAR: THE ROOT

We know that sin entered the world at the garden through Adam. We know that the end result of sin has been all manner of destruction and evil. But there is a possibility that our core concepts of sin are not as accurate as we have believed in the past. Once again our faulty religious concepts not only cloud the truth but also feed the root problem.

Adam's act of disobedience introduced sin into the world. From the time of Adam all men were born with a sin nature. But what does that really mean? Roman 5:14 tells us that Adam's sin was a transgression. In other words, it was a violation of God's truth. Romans 5:12 tells us that through this act of disobedience, sin entered the world. But the Greek word for the sin that entered the world is not the word *violation*; it is the Greek word which means "to miss the mark of the reward and not share in the prize."[1]

When man became a sinner, he didn't run wild seeking every manner of evil. The transgression of Adam was the result of not believing who he was in relation to his Creator. That which entered the world through Adam's transgression was not a passionate desire to commit transgression. What entered the world through Adam's transgression was the type of sin that caused man to lose his sense of who he was in relation to God, thereby defaulting on his capacity to share in all that

God had in store for him. No doubt, this failure to share in the prize would cause man to miss the mark and compel him to disobedience. But to confuse the fruit and the root allows our religious solution to facilitate the real problem: identity!

Adam's Sin Introduced Fear

After the fall of man, when man became a sinner, his first emotional reaction was not one of unbridled passion for evil. His first new emotion was fear. Adam, for the first time in his existence, was afraid of God! Adam expected pain and judgment, so he hid from God. Fear led to a lack of trust; absence of trust led to hiding from God; and hiding from God led us to dependence on sources other than God to meet our deepest needs. Having a sin nature may in fact mean having an inherently fearful and untrusting nature.

> THE TRANSGRESSION OF ADAM WAS THE RESULT OF NOT BELIEVING WHO HE WAS IN RELATION TO HIS CREATOR.

Fear and love are the two opposing root emotions. Some say that every emotion and thought stems from either fear or love. Interestingly, fear and love are completely incompatible. The two cannot coexist. *"There is no fear in love; but perfect love casts out fear, because fear involves torment. But he who fears has not been made perfect in love"* (1 John 4:18). The moment fear entered, love, which is the basis of trust, vanished. Fear and unbelief are so intertwined that they are hard to separate. One produces the other in a never-ending, ever-growing syndrome of dysfunction and self-destruction. It doesn't matter which comes first; one always feeds the other.

God has called us to a relationship of love. He has made it possible for all of our needs to be met in Christ. We should lack nothing. We should be whole in spirit, soul and body. *"His divine power has given to us all things that pertain to life and godliness, through the knowledge of Him who called us by glory and virtue"* (2 Peter 1:3). Fear and unbelief, however, make that an impossibility.

With all that God has freely given to us, how could we walk about in such desperate need? Simple! The need is not real. It is an illusion. Like Adam, we don't believe who we are and what we have; therefore, we feel fearful and lacking. Adam didn't trust how God had created him in the garden; we don't trust how God has created us in Christ!

There is a reason we don't trust Him; we are afraid of Him. There is a reason we are afraid; we don't believe He loves us with a perfect love. One cannot be made perfect in love and still have fear. The scales are always perfectly balanced by love and fear. To the degree you're not established in His perfect love, you will have fear. It is as if there is a void that will be filled with one or the other. To the degree that one is filled with the love of God, fear is driven out.

Faith + Love = Trust

The real faith walk of the believer has nearly nothing to do with trying to get "stuff" from God. Faith has been perverted into a selfish indulgence of self-gratification. Our greatest application of faith will be in the finished work of Jesus and who we are in Him. From this the promises are trusted and realized in a seemingly effortless manner.

> OUR GREATEST APPLICATION OF FAITH WILL BE IN THE FINISHED WORK OF JESUS AND WHO WE ARE IN HIM.

Our traditional approach to faith actually epitomizes unbelief: Since I have fear in my heart, I don't believe that God has freely given me everything I need in Christ. I am like Adam; I somehow think He is keeping the best back from me. So I'm going to get enough "faith" to get God to give me something that He says I already have. Let's face it, if I had faith, I would believe what I already have in Christ. We, like Adam, are always trying to get something God has already given us, thereby testifying to our unbelief in His finished work!

When faith works by love, it trusts the love that God has for us. We look to the finished work of Jesus and are fully persuaded of His limitless love. *"In this the love of God was manifested toward us, that God has sent His only begotten Son into the world, that we might live through Him…to be the propitiation for our sins"* (1 John 4:9-10). The word propitiation means satisfying of wrath. Because Jesus satisfied the wrath of God against our sins, we never have to fear God hurting or rejecting us. This realization of love drives out fear and faith blossoms.

Real faith is a response to what God has done in Jesus. It is not what we do to get God to respond to us. Real faith and confidence in every area of life comes because it is rooted in the love of God and the finished work of Jesus. Real believing doesn't look to how strong our faith is as much as it looks at how strong and perfect God's love is.

Control Is Preferable to Trust

Among the many things fearful people cannot do is trust the one they fear. Those who have not established their hearts in the love of God cannot trust God. Codependent people never operate from love and trust; they always work from manipulation and control. "Yes, I want to be god of my world. I want control of my world." If I am in control, it sets me free from one thing I cannot do, which is trust. If I can control my environment, I don't have to trust God. If I can control my relationships, I don't have to trust God with those relationships. If I can control you, I do not have to trust you!

If I am god of my world, I have the right to form everyone and everything into what I desire. Everything exists to serve me. I will not trust God to work in your life; after all, He may not make you into what I need you to be. He might make you into what He wants you to be. That may require change on my part and I am not going to change because I am at the center of my world. Everything revolves around me and my desires. Now, these are not words that are ever spoken. In fact, the very opposite is proclaimed. But through perverted concepts of authority, submission and righteousness, we violate every vestige of the identity of man and his relationship with God!

The codependent, whether an aggressive controller or a passive controller, is paralyzed, rigid and inflexible. Change is very threatening to the codependent.

The unspoken deception is that it is easier to change the world arou.
it is to face the possibility that I must change. I have found my comfo.
must convince everyone that this is normal and that everyone else must c.   .

The aggressive codependent doesn't look fearful. He (or she) may look like the most confident individual you've ever seen. He looks like he's got it all together. But he desperately fears things getting out of his control. It has been said that two of the greatest signs of maturity are flexibility and adaptability.[2] Truly confident and emotionally mature people are flexible and adaptable; they are not threatened by the changes that occur around them. They welcome internal change as healthy growth. The mature individual yields to others and adapts to the expressions of love that are most effective in the environment. Thus, he or she is at peace and able to function in any situation.

The codependent controller is neither flexible nor adaptable. He (or she) must be in control. Everything must conform to his control so he will not be threatened. Even the passive controller who appears to be a victim is maintaining control through passive aggressive dysfunction. He is simply doing it in the way he feels comfortable. Our lack of self-control is best demonstrated in our inability to be flexible and adaptable. Our lack of self-control becomes aggression when we allow it to thrust us into controlling others. Controlling others whether passively or aggressively is an outward expression of being the god of our world.

> THE TRULY CONFIDENT AND EMOTIONALLY MATURE PERSON IS FLEXIBLE AND ADAPTABLE.

If I entrust you to God and allow you to become who God would have you to be, I will be faced with a tremendous challenge. I will have to adapt and adjust. I will have to love you, find value for you. I will have to allow trust to grow through the free expression of your identity. If I do not allow you to be who you are in Christ, I will never be faced with the real challenges of life. I will not have to grow if I can keep you from growing. I will not need the grace (ability) of God working in my life if you never grow beyond my ability to control.

If my world or any part of it changes, I will be forced to do the one thing I do not want to do: trust God. I will be forced to trust God for the strength to love and accept others. I will be forced to find joy and contentment in the Lord. I will no longer be able to use others for my own purposes. I will no longer be god of my own world!

Endnotes

1. *Biblesoft's New Exhaustive Strong's Numbers and Concordance with Expanded Greek-Hebrew Dictionary* (Biblesoft, Inc. and International Bible Translators, Inc., 1994, 2003, 2006), NT:264, *hamartano* (ham-ar-tan"-o); perhaps from NT:1 (as a negative particle) and the base of NT:3313; properly, to miss the mark (and so not share in the prize).
2. Tony Alessandra, Ph.D. and Michael J. O'Connor, Ph.D., *People Smart* (La Jolla, CA: Keynote Publishing Co., 1995).

8

Toxic Love

Love is the deepest need of a human being. All healthy emotions, beliefs and feelings emerge from the degree that we experience love. Volumes have been written on the topic. But much of what has been written focuses on concepts of love that actually undermine healthy emotions. The Bible presents us with the only type of "love" that has the power to fulfill the deepest needs of a human being: *agape!*

Agape is the type of love God offers man. Among the unique characteristics of *agape* are the following: *Agape* is never conditional. *Agape* is not self-seeking. It is not what one does to provoke a response. More than anything else, *agape* is about value. Agape, which is unconditional, has unconditional value for the object of its affection. It holds that object in high regard and considers it precious.[1] This type of love alone has the capacity to create a healthy sense of self. It is this love for which man constantly searches. It is this love that all too often is substituted with toxic love, which has just the opposite effect!

It is inherent in man to look to an outside source to find his value. *Agape* love expressed by our Creator is the immovable foundation of a healthy self-worth. This "self-worth" is not egotistical. It is not performance-based. It is the acceptance of our value to the Creator. It is this love that stimulates positive healthy personal growth. This incredible love is the basis for our faith (Galatians 5:6). Walking in love will fulfill the perfect will of God for your life (Galatians 5:14). Loving God and loving people is the fulfillment of all of God's Word (Matthew 22:36-40). Yet, it is one of the most perverted and misunderstood subjects in the earth.

We Have Redefined Love

We must remember that, since Adam's fall, man has determined good and evil for himself. As god of our own world, we claimed the right to define good and evil. In so doing, we have redefined love. We have rejected God's concept of love and developed our own. It is our definition of love, however, that is causing most of our pain. We are drinking water from a poisonous well. It tastes good going down, but once consumed, it rots our heart!

> MORE THAN ANYTHING ELSE, *AGAPE* IS ABOUT VALUE.

Love is the deepest and most essential human need. Every person is always in pursuit of being loved, i.e., valued! Only God's quality of love can ignite our sense of self-worth. We can't deny the need. However, we have so redefined love that when we find our definition of love, it usually destroys us. No matter the pain, we can't give up our search because it is such a deep need. But remember, when we talk about love, our first thought is romantic love. Romantic love, which is important, is only a weak substitute for *agape*, the sense of being valuable!

It's like a starving man finding a poisonous berry that has a sweet taste. He refuses to believe that it is poison. After all, when he eats it, it tastes good. Later, however, it makes him sick. Our hunger, our love of the taste, keeps compelling us to eat it again and again. So we convince ourselves that it is a good plant for food. We eat, enjoy the taste and become sicker and sicker. We swear we will never eat it again, but when hunger returns, we give in to the need.

Our need to give love is almost as intense as our need to be loved. We were created in the likeness and image of God. God is love. Therefore, if we are to live as "human beings," we must be love. Love must be the first quality we seek to develop and give. Yet, we approach it from an unbiblical perspective and get hurt. But our need for love keeps driving us back. Since we only know love the way we have defined it, we do the same thing over and over, only to be hurt over and over. Because we think that receiving love is the key, we reject the idea of giving love. We fail to see the dimension of joy and fulfillment that giving love will bring us. We fail to understand that receiving love without giving love is a virtual impossibility!

Toxic love is a poisonous perverted imitation of God's love. It violates God's definition of love. It was born in the garden when man believed a lie and felt lack for the first time. It developed through the years as men became inventors of evil, creating all manner of substitutes. It was nurtured by the movie industry. It is peddled by every opportunist seeking to exploit man's deepest need. Because this toxic love works by gratification of the senses, it is like any other addiction. The more we get the more we need. The more we need the more destructive we become in our pursuits. Only the love of God can give the positive results that we vainly expect from our relationships. Anything else will bring pain and destruction. All the substitutes are poisonous, addictive and deceptive. It may seem to momentarily meet the need, but in the end we are left vacuous and hurting.

> ONLY THE LOVE OF GOD CAN GIVE THE POSITIVE RESULTS THAT WE VAINLY EXPECT FROM OUR RELATIONSHIPS. ANYTHING ELSE WILL BRING PAIN AND DESTRUCTION.

Examples of Toxic Love

One form of toxic love is giving to get. We flatter to be flattered. We buy gifts to be repaid sexually. We do the little things to be repaid with the big things. The person giving this kind of toxic love is not motivated by the value he (or she) has for the other person. If that were the case, he would do things that express value. Instead, he is motivated by how the other person can make him feel valued and precious. It is being done for self! The ultimate goal is not how it contributes to the other person's sense of self, but how it brings about the desired response. This "love" is nothing more than manipulation. It is a way to get what we want. We may pour on all the charm, kindness and gifts one could imagine, but it is nothing more than bait.

The motive for a person's action is often revealed when he (or she) does not see the desired response. Anger is the most common indicator of corrupt motives disguised as love. Or possibly, it could be guilt. The person reminds you of all he has done for you. He points out how good he is to you, implying that you should do what he wants you to do. If these tactics fail, he may resort to punishment. He may stop doing any good things until you respond according to his desires. The codependent manipulator shifts from one emotional manipulation to another, seeking to find the right "button" to get the desired response!

A MANIPULATED RESPONSE DOES NOT SATISFY THE HEART LIKE THE UNCONDITIONAL LOVE OF GOD.

The person who gives toxic love is a "user" who will never be satisfied. Even when you respond in the way he (or she) desires, it doesn't satisfy the hunger in his soul. A manipulated response does not satisfy the heart like the unconditional love of God. We actually need someone to love us in a way that only God can. The user knows that you are just responding to manipulation. Therefore, he is never really confident in your love. After all, if the manipulation stopped, would you give what is demanded?

This can cause the user of toxic love to swing from one extreme to the other. The resentment that you are not meeting the need for true love will overwhelm him (or her) at times. Even if your love is true, it will never really be trusted. Because (in the mind of the manipulator) your love is being bought by his actions, it is not unusual for the user of toxic love to place more and more demands on you to prove your love. Often, sexual demands will become quite extreme. He expects an unrealistic loyalty. Your entire life becomes consumed with the demand to prove your love.

Any time you fail to meet the need, the tools of manipulation come out! Statements like, "Can't you just support me… After all I've done for you, you're going to leave me… I need for you to show me you love me," become a barrage. If that doesn't work, there is the silent treatment. There are hundreds of guilt-producing, self-centered statements that the users of toxic love will make. If those tactics fail, they may even resort to aggression or violence. Their intention from the very beginning is just to get the desired response.

The users of toxic love are prevented from ever trusting your response. "Does she love me, or does she just love what I do for her?" They are haunted with the lack of certainty! It is a tormenting existence that spills over onto everyone in their environment. The toxic lover can never be satisfied. Sometimes extramarital affairs are the desperate search for the sense of value.

When toxic love is the driving force, there is little respect for the boundaries of others. Violating a person's will becomes part of the test for love. Sexual demands that are not satisfying or are even humiliating for the other person may appear. All of the bizarre demands are the way you must prove your love. "If you love me, you will…" is the famous line of the toxic love user.

Remember, the codependent person can be an aggressive or passive controller. You may be the one forcing your desires on another person. Or you may be the one who feels you must violate yourself to prove your love. You may feel a duty or obligation to violate your dignity. "After all," you think, "it is my duty."

Many scriptures from the Bible have been twisted to create obligation and guilt for the purpose of manipulation. "Wives submit!" is the favorite scripture of the male controller. This becomes his justification to force his wife into his every desire. This scripture does not, however, override every other scripture in the Bible. It does not void out, *"Husbands, love your wives, just as Christ also loved the church"* (Ephesians 5:25). It does not void the ultimate command that all things should be done in love and nothing should be done in selfishness. There are hundreds of scriptures that must be violated in order for this submission scripture to become the pivotal point of the marriage.

Real love never oversteps certain bounds. It never violates another person's will. It doesn't demand; it compels. It never takes another person's freedom of choice away. It is never given with me in mind. It is always given with you in mind.

The love we are called to give to others is a love that says, "At the end of our involvement, with the way I have handled this, you will feel valuable and precious and your dignity will be intact!"

Endnote

1. Kenneth S. Wuest, *Word Studies in the Greek New Testament, Bypaths in the Greek New Testament* (Grand Rapids, MI: William B. Eerdmans Publishing Company, n.d.), 112.

9

WHAT IS LOVE?

This seems like such a mystical question. It is only mystical, however, because we have refused to look to the Author of love to find its true meaning. We have looked in all the wrong places only to find all the wrong meanings. God is the Author of love because He is Love. *"And we have known and believed the love that God has for us. God is love, and he who abides in love abides in God, and God in him"* (1 John 4:16).

Only the type of love embodied in God's character and described in His Word can produce the results we so desperately desire. The degree we move away from God's definition of love is the degree we will experience pain and difficulty not just in our relationships, but also in our own heart. A life not lived in love is always void, it always hurts, it always longs. Sadly, a heart not giving and receiving genuine love will either die from sorrow and emptiness or fill its void with some type of addiction. In the treatment of addictions we have a saying that "codependency is the mother of *all* addictions!"

Love According to God

The Bible describes the attributes of God's *agape* love as follows: *"Love suffers long and is kind; love does not envy; love does not parade itself, is not puffed up; does not behave rudely, does not seek its own, is not provoked, thinks no evil; does not rejoice in iniquity, but rejoices in the truth; bears all things, believes all things, hopes all things, endures all things. Love never fails"* (1 Corinthians 13:4-8).

In *The Prayer Organizer*[1] I have expanded the definition of these words used in First Corinthians 13 to make them a little closer to the original meaning.

Love is patient; it does not become pushy or demanding. It endures and remains consistent under pressure. Codependent, toxic lovers are never patient. They need for you to respond to their needs at their every whim. They demand a specific response. True love, however, is longsuffering. It allows you the time to work through your problems. It is not reactionary.

Love is kind. Kindness is essential to love. Toxic love can be harsh and hard. Gentleness is only employed when it is the most effective manipulative tool. Toxic love views kindness as something that is given as a reward or used as a tool. When you please codependents, they will reward you with kindness. When you fail to please, kindness is withdrawn. With God's love, kindness is a frame of mind. It is an attitude and a manner in which you treat all people because of the value you have for them. It is the "package" that holds all expressions of love.

> A HEART NOT GIVING AND RECEIVING GENUINE LOVE WILL EITHER DIE FROM SORROW AND EMPTINESS OR FILL ITS VOID WITH SOME TYPE OF ADDICTION.

Love does not envy. It is not jealous or possessive. It does not seek to control. It gives room for freedom of expression apart from self. In toxic love, jealousy is offered as proof of love. "I love you so much I just can't stand to see you talking to someone else." What this really means is, "I don't want you to have any friends, I don't want you to have any fulfillment, apart from me." I envy your involvement with others. I fear you might realize that you could be happy without me! My security is not in the fact that you are receiving true love from me; it is that you are not allowed to experience anything good from anyone else. I can't allow you to have satisfaction apart from me.

Love does not boast. In other words, it is not obsessed with drawing attention to self by bragging or exaggerating about self and personal accomplishments. Braggarts build a false sense of security through vain deceit. They have an extreme overestimation of self. They try to convince others of how great they are as a way to earn the desired response. They are very anxious to impress. A braggart needs for you to see him as Mr. Wonderful!

The love of God is not proud. The proud person is an unteachable fool who delights in airing his (or her) own opinions. He can't admit that he needs to be taught. To do so would be tantamount to admitting weakness. And since, in his mind, people will only love and respect him when he is right, he can't admit to being wrong. The proud person is always surrounded by strife and conflict. *"By pride comes nothing but strife, but with the well-advised is wisdom"* (Proverbs 13:10).

> WITH GOD'S LOVE, KINDNESS IS A FRAME OF MIND.

The proud person is driven by the need to be right. Really, he doesn't need to be right as much as he needs for everyone else to perceive him as being right. Many of the conflicts in his life are brought about by his need to prove himself right.

The love of God is not rude. It has good manners. It is able to show proper respect. The need to dominate is always rude. A dominator has no real value for the other person, his or her feelings or his or her boundaries. A dominating person seeks to be understood with little desire to understand others. Regardless of how cordial and diplomatic he (or she) may be in the pursuit of his quest, in the end the other person's feelings don't matter. When we walk in the love of God, we have a value for good manners. We consider how our words and action will affect the other person. We are interested in protecting the feelings and worth of other people. Our style of communication and our treatment of others always reflects worth and value for them as people.

One of the greatest aspects of God's love working in our life is that it is not self-seeking. Self-centeredness is always at the heart of every sinful, negative, destructive action. True love does not use others for personal gratification. Instead, it seeks to give of self for the benefit of others. The self-centered individual has one primary question about all of his or her effort: "What do I get out of this?" This is always his or her personal and often secret motive. The self-seeking person is always working an agenda.

God's love is not easily angered. It is not explosive. It doesn't take things too personally. The codependent, on the other hand, is always angered when things are out of his (or her) control. When people do not respond the way he wants them to, when he is threatened or embarrassed, he becomes explosive. You find that you must always guard your words and actions when he is around. You feel like you are "walking on eggshells." When everything is about you, there is a lot that can make you angry!

> TRUE LOVE DOES NOT USE OTHERS FOR PERSONAL GRATIFICATION.

"I'm sorry I blew up on you like that" or "I didn't mean to hurt you; I just love you so much I get a little crazy sometimes"…the codependent justifies his extreme, unacceptable behavior as some expression of extreme, precious love that is so great, it just sometimes loses control. The passive codependent tries to believe it is love. "Sure he gets mad and beats me up sometimes, or sure he embarrasses me in public, but he loves me so much and I do such stupid things."

God's love keeps no record of wrongs. It does not dwell on past hurts nor does it use the past as a way to manipulate. Love doesn't use past failures as a way to create guilt. It is anxious to forgive and move on. Love always operates in the now! Because the codependent views himself as a victim, he is ever aware of past hurts. There seems to be no willingness to leave the past behind.

God's love does not rejoice in evil. It does not find satisfaction when others are found to be wrong. It does not use the faults of others as a way to justify self. The codependent often delights in seeing the faults of others. He (or she) seems to look for the dirt. This is a pathway to empowerment over the one found in fault. His fault justifies my wrong actions.

Instead of looking for fault, true love rejoices with the truth. True love is always happy when others find and live in the truth. It delights when others come into a healthy trust for God. *Love protects*. This doesn't happen in an unhealthy, overprotective manner. There is a difference between protecting and defending. Love protects not only with encouragement and acceptance, but also with correction when necessary. Love doesn't try to isolate people from the pain they create for themselves; it simply accepts people while they are in those situations. Love realizes that people must face the consequences of their actions, otherwise they will never grow and become responsible. But love also realizes that people's self-worth needs to be protected, even when they must be confronted. Therefore, love doesn't attack the individual; it merely addresses the actions of the individual. Love always protects the other person's sense of dignity and worth!

> LOVE ALWAYS PROTECTS THE OTHER PERSON'S SENSE OF DIGNITY AND WORTH!

Love always trusts. Many think this is a naive, blind trust, but this is not the case. Love desires to trust. It looks for the best in others, but it yields to the biblical admonition that says, *"A righteous man is cautious in friendships"* (Proverbs 12:26a NIV). Some people who are afraid of love think it will make them vulnerable to manipulation. They think that love is being a doormat. Much to the contrary, it takes great strength to walk in love. A person who loves never allows another to define love for him. I will not love you the way you say love is; I will love you the way God says love is.

Love is given; trust is earned. We can only trust a person to the degree that we know him or her and his or her track record. If the person is not worthy of trust, it should not be given. Yet love always allows one to have the opportunity to establish a new track record. Love that is given to trust is not given to suspicion!

Love always hopes. Hope is the expectation of good. When we love someone, we never lose hope of what God can do in his or her life. People tend to live up to our expectations. To some degree our expectations can play a role in forging their future. If we expect the worst, we treat them accordingly. Our treatment of them can bring out the worst. It becomes a self-fulfilling prophecy. When we have hope, we treat people differently. After all, our hope is not in them; our hope is in God who, when given the opportunity, can work mightily in anyone's life.

Love never fails. Many things will fail to work, but the one thing that will never fail or cease to be effective is love. If anything has the potential to affect a person's life, love does. People who will not respond to miraculous gifts like tongues and prophecy will still respond to love. When we can't find the knowledge to answer their questions and meet their needs, love can still work. Love can affect a person beyond the realm of knowledge. Knowledge answers questions and sometimes makes the person feel belittled for not knowing. Love makes a person feel special regardless of what he knows. Long after people have forgotten what we have told them, they will remember how we made them feel.

Because love never ceases to be effective, it is the one place where we should put our hope and our efforts. Love can do what control cannot do. Love can do what no other force can do. The person who walks in love realizes that he or she does not want what comes by force or control. It isn't real. If *agape* isn't enough to draw and bond the other person to you, there isn't enough!

These expressions of love come from value for other people. Because they are precious to us, because we hold them in high regard, this is the way we communicate and express ourselves. But more than anything else, we share this kind of love because of who we are. Agape can only come from a heart that is experiencing agape. We cannot give what we do not have. As we experience the love of God, we become capable of giving the love of God. As we experience this quality of love from God, it becomes our nature to express this love to others!

Endnote

1. Dr. James B. Richards, *The Prayer Organizer* (Huntsville, AL: Impact Ministries, n.d.).

10

LOVE ON DIFFERENT LEVELS

The world around us and its current effect on our life is basically a reflection of the beliefs and attitudes that drive our reactions. Most of our expressions to others are not deliberate choices made with intention. They are impulsive responses! More often than not these reactions not only fail to produce a desirable response, but they also provoke the complete opposite of what we desire. These destructive exchanges are usually subconscious reactions based on beliefs that were forged at a very early age. They were probably forged out of our attempts at emotional survival when we were children.

We had no choice what kind of family we would be born into. We didn't have a choice about our siblings. No one asked us what school we would go to. It was unfortunate that we sat next to the most sarcastic, cruel, hurtful boy in school. There are things about our appearance that may be less than desirable. There are so many things in the formative part of our life about which we had no choice. We can, however, choose how we will relate to and communicate with the people and circumstances in our world today. This is one arena wherein we do have choice!

Today, I can choose how I will relate to my past and my present, all of which will determine my future. I can decide if I want to suffer or move past the pain. I have the freedom of response. I can respond to the things over which I had no control in a way that keeps my present life out of control. Or, I can take control of my responses and have the life I choose instead of the one imposed on me.

Taking Self-Control

My world is a reactionary world; it reacts to me. Just as I have spent most of my life unconsciously reacting, so is everyone else. Every minute of every day I stimulate reactions in the people around me, which means I am in control of my life. Controlling my reactions is controlling my life. People's reaction to me is like a garden I have planted. If I don't like what's growing in the garden of my life, I should consider planting different seeds. The codependent, however, doesn't want to be in control of his (or her) own life. Instead, he wants to be in control of yours. The codependent puts forth every manner of vain effort to control others while putting forth little effort in controlling himself. Instead of controlling others, we should consider what kind of reactions our behavior and communication will provoke! Begin making conscious choices about how you intend to communicate, thereby increasing the likelihood of a better outcome.

> CONTROLLING MY REACTIONS IS CONTROLLING MY LIFE.

Proverbs 25:28 in the New International Version says, *"Like a city whose walls are broken down is a man who lacks self-control."* In those days, a city without walls didn't stand a chance against being destroyed by invasion. Likewise, pain and destruction are imminent for the person who refuses to exercise self-control. Self-control is not something you have or do not have. Self-control is something you choose. It is a fruit of the Spirit, and when you commit your life to love, the power for self-control grows. But it all starts with a choice.

Just as others react to us, we react to them. Just as we believe their reaction is the source of our problems, they believe our reaction to them are the real problem. Everyone is blaming others but no one is taking control over the one and only thing we can control: ourselves! Our foolish reactions to one another keep us on a course of devastation and pain. Our pain grows exponentially with every reactionary response. But what we fail to accept is that we are the creators of our pain!

The codependent didn't create the pain and suffering that came to him (or her) as a child. He did not create pain in those areas over which he had no control. But today he is creating his pain because he refuses to control the one area that he can control: himself. Today I can choose how to react to the pain of the past. I can end the pain and its relentless control of my life.

Codependent Christians are always focused on how everyone else should treat them. *You* should walk in love; *you* should be kind; *you* should understand my unique problems; you, you, you. The moment you ask, "Well, what about *you?*" Their typical response is, "You're judging me! You're violating my boundaries, you're in my space, you're trying to control me." Our insistence that we will only become responsible when the other party becomes responsible is emotional suicide.

Like it or not, fair or unfair, we cannot expect the people around us to be perfect. We can't even expect them to be who we think they should be. We don't even have the right to demand that they act godly any more then they can demand it of us. They have hurts, pains and a past just like we do. What we can certainly expect is that the people around us will react to our actions. If we sow bad seed, we'll reap a bad crop.

> OUR INSISTENCE THAT WE WILL ONLY BECOME RESPONSIBLE WHEN THE OTHER PARTY BECOMES RESPONSIBLE IS EMOTIONAL SUICIDE.

What We Sow, We Reap

One of the most misquoted passages in the Bible is Luke 6:38: *"Give, and it will be given to you: good measure, pressed down, shaken together, and running over will be put into your bosom. For with the same measure that you use, it will be measured back to you."* This passage has little if anything to do with money. When taken in context, it is talking about the way we treat people. If you give judgment, you'll reap ten times as much judgment. If you give condemnation, you'll reap ten times as much condemnation; but if you sow mercy, kindness and peace, you will reap that as well.

Jesus very poignantly brought this into context in verses 41-42 where He said, *"And why do you look at the speck in your brother's eye, but do not perceive the plank in your own eye? Or how can you say to your brother, 'Brother, let me remove the speck that is in your eye,' when you yourself do not see the plank that is in your own eye? Hypocrite! First remove the plank from your own eye, and then you will see clearly to remove the speck that is in your brother's eye."* Our tendency is to want to fix others when we are not in fact seeing clearly ourselves. The plank that is in our eye causes us to gouge our brother's eye while trying to remove the speck of sawdust. But we insist the problem is not the plank in our eye—it is the sawdust in our brother's eye!

A lady came to me lonely and struggling because she had no real friends. I attempted to tactfully share some helpful insights, but she interrupted and said, "You could not possibly understand my problem because you always have friends." Attempting to be patient I encouraged her to invite people into her home, to take the initiative. She argued, "I don't have the money to feed people like you do. I can't have people into my home. I can't, I can't, I can't."

I explained, "Many times Brenda and I will feed people when we don't have any food left for ourselves." She continued that she had occasionally invited others into her home, but they didn't repay the kindness. I explained, "We have people in our home to help them, not buy their friendship. Those who are emotionally capable of responding sometimes become our friends. But we are reaping what we are sowing." She continued to justify and defend her position and I finally read this scripture and explained, "You are reaping what you are sowing. You are giving to get, so that is the kind of people you attract. You give with expectations, and the magnitude of your pain is the degree your expectations are not met!" Like the rich young ruler who came to Jesus, she went away very sad. The young man was not willing to give up his possessions; she was not willing to give up her offenses.

Jesus warned that it would be this way. A warped Christian community has interpreted the passages about sowing and reaping into something God does in response to what you do. The implication of the context is not that God will do these things to you but that men will heap these things unto your bosom. This is the reaction of people to you. What you do and why you do it affects how people respond to you.

Reactions are real anomalies. How is it possible that I could do the same kindness that another person does and the reaction be so different? There are so many things communicated by nonverbal behavior. So we know on a physical level we are communicating things that say much more than our actual words or behavior. But the more we understand about the heart, the more we understand that our heart sends signals to the world around us with every beat. For me that gets down to one heart wave per second that is encoded with everything about me, who I am and my true intentions. It is not enough that we do the "right thing"; we must do it from a heart governed by healthy motives!

To Give Love, We Must Experience Love

We have already discussed the definition and behavior of *agape*. *Agape* is not self-generated. It is something you cannot give if you are not experiencing it! *Agape* is how we relate to the world as a consequence of what we experience from God. In a sense it is our response and expression to what we believe and experience about God. The ability to walk in kindness, patience and the other qualities of First Corinthians 13 is the result of what is happening between us and God. When we believe and accept the unconditional love of God, it becomes very difficult to stay bitter and angry. First John 4:8 explains, *"He who does not love does not know God, for God is love."* The word know comes from the concept of interaction and experiential knowledge. In other words, the one who is not walking in love is simply not experiencing love at the moment.

> WHAT YOU DO AND WHY YOU DO IT AFFECTS HOW PEOPLE RESPOND TO YOU.

There is an even bigger concept of this Greek word we translate as "know" in relation to God! One of my favorite tools for language research emphasizes "understanding rather than sensory perception...It is a perception of things as they are, not an opinion about them."[1] In other words, if we simply believe in the negative concepts of God handed down to us by religion, *agape* will not and cannot be the fruit.

We must see Him as He is, especially as He expressed His unconditional love through the death, burial and resurrection of the Lord Jesus.

When we believe the love of God, we can know (experience) the love of God. When we experience the love of God, the fruit, i.e., that which grows organically and effortlessly, will be to love others with the quality of love we are experiencing. We are experiencing that upon which we place our focus. By continually making ourselves aware of past hurts, we experience them anew! As that experience grows in our emotions, we respond to others from what we are currently experiencing. If we were to make ourselves aware of the love of God, focus our attention on His love, then that would become the emotional resource from which we would respond to others. Whatever we choose to hold in our thoughts is what we choose to experience. What we experience is what determines the way we relate to the world around us. Romans 8 explains this as the choice between a spiritual mind and a carnal mind.

> WHATEVER WE CHOOSE TO HOLD IN OUR THOUGHTS IS WHAT WE CHOOSE TO EXPERIENCE.

Brotherly love, *phileo*, is a response to the way someone treats you. When we relate to others with the agape love of God, they are more likely to respond to us in brotherly love. We reap what we sow. There will be some who are so dysfunctional that they cannot respond properly. The codependent, who is not experiencing God's love, is negatively reactionary to those who are incapable of giving back. But the person who has been made whole through the love of God realizes that other people respond based on who they are and what they are currently experiencing, not on who he or she is! But, as a whole, we will reap the love that we are sowing. It will come back in *phileo*, i.e., friendship or brotherly love!

In our marriages, we want to experience a degree of *eros*, erotic love. We want to have a passionate relationship with our mate. We want the affection and excitement that we had in the beginning. We fail to realize, however, that if we treated one another the way we did in the beginning, we would still have *eros*. That passion was a response to the way we were treating one another at that time.

When we found our mate, we treated them as a pearl of great price. They were precious (*agape*) and it showed in the way we treated them. Because the love we expressed for them was conditional, they would only remain precious and valuable as long as they consistently did those things we valued. This is conditional love. Conditional love sends a message that says, "I do not value you as a person. I simply value what you do for me." When they let us down or fail to meet our expectations, instead of reinforcing our value for them, we usually express our lack of value. Self-centeredness raises its ugly head and reveals the true motives of our heart. Sometimes it's not even because they disappoint us; we just say in our hearts, "The chase is over, she's mine, now I can relax." Regardless of the reason, they are no longer treated like a pearl of great price. Then we reap what we sow.

What Will You Choose?

All of life is a series of choices that stimulate people around us in a positive or negative fashion. If I treat people well just for the desired result, that will be little more than manipulation, which will soon be exposed and despised. It will be something I stop when I don't get what I want. Often, through our own warped upbringing, we think that if we express lesser value for others when they are failing it will motivate them to act better. But the Scripture teaches just the opposite. *"Every seed bears after its own kind. Harsh words stir up wrath."* If they are acting in a less than desirable manner, it is because in their hearts they are not experiencing the value God has for them. These are the times we should reinforce our value for them. We should remind them of their strengths and all we appreciate about them. We should prove that our love is not conditional. Just like the goodness of God draws people to repentance, our goodness can also facilitate change of heart.

In the face of rejection or hurt, we must turn to the one source of unconditional unwavering love…our heavenly Father. As we focus on, think about, ponder and meditate on the love of God, we will begin to experience that love anew! Then, in the face of what could be devastating pain, we will have mercy and compassion. We will pour out the sweet wine we ourselves are drinking! When the people around us experience the love of God through us, they will be more likely to respond in a loving manner. When we can give our spouse *agape* love, it creates *phileo*, or friendship love, and friendship loves then blossoms into *eros*.

Love can be experienced on all these different levels, but it must start with a choice to focus on and experience God's perfect love. As we experience that love, it matters little how those around us respond. As a whole, however, they will respond with all the different levels of love.

Therefore, the world around me is reacting to the way I relate to it. I can sow love, kindness and patience, or I can sow control, manipulation and selfishness. Whatever I give, I can be sure the world will give it back to me… *"pressed down, shaken together, and running over."*

Endnote

1. *Theological Dictionary of the New Testament*, abridged edition (Grand Rapids, MI: William B. Eerdmans Publishing Company, 1985).

DESTRUCTIVE ASSOCIATIONS

What would ever make people expose themselves to painful situations over and over? How could someone allow him or herself to be humiliated and yet feel the need to stay? Why do so many feel the need to cling to a destructive relationship? Logic would seem to say, "Anyone can see what's happening here. You need to make better choices." If logic were the driving force, this would be an easy fix. But it's not logic that keeps us in this painful cycle. It's beliefs...and specifically beliefs about ourselves!

We know God created every person to be a social, emotional, relationship-oriented being. We know that people's physical and mental health thrives in a healthy, loving environment. We know that everyone has, at the seat of his or her being, the need to be loved and accepted. We know that every desire man has comes from a God-given root, however perverted and twisted that desire may have become. However, all of those factors are molded to our beliefs. We didn't choose most of our beliefs and, sadly, we are resistant to the biblical process for changing beliefs.

The Pattern of Our Belief

Our distorted concepts of love and our negative sense of self are the major factors in the codependent cycle. We all want to be loved. The problem is often found in our beliefs about love and what we believe we deserve. Because we have not accepted God's definition of love, we have, by default, accepted definitions imposed upon us by others. The manner in which we have experienced love has become our definition of love! We have established certain psychological associations with love. However dysfunctional our concept of love, that along with our self-worth will play the primary role in determining how dysfunctional we will become in our attempts to acquire love.

> OUR DISTORTED CONCEPTS OF LOVE AND OUR NEGATIVE SENSE OF SELF ARE THE MAJOR FACTORS IN THE CODEPENDENT CYCLE.

For example, if a child grows up in a physically abusive home, she may accept a distorted concept of love. Let's say her father beats her, then in his need for justification, convinces her that it is an act of love. Now she considers beating to be a normal expression of love. There is now an association between being beaten and being loved. She may even go as far to think that if a man loves her he must beat her. Her need to be loved will draw her into and cause her to remain in an abusive situation. In her mind, it is the only way to feel loved. In extreme cases, she may agitate physical abuse, since it is part of her association of love!

Then there is modeling. That which is modeled to us by our parents becomes the standard, what we accept as normal. The way our parents relate is the way we think everyone relates. We expect our relationships to be like theirs. If our father is a dominator, the male child will likely follow that pattern. If our mother is passive, the female child is prone to duplicate that dysfunction.

Through associations we develop a "this is that" paradigm. When we think of love, we think of "that." In her book, *Emotional Alchemy*,[1] Tara Bennett-Coleman presents the idea of schemas. The word *schema* is the root of the word *schematic*. A schematic shows the pattern that electricity follows in any given device. The moment we turn on the switch, the electricity will always follow the same pattern. That's exactly what happens in associations. The moment I hear, smell, feel or think anything about a given topic, the switch is turned on. My thoughts, feelings and behavior then run a pattern that follows all the beliefs, thoughts and feelings I associate with that situation.

When an association is made, I do not think or feel based on the current situation as much as I do on everything I believe about it based on past experiences. Before the conscious mind can direct my thoughts, feelings, behaviors and choices, my other-than-conscious mind is moving me down paths I may not consciously desire. It is as if I am being swept downstream by a strong current without the strength to correct or choose my course! How you and I developed our schemas is not the major concern. For the codependent, that simply gives him or her someone to blame. Knowing we have those schemas and finding the empowerment to change them is the main issue!

> UNTIL WE HAVE ESTABLISHED OUR HEARTS IN GOD'S LOVE, WE WILL FOLLOW THE PATTERN FOR LOVE THAT WAS IMPOSED UPON US.

Love is the deepest human need. Until we have established our hearts in God's love, we will follow the pattern for love that was imposed upon us. The legitimate need for love coupled with our destructive associations can potentially expose us to every imaginable abuse. If, however, we accept God's definition of love, it enlightens us to know the difference between real love and toxic love. We can then make a rational decision to reject any abusive treatment and pursue real love. But that is only the starting place. Dealing with the beliefs of our heart is the ultimate key.

Explaining Aberrant Behavior

Long before we have the mental and emotional maturity to make rational choices, we had someone program our minds that love is expressed a particular way. At a subconscious level, far below the ability to reason, a destructive association is established. It is not rational. It makes no sense at all. It is painful, but it is what we believe to be the pathway to love. In order to have love, the thing we desire the most, we must endure this, the thing we hate the most! Therefore, we find ourselves locked into destructive patterns in the pursuit of love, the ultimate need.

The same thing can happen with sexual situations. It has long been my observation that many sexually abused children become very promiscuous. While there are many factors involved in this scenario, the concept of love plays a major role. I have seen women and men do things that bring them so much pain and shame that they become suicidal. As soon as they "pulled themselves together," they would be right back into the same destructive behavior. Why? A destructive association. They are looking for love but destroying themselves in the process!

> ANY INFORMATION RECEIVED DURING TIMES OF STRONG EMOTION CREATES AN ASSOCIATION.

Let's say someone is sexually molested as a child. At a time of great emotion, the offender tells her it is because he loves her. Any information received during times of strong emotion creates an association. Or as the Bible says, it is written *"upon the table of thine heart."* Once something is written on our heart, it becomes second nature. It becomes a part of our subconscious beliefs. It directs our decisions without conscious thought.

Even though promiscuity is a degrading, shameful experience, it is the "believed" pathway to being loved. She is convinced that sex is what will make her lovable. Until she breaks that destructive association, she will continue to degrade herself with the thing she hates, searching for the thing she needs...love.

Some research says that most of our basic beliefs are established by the time we are five years old. We have associations, beliefs and concepts that were established at such an early age, we don't know where they came from, yet they are driving our life today. Think of it—most of our destructive behavior is because we are using the rationale of a three-year-old. These beliefs were developed when we were children. Most of our core beliefs were established at such an early age, we think we were born with them. We think, "This is who I am."

The Importance of Self-worth

The world, especially the church world, has failed to grasp the human need and the biblical agenda for positive, healthy love (*agape*). We all need to know we are loved. That is the basis for our self-worth. The worth we place on ourselves is directly proportional to the worth we perceive that others have for us. Those who do not find this worth from God will look to people. Self-worth then determines the quality of our every decision.

A healthy self-worth is our only protection against destructive associations. Our behavior will not consistently sink below our sense of self. Even when we have a dysfunctional concept of love, if we feel good about ourselves, i.e., we value ourselves, and we know we are precious to God, then we cannot allow others to violate our sense of self. It is our sense of self-worth that determines our boundaries!

> A HEALTHY SELF-WORTH IS OUR ONLY PROTECTION AGAINST DESTRUCTIVE ASSOCIATIONS.

People with low self-worth do not feel worthy of love. They do not feel valuable or precious. They may not believe they can be loved. As a child, I spent most of my days with my grandmother while my mother worked. My grandmother had deep emotional problems. They were not obvious to most people. They only became obvious behind closed doors. When other adults were not present, she transformed into a manipulative sociopath.

Through manipulative calculation, my grandmother convinced me that I was unlovable. Most of my life that's what I believed. As a result I would destroy every relationship. As soon as the relationship began to look like love, I would sabotage it. If I was unlovable, then the moment I began to feel loved, I could no longer function. I was operating on a belief established in my heart before I was five years old. I didn't realize where it came from. I never even understood why I did the things I did until later in life.

This meant that every relationship ended in pain. Yet, my need to be loved drove me to keep getting into relationships. My need to be loved was stronger than my dread of the pain, so I repeated the cycle for years. God created us to live enjoyable lives of pleasure and fulfillment. Therefore, our desire for pleasure is stronger than our fear of pain. It is the need for a fulfilling life that drives us to repeat the cycle of pain. We will face pain in the hopes of meeting our deepest needs.

We all want to be loved and accepted. God wired that into our emotional makeup. But He intended for us to look to Him to find that perfect love. In so doing, we would have complete emotional stability and peace. Believing and experiencing the great worth He has for us would then translate into an incredible sense of self-worth.

What the Church Did

Instead of the church proclaiming the love of God, it has traditionally proclaimed the wrath of God. Because we do not believe that the goodness of God brings us to repentance, we have determined good and evil for ourselves. We try to bring people to God through fear instead of through love. We try to manipulate instead of compel. We do not preach the gospel (good news) of Jesus delivering us from the wrath of God; instead, we preach bad news.

> WE PUSH PEOPLE AWAY FROM GOD BECAUSE WE DO NOT BELIEVE OR PROCLAIM THE LOVE OF GOD.

Think of it! We tell people that if they don't get saved, God hates them and has no value for them. Then when they do get saved, we tell them that if they don't live right, God still has no value for them. This means people have to look somewhere else to find the love that God desires to give them. We push people away from God because we do not believe or proclaim the love of God.

Yet, the need still exists—the need to experience perfect, unwavering love. We have to have it from some source. Our beliefs determine what that source will look like; our self-worth determines the degree of destruction we will allow ourselves to experience. The problem is, there is no one on this earth who can meet that need. Yet, our only source for perfect love has been so slandered that we also have destructive associations with God.

When bad things happen, because of what we have been told, we say, "God did it," or "God allowed it." When good things happen, we say it is luck. If a tornado destroyed five houses in a row and skipped one, we would say the five destroyed was an act of God, but "Man, wasn't that sixth guy lucky." A dread has been put in the hearts of children about God. When they are grown, they still have this infantile belief that God is the source of pain and rejection.

One of the most difficult tasks I face as a minister is getting grown people to believe God is a good. They will read the New Testament. They intellectually acknowledge that Jesus represented God, yet there is still a mentality of a good Jesus and a bad God. This destructive association will drive a person away from the only source of complete love and acceptance to a lifetime of pain and rejection.

Negative, destructive associations must be identified and eradicated. We must write the truth about God on our hearts. We must establish our hearts on the biblical concepts of love.[2] The Bible teaches that all of our life is the product of the beliefs of the heart. Beliefs of the heart are not just about the world around us. Beliefs of the heart reflect what we believe about us in the world. By changing our sense of who we are, our boundaries change to align with our sense of self!

Changing beliefs of the heart will not happen automatically or accidentally. We must invest in our beliefs just like we invest in our retirement. Reading, praying and meditating on the Word of God have to be more than ritual. They must be the deliberate process whereby we renew our mind and heal our heart. By using effective heart tools,[3] old associations can be replaced. Your every thought of God, life and love can lead you to something positive and rewarding.

Endnotes

1. Tara Bennett-Coleman, *Emotional Alchemy: How the Mind Can Heal the Heart* (New York: Harmony Books, 2001).
2. Dr. James B. Richards, Heart Physics®, www.heartphysics.com.
3. Ibid.

12

VICTIM'S MENTALITY

At the seat of all abuse issues you will find a person who is inept in personal relationship skills and incapable of expressing negative feelings in a productive manner. His or her emotional perceptions create interpersonal conflicts that make it impossible for him or her to have healthy relationships. The resulting vacuum can lead to all types of dysfunction and addiction. As is said in treatment circles, "Codependency is the mother of all addictions." No matter what type of addiction you face, the root cause is codependency and the root of codependency is the attempt to meet needs outside of you that only God can meet in your heart!

We attempt to fill our God-given interdependent need for meaningful relationships with all manner of codependent substitutes. The need for love and acceptance dominates our deepest needs. The need for meaningful socialization drives us. But faulty beliefs give rise to destructive attitudes, which lead to behaviors that make it nearly impossible to have good relations. So the void grows! We attempt to fill the void with every imaginable substitute, thus allowing for some type of addiction. Sex, drugs, power, eating and violence are just a few of the many ways we try to fill the void!

Playing the Role of Victim

Instead of realizing how his (or her) behavior is negatively affecting the relationship, the codependent assumes the role of the victim. He often feels that the entire world is against him. The victim's response to the world can be vast. It can include feelings of helplessness that promote passive behavior or it can invoke a reaction of aggression and violence. Either way the behavior is falsely justified because he believes himself to be a victim.

> SEX, DRUGS, POWER, EATING AND VIOLENCE ARE JUST A FEW OF THE MANY WAYS WE TRY TO FILL THE VOID!

People with a victim's attitude feel that others unfairly inflict pain upon them. They never see the part that their choices play in the scenario. It almost seems as if the world had a secret meeting and did not invite them. In this meeting, everyone agreed to make them miserable. Regardless of which way the victim's mentality "tilts," it basically concludes that they are in no way responsible for how others react to them. Nor do people with a victim mentality feel they can do anything about it.

The Bible says, *"Fools' words get them into constant quarrels; they are asking for a beating"* (Proverbs 18:6 NLT). In other words, the way one talks creates contention, which leads to pain or aggressive reaction. The victim only focuses on what others are doing to hurt him (or her). The person cannot allow himself to focus on what he is doing to create these types of responses. To do so would force the person to face his own issues, something his low self-worth cannot afford. The need to be right produces a false sense of being in control. That deception of control is the only sense of security the victim has.

People in prison are outraged at how unfair the system is treating them. They consider themselves to be victims of the system. Yet, they seldom consider that they took someone's life or they stole or they broke laws that put them in the prison. The codependent victim focuses all of his attention on others with no consideration for his personal actions.

The Government Cannot Fix It

Our society has nourished the codependent victim's mentality by focusing the blame for unacceptable behavior on society. Over the past 50 years there has been a tendency toward the socialist idea that society is to blame for the actions of the individual. This type of thinking leads us to the delusional concept of a social salvation instead of individual salvation. We attempt to change all of society instead of making the individual responsible for his or her actions. Ronald Reagan said, "We must reject the idea that every time a law's broken, society is guilty rather than the lawbreaker. It is time to restore the American precept that each individual is accountable for his actions."[1] The false concept of social salvation feeds the victim's mentality by reinforcing the idea that everyone else is to blame.

> WE HAVE A TENDENCY TOWARD THE SOCIALIST IDEA THAT SOCIETY IS TO BLAME FOR THE ACTIONS OF THE INDIVIDUAL.

Many times, I counsel people who have gone through years of therapy, spent tens of thousands of dollars, and all they have done is determined who they would blame for their problems. The victim always has someone to blame. Placing blame gives a false sense of justification for our unacceptable behavior. As long as I have someone to blame, I'm okay! Right? No! You're not okay, you still have no friends, no meaningful relationships and no self-worth. Finding someone to blame has never healed one emotional pain, but it has been known to keep the pain alive for a lifetime. Learning how to live responsibly in society is the only thing that will make your world a fit place to live.

I must realize that my dysfunctional behavior creates reactions in others. I can idealistically talk about how they should love me, accept me and respond to me, but that is mere idealism. If I want friends, I must learn to be a friend (Proverbs 18:24). People respond negatively to my inappropriate behavior, just like I respond negatively to theirs. I want them to overlook and justify my dysfunction, but I will not overlook theirs. God created me to be a social being; I must learn to function as one.

The government cannot pass laws that make others relate to me properly, nor should I expect that. The preacher can't make the church love me. No one else can create the kind of responses that I desire from others. I alone possess the power to initiate positive responses. I will live in the world that I create by my words and actions and I must be happy with it. It's all I'll ever have. If I do not like what is growing in the garden of my life, maybe I should consider planting different seeds.

Proverbs 18:20-21 in the Amplified Bible says it this way: *"A man's [moral] self shall be filled with the fruit of his mouth; and with the consequences of his words he must be satisfied [whether good or evil]. Death and life are in the power of the tongue, and they who indulge it shall eat the fruit of it [for death or life]."* On the street they say, "You better make those words sweet when they come out, because you'll eventually have to eat them."

The wisdom of Proverbs continues with this incredible advice: *"A fool's mouth is his destruction, and his lips are the snare of his soul"* (Proverbs 18:7). The codependent creates strife and destruction with words and actions. He (or she) enters into the realm of sowing and reaping. Sometimes he actually tries to be extreme. Extreme behavior can be a way to test the boundaries. Possibly it will force others into giving him the unconditional love that only God can give. It is as if he wants the world to prove to him that he is loved. Yet, when he has to experience the negative consequences of his actions, he feels that he is being victimized.

It's the Law of Sowing and Reaping

There is a law of sowing and reaping that continues every day, whether we believe it or not. We reap the results of our actions daily. The way people treat us today is a product of how we treated them yesterday. (The exception is when we are in relationship with an abusive person. The abuser's treatment of us is the overflow of his or her codependent issues. Our willingness to remain in that relationship is an issue of our lack of boundaries.) The religious teaching concerning sowing and reaping has led us to believe that when we do something, it creates a reaction from God. So we believe the pain in our life is some reaction from an angry God. Not true! God loves us unconditionally, yet we still must live with the consequences of our actions. Reaping is not about God; it is about people. God can no more force people to be kind to you than He can force you to be responsible with your behavior.

Sowing and reaping happens on the horizontal plane, not the vertical. God is always good to me, but the people I hurt and insult are not. They react to my unacceptable behavior. They react to my lack of tact. They react to my harsh words. They do things that hurt me in response to my actions. But that does not make me a victim. It makes me the sower!

I once had a preacher friend who made bizarre statements from the pulpit. His statements would solicit negative reaction from the people. He felt that there was some great value in shocking people. But when people would respond to him negatively, he felt victimized. He felt people were doing him wrong. He was quick to point out how unfair others were to him, but he never accepted his part in creating the problem. More than once I tried to warn him, "If you're going to take that approach to ministry, you'll have to live with the consequences." We all have some personal agenda driving our unacceptable behavior, but the outcome is never what we hope!

> GOD IS ALWAYS GOOD TO US, BUT THE PEOPLE WE HURT AND INSULT ARE NOT.

It's like a girl who attended my church. She would come to church with her hair dyed green and wearing strange clothes. Sometimes she would have on no shoes and two very different colors of socks. She would complain that she didn't feel close to anyone. She did not want to accept that just as she had the freedom to dress how she desired, they had the freedom to respond how they desired. When you violate culture or what is socially acceptable—right or wrong—you had better be ready to live with the response.

The codependent is quick to point out how everyone else should have the love of God, with no consideration that he or she is not walking in love. I have often had people complain that they had no friends. They bemoaned that no one loved them. "If these people really were Christians, they would treat me right." More than once, all I could say is, "You're not a very friendly person. No one is obligated to be your friend. If you want friends, you've got to change."

Count the Cost

Our country is based on the godly principles of equal opportunity. But equal opportunity does not equate equal outcome. We have the opportunity to have friends, work and enjoy a good life. How we manage that opportunity determines the outcome. The progressive doctrines that have crept into political and even Christian thinking suggest that we should guarantee everyone the same outcome. Even God does not promise you a controlled outcome. He gives us the teaching from His Word and He gives us the grace (strength) to apply that wisdom. We then have a somewhat predictable outcome. But the choice to be wise or to be a fool is ours! A fool, by the way, is not someone who is stupid. A fool is someone who will not learn from instruction!

> EQUAL OPPORTUNITY DOES NOT EQUATE EQUAL OUTCOME.

I had a young man in my church who had come out of a homosexual background. He did very well for a while. Later, he began to dress effeminately and wear his hair in an effeminate way. He came to me complaining that people thought he was still gay. He also complained that gay men were "hitting on him." All I could say was, "You're dressing like you're gay; you're acting like you're gay. If you don't want society to think you're gay, you must make the changes that are necessary." He complained, "Well, they have no right to think I'm gay just because of the way I dress!" And I responded, "You're right, but you have no right to expect them to think anything other than what you show them."

I am very compassionate for homosexuals who desire a different lifestyle. I have had the opportunity to witness many come out of that background and find a new quality of life. I have seen a common denominator when helping people from a homosexual background: the victim's mentality. This one factor is the most common failure factor I have seen in those seeking to establish a new life. A homosexual lifestyle defies nature, it defies God and it defies society. It is a life of extreme behavior. When society doesn't respond to the homosexual the way he (or she) desires, the tendency is to feel victimized. This seems to be the attitude that is carried forward into his new life that ultimately causes his downfall.

I have seen very few ex-homosexuals fall simply because they wanted to have a homosexual lifestyle; it is usually the victim's mentality that causes them to have offense against the church. They still have a tendency in daily life to yield to the bizarre or flamboyant and feel victimized by the reactions of others. I am by no means implying that we should always conform to society. But I am saying we must accept the natural consequences when we choose to break the mold. I saw the same types of reactionary behavior with hippies back in the 1960s and '70s. The result was the same: an inability to fit into society and an irresponsible victim's reaction!

I am not saying society is right in all of its responses. I am saying, however, that we should count the cost before we act and speak. Are we really ready to accept society's reaction to our behavior? Do we really understand how it will affect us to lose the acceptance of our friends?

Proverbs presents an insight into a specific mindset. *"The slothful man saith, There is a lion without, I shall be slain in the streets"* (Proverbs 22:13 KJV). Sloth is an attitude. It is an attitude that produces laziness. But it is deeper than simple laziness. It is an attitude that discourages responsibility. The person with this attitude is paralyzed. He (or she) feels that he cannot go out and pursue life because there is some undefined, nebulous danger…out there. This can be applied to the victim. He fears he will be victimized. He feels he has no control over what will happen to him. He has no sense of responsibility.

The slothful man chooses to live an irresponsible lifestyle and blames others for the undesirable reactions. His low self-worth is the real issue. He fears there would be more pain in change than there would be in rejection. The passive victim stays in the destructive relationship afraid to venture out into the unknown. The aggressive victim attempts to force others to respond the way he wants.

The only solution for the victim is to become the person he or she really wants to be. Those who leave you for being true to yourself need to leave. As someone has said, it is better to be rejected for being yourself than to be accepted for being someone else! You attract the people who support the view you hold of yourself. If you reject yourself, you will attract those who reject you. If you see yourself as a failure, you will attract those who see the same thing. As you begin to embrace the "you" you truly desire to be, the real you "in Christ," you will attract those who will love and accept the "new you."

In closing I must give a word of warning. There is a paradox in accepting responsibility for how we provoke others. Those who tend to blame themselves may tend to substitute personal blame for personal responsibility. Each person is responsible for his or her own actions, and in fact the way a person responds is a reflection of his or her own character. Most of the world is out of touch with their feelings and have no experience with unconditional love, so the likelihood of healthy responses is low. However, my behavior is not the only factor in how others react, but when I act responsibly I can produce the probability of a good response.

Endnotes

1. Ronald Reagan, http://www.brainyquote.com/quotes/authors/r/ronald_reagan5.html, (accessed July 18, 2011).

13

BLAME VS. RESPONSIBILITY

One of the crippling paradigms of the codependent lies in his or her inability to distinguish the difference between responsibility and blame. This perceptional problem paralyzes an individual in a place of irreconcilable conflict. It makes every trap a snare from which there is no escape. Every attempt to free one's self only causes the jaws of destruction to grip tighter. When the wrong question is asked, it always leads to a wrong answer. "How can I take responsibility without making this my fault?"

Blame points to the past. It points to the wrong. Blame determines who should be punished or penalized. Blame has absolutely no value in solving the problem. It actually becomes part of justifying the problem. The entire "blame mentality" seems to think the one who is to blame is the one who is responsible. In other words, "You broke it; you fix it." The futility of this thinking is that it leaves a person in pain waiting for someone else to take action. The people who hurt you will seldom be the people who will fix you. Waiting for them to see the error of their ways and assume responsibility is personal sabotage at its best!

Responsibility, on the other hand, determines who will solve the problem. It looks to the solution, not the offense; to the future, not the past. You can blame who you want for the problem, but that does nothing to solve the problem.

The real question is, "Who will assume responsibility to *solve* the problem?" Responsibility assumes the obligation to find the cure.

There are few cases where the one who is to blame for the damage will be the one to assume responsibility for the recovery. Waiting for someone else to resolve your pain makes you a perpetual victim. You may have been victimized, but your life does not need to be reduced to that of a victim. A victim feels helpless to do anything about the problem. But we are never helpless. We may lack the courage to take the appropriate action, but that is a choice, not a condition! Someone else may have caused my pain. I may have caused my pain. But who caused it does not matter. If I am hurting, I am the only one who can do anything about the hurt. If I surrender my responsibility, I have surrendered my choices and my power! Refusing to be responsible is a self-imposed sentence to live the rest of my life as a victim. I can only have freedom to the degree that I assume responsibility.

BLAME HAS ABSOLUTELY NO VALUE IN SOLVING THE PROBLEM.

Proverbs 18:9 in the Amplified Bible says, *"He who is loose and slack in his work is brother to him who is a destroyer and he who does not use his endeavors to heal himself is brother to him who commits suicide."* Refusal to assume responsibility and engage in my own healing is to become a conspirator in my demise. I join the team and multiply the efforts of those who hurt me! Far too often this happens because of a deceptive twist in people's concepts of responsibility and blame.

If the codependent confuses blame for the problem with the responsibility to solve the problem, his (or her) low self-esteem will not allow him to find the cure. The codependent already feels too guilty for too many things. He can't bear to lay another brick on the load of his emotional burden. One more straw may not break the camel's back, but it could break his heart! In his mind, to accept responsibility may generate greater feelings of guilt than he can bear, so he seeks to find relief by identifying a source to blame.

Keep Your Footing in Peace

Codependent people do not realize the unconditional love of God. They do not know that God can love them even if they are the source of their own problem. Not only would God continue to love them, but God also would deliver them. God would give them the strength they need to overcome and lead them into a life that is better than they deserve. But codependent people must justify themselves before God and man. They must be proven right. They cannot bear being wrong. They wrongly think God only helps people when they deserve it, i.e., when it is not their fault!

There is, of course, those who swing to the other extreme and assume blame for everything! Posturing in their victim's pose is yet another self-destructive game of avoiding true responsibility. This is nothing more than a defense mechanism to keep from dealing with problems on any serious level. After all, if everything is my fault, then it is obviously too big to solve…and besides, there is the outside chance that I may experience some sympathy if I take blame! Many times sympathy is the closest thing to love the codependent has ever felt.

The Bible says in Ephesians 6:15 that one should have *"your feet* [shod] *with the preparation of the gospel of peace."* Our feet provide our foundation, our stability. *Thayer's Lexicon* translates preparation as "a firm foundation that comes from a readiness of mind."[1] In hand-to-hand combat, it is essential that one never lose balance. One must have a readiness of mind and be able to respond to an attack that comes from any direction without losing his or her footing.

> IF I SURRENDER MY RESPONSIBILITY, I HAVE SURRENDERED MY CHOICES AND MY POWER!

In the martial arts, one is taught to move in a circular motion away from every attack in a way that not only maintains his or her balance, but also throws the opponent off balance. To do this requires a readiness of mind. One must respond instinctively and instantly. It also requires the knowledge of how to respond. The same is true emotionally. Before you make a quantum leap into misinterpretation, this type of vigilance is not the product of a tense, fearful, reactionary mindset. No! This readiness of mind is rooted in peace. Paul employs the perfect example. Spiritually this readiness of mind is a result of believing the gospel of peace.[2] Everything we know about the human mind and body shows us that the ability to respond quickly and accurately always flows from the place of peace.

When guilt, condemnation and shame hit me, I must maintain my footing in the gospel of peace.[3] My first response cannot be to blame shift. While I am looking for someone to blame, I am being destroyed. My first response should always be, "No matter what is happening, God is at peace with me through the Lord Jesus Christ. God is not doing this to me. God is not blaming me."

> BEING WRONG IS NOT A BIG ISSUE FOR THE ONE WHO IS ESTABLISHED IN PEACE.

This causes me to keep my footing, both emotionally and spiritually. Paul clearly points out that this kind of peace comes from knowing we are righteous before God through the Lord Jesus, not from whether we are right or wrong. *"Therefore, since we have been made right in God's sight by faith, we have peace with God because of what Jesus Christ our Lord has done for us"* (Romans 5:1 NLT).

Even if I am the problem, I can face it and admit it if I know that I will not lose the love and acceptance of God. Being wrong is not a big issue for the one who is established in peace. Unfortunately, religion has tried to make everything revolve around being right. In Christianity, however, everything revolves around the finished work of Jesus. The religious codependent must prove himself (or herself) right in order to maintain his footing (his standing with God); therefore, he can rarely ever work through any major problems. To do so would require owning his problems. From his perspective, being wrong would bring rejection and punishment from God. So all of his emotional energy revolves around trying to prove he is right.

If I know there is peace between me and God because of Jesus, I have the freedom to deal with getting healed and getting free. I can figure out whose fault it is later. When someone wrongs me, I don't consider myself a victim; I can do something about it. I have a God who will never leave me, never forsake me and never fail me. My highest priority when hurting is to get healed, not determine blame!

"But it's not fair. It's not! If it's not my fault, why do I have to be the one to do something about it?" Who said life was fair? The idea of life being fair is nothing more than a socialist ideology that has crept into our society and undermined responsible living! The reason I must do something about what is affecting my life is because I am the only one who can.

Wash Your Face

I once read an amusing story about a man walking down the beach. A seagull flew over and "pooped" on his nose. He became so angry at the seagull. He reasoned within himself, "That seagull did this to me, and he's going to have to come back and get this off of me!" When he returns to his group of friends, they are all repulsed. "What is that smell? Stay away from us!" they all shouted. Then they ran away from him. He became even more angry at the seagull, "Look what you've done to me," the man cried. "You come back right now and get this off of me."

When he goes home that night, he wants to be intimate with his wife. She immediately kicks him out of bed and demands that he go wash his face. He lies on the couch lonely and rejected, contemplating how the seagull was ruining his life. His friends had run away from him and his wife had rejected him, and he didn't do anything. All he could think was, "It's not my fault!"

When he goes to work the next day, people quickly go to the other side of the room to avoid him. The odor has become unbearable. The man had stopped bathing because, if he bathed, he might remove the poop from his nose—and then the seagull would have gotten away with his unfair treatment.

Finally, his boss called him in and said, "None of the clients want to do business with you. None of the coworkers can stand to be in the same room with you. Either you wash that poop off of your nose or you're fired." The man's response was, "How unfair can you get? Why are you all persecuting me? I didn't do anything. I didn't put this on my nose; I shouldn't be the one to have to wash it off."

So now he sits alone under an overpass, victimized by the world. And every day he looks out at the sky because he knows who is to blame. And one day that rotten seagull will have to come and clean up his nose.[4]

This story seems so utterly foolish, yet I have seen many marriages end in divorce around this kind of logic. "He is the one who caused the problem; I'm not going to do anything about it." Millions of people go through pain every day feeling that someone else should come and fix the pain he or she inflicted on them. The truth is, it will never happen. If you want to be free from the past, quit living for the past. The past has no power to affect your life today beyond the significance that you attach to it or your unwillingness to change.

Maybe you didn't do it, but I'm sure that if it is affecting you, you can do something about it! At the end of the day, responsibility is simply the ability to respond. Usually the person who sees and feels the pain is best able to respond. The offender rarely has any idea of how bad you are hurting. In fact, he may be so self-indulgent he doesn't care. In either case, the offending person would be emotionally incapable of responding in a way that would free you from the pain. You will either respond to the pain to find healing or become the co-conspirator with the person who hurt you.

Endnotes

1. *Thayer's Greek-English Lexicon of the New Testament* (Grand Rapids, MI: Baker Book House, n.d.).
2. Dr. James B. Richards, *The Gospel of Peace* (New Kensington, PA: Whitaker House, 1990).
3. Ibid.
4. Adapted from a story in Wes Daughenbaugh's *Foundations of Intercession* (Omaha, NE: Gospel Net Ministries).

14

DESTRUCTIVE EXPECTATIONS

The codependent has unrealistic expectations of people, circumstances and life in general. Because he or she is looking to others to meet the needs that can only be met through a meaningful relationship with God, every relationship becomes a disappointment. No one and no thing lives up to the expectations of the codependent. Every relationship is doomed for failure and disappointment at the outset.

There are probably few attitudes that are as mean and hurtful as the expectations of the codependent.[1] Because he (or she) expects things of others, he enters every relationship poised to reject the other person when he or she fails to meet his expectations. He does not get to know the other person and allow the relationship to develop. He goes in expecting that other person to meet certain needs. Before he ever knows the other individual, before he has ever given that person an opportunity, he has rejected him or her because the person did not meet his expectations.

The codependent misses out on much of life and its opportunities. Every person he meets, every relationship, every circumstance holds new opportunities to learn and grow. He is given the opportunity to meet different kinds of people in different settings. He has the opportunity to have friendships on every different level. Each of these friendships has the potential to develop his relationship skills and prepare him for a life of happiness. But the codependent will never experience most of these joys of life. He is too busy attempting to find the person or situation that will meet his need.

Relationships on a Codependent's Terms

Relationships provide the framework for incredible growth. But if we have a static definition of "friend," we will never change or adapt or learn how to relate to others. We simply demand they be what we expect. Consequently, we never develop the relationship skills we need to have the meaningful involvement we desire.

> RELATIONSHIPS PROVIDE THE FRAMEWORK FOR INCREDIBLE GROWTH.

We can never truly know the person upon whom we have imposed our expectations. We cheat ourselves out of the opportunity to grow and develop character because we expect everyone to conform to our expectations instead of us yielding enough to have a variety of friendships.

The codependent thinks the opportunity for happiness simply never comes his (or her) way. Sadly, although he has the same opportunities as everyone else in life, he simply does not see them because he rejects everything and everyone who does not fit into his paradigm. In his pursuit of the ideal friend, the perfect mate and the utopian job, all other opportunities are excluded from sight!

The codependent thinks he knows what will make him happy. Therefore, he develops a type of selective reasoning. He defines a friend as "this kind of person." So, if you're not "this kind of person," he doesn't give you a chance. The irony is that "this kind of person" has never made the codependent happy. Because he is convinced, however, that this is what he needs, he searches for it relentlessly, rejecting all other possibilities.

The codependent says, "I need you to make me happy. I expect things of you so I will be happy. The entire purpose of this relationship is so you can make me happy. If you fail to meet these needs, I will reject you." Our expectations of others cause us to reject them before we even know them. The codependent actually believes others can make him happy. Just as ludicrous is his belief that he should be the sole source of someone else's happiness.

One of the sickest motivations for a relationship is need. "I need you!" is the mating call of the codependent. In other words, he or she is saying, "I have needs I expect you to meet. This relationship is all about me and my needs. I want you to live up to my expectations." To compound the twisted expression of codependent love, he wants you to need him. In other words, "I don't want you getting any joy, happiness or benefit from anyone else. I want you to be weak and crippled without me. Make me your source so I can feel secure in the relationship."

The Problem With Expectations

These expectations form the basis of the majority of interpersonal conflict for the codependent. It fuels hurt and disappointment with life. It may be rare that anyone actually creates a real offense against the codependent, yet, in his mind, it happens regularly. A codependent feels that people regularly and deliberately hurt him, but many times what he interprets as acts of aggression are really just those times when people fail to meet his expectations.

> OUR EXPECTATIONS OF OTHERS CAUSE US TO REJECT THEM BEFORE WE EVEN KNOW THEM.

Jesus told a parable about a man who hired workers out of the marketplace. He hired some of them first thing in the morning and promised to give them "a penny" (a day's wages). The man goes out about an hour later and hires more workers and offers them the same pay. He does this throughout the day and about the last hour of the day he hires even more. When he begins to pay the workers, he pays the ones he hired last. He gives them a full day's pay. *"But when the first came, they supposed that they would receive more; and they likewise received each a denarius. And when they had received it, they complained against the landowner"* (Matthew 20:10-11).

The key word in this passage is *supposed.* They *supposed* they would receive more. They were not promised more; they expected more. They had a logic they worked from, but their logic was wrong. The man paid them just what he had committed. Although he had done them no wrong, they became offended. Their offense, however, did not come from the person actually wronging them; it came from their failed expectations.

What this story doesn't tell is how these codependent workers went forth and told this story to their friends. "It was so unfair. We worked all day long in the sun. We did ten times as much work as those other guys, and he only paid us one hour's wages." By the time it's over, people are afraid to come and work for this employer because they think he will cheat them out of their pay. Codependents attempt to spread their feelings to everyone they know. In the process they actually become the perpetrators. Additionally, every time they repeat and relive this incident, it grows in their own mind. Through their imagination they create the prison bars that hold them captive.

Because control is the goal of the codependent, it is impossible for the codependent to stay in a relationship he (or she) cannot control. He seeks to control the other person to meet his expectations. The codependent will often despise a kind, loving person simply because he can't control that person. People often tell me stories about some pastor who offended them. They may even have horror stories of how he controlled them. When we get to the root of the problem, the codependent is actually angry because he couldn't control the pastor. Such people had expectations that were never met. They may have made sacrifices, they may have served faithfully or given large amounts of money. They may have even been used and manipulated. But the real issue is, their actions did not bring about the expected responses. Their sacrifices were simply veiled attempts at control.

Jesus faced the false expectations of the people daily. It was not the things that Jesus did that caused the religious world to reject Him as much as it was the things He didn't do. He didn't live up to their expectations and, true to the codependent code of ethics, when He failed to meet their expectations, they rejected Him and killed Him.

Listen to people in the Bible express their false expectations of what the Messiah would be like. The woman at the well said, "We know that when Christ comes, He will tell all things." There was not one scripture in the Bible that said this. The Pharisees said, "If You are the Christ, show us a sign." They had seen every sort of miracle, but they just had not seen the one they wanted...more free food. In Jerusalem the Jews said, "We know where this man came from. When Christ comes, no one will know where He comes from." The Bible was very clear about where Christ would come from and they only thought they knew where Jesus was from. Even the thief on the cross said, "If You are the Christ, come down from the cross." Everyone had their expectations, but they didn't get them from what God had committed in the Scriptures. They assumed what it would take to resolve their unbelief.

God had promised a Messiah who would come the first time as a man who would suffer and die for their sins. That was not the kind of Messiah they thought they needed. They thought they needed a Messiah who would be a military leader and break the yoke of Rome from their necks. Like so many codependent people, what they thought they needed and what they really needed were worlds apart.

> LIKE SO MANY CODEPENDENT PEOPLE, WHAT THEY THOUGHT THEY NEEDED AND WHAT THEY REALLY NEEDED WERE WORLDS APART.

In one situation, Jesus healed a crippled man. To experience such an act of kindness must have been overwhelming. I'm sure the man reasoned, "I've got sin in my life, I have problems, but Jesus healed me anyway. I'll bet He doesn't even care about the sin in my life." In the face of unbelievable mercy, the man reasoned until he reached an unrealistic expectation. John 5:14 says, *"Afterward Jesus found him in the temple, and said to him, 'See, you have been made well. Sin no more, lest a worse thing come upon you.'"*

With Jesus' statement, this man's paradigm was broken. Although Jesus had healed him and shown him great mercy, He still wanted to deal with this sin issue. Jesus wasn't angry with him because of his sin; He was concerned. He knew how sin could affect the heart of this man. The man totally misinterpreted what this meant. In verses 15 and 16 the Scriptures continue, *"The man departed and told the Jews that it was Jesus who had made him well. For this reason the Jews persecuted Jesus, and sought to kill Him, because He had done these things on the Sabbath."*

A man who had just received healing now brought about the persecution that ultimately led to Jesus' crucifixion. Was any of this because Jesus had wronged him? No! It was all because Jesus failed to live up to the man's expectations. He believed he had been wronged. He probably went out and told people how critical and judgmental Jesus had been.

Jesus, like most preachers, was betrayed the most by some of the ones He helped the most. We fail to realize people who need the most help are usually where they are because they have the most distorted view of life. It is idealistic to think rescuing a person with deep codependent issues will solve any of those heart beliefs. Jesus, however, did not fall into the codependent leadership trap. He did not develop expectations of the people because of what He had done for them. He knew they were still people with problems. True servants don't help people as a way to get the desired response; they help them because they love them.

Reasoning Beyond Reality

The Bible explains a little about Satan's fall. Ezekiel 28:17 says, *"Your heart was filled with pride because of all your beauty. Your wisdom was corrupted by your love of splendor. So I threw you to the ground and exposed you to the curious gaze of kings"* (NLT). Satan corrupted his wisdom and reasoned his way into his fall. But his reasoning began with something that was real. In his case, it was his brightness and splendor. The King James Version says it like this: *"By reason of thy brightness...."*

Codependent people may begin their reasoning at a point that is rational. Like Satan, however, we can reason beyond reality. Satan's reasoning was like adding one point to another point, to another point, until he surpassed truth and reality. The men in the parable of the worker, which Jesus taught, began with a reality. "Look, he paid those who worked one hour a full day's wages." This was a reality. From here they took a quantum leap and said, "He owes us more because we have worked all day." Or, they may have looked at his generosity to those who had not worked a full day. Regardless of the thought process, they reasoned until they arrived at a logic that was no longer reality. Reality could have been, "*Possibly* he will pay us more," or "We can *ask* him for more pay tomorrow." Any number of things would have kept them in reality. Instead, however, they created an expectation that they had no right to create. And instead of being thankful that they had the opportunity to work that day, they were offended and unthankful.

Instead of being thankful for what we do have, expectations cause us to be angry because of what we don't have. We put those around us under the pressure of living up to our expectations. We expect what was not promised. Sometimes we expect what is not possible. Through our expectations we become unthankful people who destroy meaningful relationships. The expectation of our friends is what so often destroys our relationships with them. The expectation of our mate is often what destroys our marriage. The expectation of my church will destroy my relationship with my church. My expectation of you makes me try to control you. In the end, codependents will feel betrayed and offended. Their expectations cause them to believe they have been wronged.

> LIKE SATAN DID, WE CAN REASON BEYOND REALITY.

It is not wrong to have expectations in a relationship. But we can expect nothing from someone that he or she has not committed. Before we assume, we should ask. If people know what we are expecting in advance, they may back away, they may offer negotiation or they may agree. But until they have agreed, we have no right to expect. To expect will only bring failed expectation and, Proverbs 13:12a says, *"Hope deferred makes the heart sick!"* It doesn't matter if it's false hope; any failed hope (expectation) makes the heart sick!

Endnote

1. Dr. James B. Richards, *My Church My Family* (Huntsville, AL: Impact Ministries, 1995), 91.

113

IDENTIFYING CODEPENDENCY IN SOCIETY

15

CODEPENDENT SOCIETY

In order to properly understand how codependency has permeated so many areas of our thinking, it is essential that we identify the very subtle ways it has been introduced into every area of our lives. Now, no one decided to make the entire world codependent. It is not a grand conspiracy. Yet, the very philosophies by which the world operates will always ultimately lead to codependency.

At this moment the world is on fire. Riots are breaking out all across the globe. In a grab for power there is the distorted concept of a class war. Those who stir chaos and conflict play on the codependent mindset that has been meticulously crafted in the emotional fabric of the common man. The spin is that capitalism is evil; this government or that government is bad. The truth is, any system is as evil as the hearts and intentions of those who lead it. But be assured that any movement based on an ideology that anyone owes anything to anyone, other than the debt of love, is built on the very message that ejected man from the garden and plummeted the world into its present chaos.

Governments Need Codependent Societies

Greed, power and manipulation can only function in a codependent society. Therefore, the attempt to set up a world economy simultaneously calls for a codependent society. Marketing flourishes by making people feel they have needs. If people aren't made to feel needy, far less merchandise can be bought or sold. Most purchases are made to compensate for the feeling of need or lack.

Don't misunderstand…there is nothing wrong with prosperity. There is nothing wrong with material possessions, until those possessions are used to create a sense of security, identity or self-worth. Then those possessions become the corruption that feeds the needs they falsely offer to meet. It might be worth mentioning that the last thing that has to be removed from planet Earth in order for Jesus to return is Mystery Babylon, which the Bible calls the mother of all abominations (Revelation 17:5), and it is directly tied to governments and economy. Its seductions have affected all people and all nations for nearly all times.

> GREED, POWER AND MANIPULATION CAN ONLY FUNCTION IN A CODEPENDENT SOCIETY.

What people once considered to be luxuries are now considered to be essential needs. Happiness is sold by the advertisers, forming the thoughts and values of the young and old alike. The Bibles says in First John 2:15-16, *"Do not love the world or the things in the world. If anyone loves the world, the love of the Father is not in him. For all that is in the world—the lust of the flesh, the lust of the eyes, and the pride of life—is not of the Father but is of the world."* As so aptly pointed out by the Apostle John, the entire world's system is driven by lust, i.e., desire! It is the desire for things to make us happy!

When a person longs for the things of the world, the love (value) for the Father cannot find a place in him or her. When a person is looking to the things of the world to meet the need that only God can meet, he or she can never really get the need met. Advertisers put the love of the world in the hearts of men. Governments put the love of the world in our hearts. They do it through the process of education…education in schools, education on television, education through marketing and education through just about any other type of media. By so doing, they make the human race dependent on their merchandise for fulfillment. Governments can only maintain power through force or economy. Even force will fail if the economy is not stimulated!

We are constantly bombarded with information that has a subtle agenda to profit by creating the feeling of lack or insecurity. In a recent news program about smoking, young teens said they were more influenced to smoke by advertising than by peer pressure. Strong associations about love, sex, happiness and self-worth are made by coupling information with images. Everyone over 45 knows what they would "walk a mile for." They all know what "tastes good like a cigarette should." We have had these images etched onto our minds.

All that the world has to offer meets the criteria for First John 2:16. It looks good, it feels good and it makes me feel like somebody. I'm hooked! I need your stuff so I can feel good about me. A heart overrun by the need for things has an addiction just as powerful as heroin. It constantly cries out for fulfillment. And those who lack the sense of dignity and worth that comes from a loving connection with their Creator race to the counter to purchase the latest magic potion.

> GOVERNMENTS CAN ONLY MAINTAIN POWER THROUGH FORCE OR ECONOMY.

The concepts that are embraced by the world's economic system most certainly interlock with the harlot in the Book of Revelation. By these concepts, the entire world is deceived. By them, wars are fought. By them, countries and their leaders rise and fall. The desire for a world economy is the one thing that has been able to unite the countries of the world into a false peace. Since the birth of Babel, the world has been lulled into a false sense of economic security independent of trust and harmony with the wisdom of God. It doesn't take much of a look at history to see what it has produced!

It's a Big Issue

The following chapters in this section in no way deal fully with all the issues involved, nor do they attempt to be an authoritative source concerning this topic. They merely attempt to look at the basic areas that influence our thinking (i.e., family, government, education and mental health). These chapters will show how the basic philosophies that touch every life have been molded to affect our life paradigm, our sense of self-worth, our view of God and, to some degree, who we look to for security. We are daily saturated with a constant barrage of information that is somewhat rational but leads us to a place of irrationality. Even when it is not rational, it is constant. As someone once said, "We'll believe a lie that we've heard all of our life before we'll believe the truth that we've only heard once." The constant message continually appears to be true but never ends as promised.

I do not desire for you to dive into hopelessness as you grasp the perils of the world system. I merely hope to open your eyes to the degree of the problem so you will fervently seek the solution. Unless we get real about the magnitude of the problem, we will never seriously deal with it. Until we open our mind to the truth, we can't see the lie. Sometimes, however, until we compare the lie to the truth, we can't see the truth. Abraham looked at the enormity of his lack and inability, but he then looked at the enormity of God...and in comparison he was persuaded to trust God. We must do the same!

> THE WORLD HAS BEEN LULLED INTO A FALSE SENSE OF ECONOMIC SECURITY INDEPENDENT OF TRUST AND HARMONY WITH THE WISDOM OF GOD.

The church is like the frog in the pot. If you were to drop it into boiling water, it would jump out and escape. But if you slowly turn up the heat, it will sit there until it is cooked. The traditional orthodox church has sat in the pot for so long it doesn't realize that it is about to boil. It has become such a part of the world system that it seldom offers us tools to free us from the system. Freedom from the system means freedom from religion. If we were freed from religion, we'd free ourselves from controlling, dysfunctional churches. If we were free from religion, we would becomes disciples who follow the Lord Jesus, build our lives on His teaching and examples and experience the grace of God to live as the Bible promises.

Be assured that there is a solution. Solving this problem may not be as difficult as it seems. God has easy solutions for difficult situations. Don't lose hope or become overwhelmed as you read. Let every frightening reality about the world's system compel you to live intimately connected to your Lord and Savior. Let this be the final call to surrender your life completely to the Lord Jesus and free yourself from the *"snare of the fowler."*

16

THE WORLD SYSTEM

All of my Christian life I have heard the stories and read the books that suggest a worldwide conspiracy. We know, in the end, there will be a one-world government. We know that it seems as if there is a monumental conspiracy, but the truth is, there doesn't have to be a conspiracy, as we know it, for the world to end up in chaos.

Those who pursue power and control always work from the same set of "rules," although their ideologies may radically differ. The leftists will conspire with the communists even though the communists violate their ideals about human rights. The feminists will ally with the radical Muslims even though radical Islam is very much against women's rights. The Chinese will find ways to work with the Russians even though they despise one another. What is it that binds these different radical groups together? We fail to grasp is that there is a system of thought that is vying for power, and these groups really don't mind with whom they align themselves as long as it is not with God or His truth! The one thing these and other groups have in common is this: they think, "If we eradicate all concept of God from the memory of mankind, we can create the world we desire." That is the conspiracy that binds them all together despite their differences.

A conspiracy entered the earth at the garden when man became a sinner. Every human being born since Adam has been born a sinner (inherently fearful and untrusting). As a sinner, man has been afraid of God. Since the day Adam hid from God in the garden, man has habitually hidden from Him. Man is afraid to trust God; therefore, man is always looking somewhere other than God to get his needs met. The need for feeling safe is usually expressed ideologically through the need to be right and functionally by taking control. Since the founding of Mystery Babylon, the birth of the first government, man has utilized the ultimate tool for seizing power: government and economy. These are the two social structures whereby massive control can be seized under the guise of promoting the well-being of the population.

> THERE IS A SYSTEM OF THOUGHT THAT IS VYING FOR POWER, AND THESE GROUPS REALLY DON'T MIND WITH WHOM THEY ALIGN THEMSELVES AS LONG AS IT IS NOT WITH GOD OR HIS TRUTH!

Gaining control of planet Earth was Satan's plan from the beginning. It became a conspiracy when he convinced Adam that he could be god of his own world, choosing right and wrong based on his point of view rather than God's. From then until now, men and women have emerged who would show man the "way." At least, it was the way as far as the people presenting it were concerned. They simply needed to get everyone else to try their way so they could prove it was right. In the end, those who benefit from presenting their way are the ones who gain control!

A Practical Example

The last generation of parents were raised under the philosophy that spanking children was unacceptable. They were taught by people who had opinions, not facts, that striking children would cause them to be violent. They believe children would come to accept violence as a way of life and would cause aggression, etc.

This all seemed very reasonable and logical, and while it had never been proven, people accepted it in great numbers. But the biggest flaw was not that it had not been proven; the biggest flaw was that it contradicted the Bible. Man chose good and evil for himself without regard to what God said.

I find it interesting to note that the children who were raised by non-spanking parents have become the most violent, aggressive, out-of-control children history has ever seen. They thrive on violence—they seem to crave it. It seems that once again man's opinion was worthless. (No doubt, there would have been great value in dealing with the issues of child abuse. Spanking and child abuse are, however, two different issues.)

The Bible doesn't teach, as some suppose, that spanking is the answer for every disciplinary situation. Actually, we should be able to teach by compelling. We should instruct, lead, encourage and affirm our children in a way that draws them into responsible living. Yet, some children are foolish. A fool is one who will not learn by instruction. Thus, the Bible says, *"Penalties are prepared for mockers, and beatings for the backs of fools"* (Proverbs 19:29 NIV). This makes a clear distinction of who should receive a spanking and who should receive a penalty.

> THE FARTHER WE HAVE MOVED FROM THE BASIC VALUES OF THE BIBLE AND OUR FOUNDING FATHERS, THE MORE CHAOTIC, VIOLENT AND DESTRUCTIVE SOCIETY HAS BECOME.

When a child is so rebellious he (or she) will not learn from instruction, he must learn from consequence. If he does not learn from consequences, he will have no boundaries in life. He thinks he will always be able to do what he wants and get by with it. Such children live their life out of control, as this generation of children are doing. So the ideology proved to be wrong. Instead of learning from the consequences, the people who believe their own version of right and wrong continue to argue their ideas totally independent of hard proven facts.

The more politicians and society depart from the wisdom of God and cram their agendas down the throat of American society, the worse our society becomes. This is not a problem of Democrats versus Republicans. This is a problem of corrupt agendas and ungodly methods from both sides of the aisle. Yet, they insist if we would blindly accept more of their ideas, everything would get better. But it doesn't. In fact, it gets worse. The farther we have moved from the basic values of the Bible and our founding fathers, the more chaotic, violent and destructive society has become.

What the Founding Fathers Knew

Our founding fathers knew one thing about government: It always becomes corrupt if unchecked by the people. Freedom was the goal of the American Revolution. The Constitution was written from the perspective that God endowed man with certain freedoms and no government has the right to come between man and those freedoms. But by accepting these freedoms, man also became responsible. He was responsible to manage his life and use those freedoms to reach his desired goals or live a life with consequences equal to his efforts.

The primary goal of the Constitution was not to show the government how to rule people. It was written to protect the people from the government. But for more than 100 years there has been another American revolution that says, "Life is not fair; society owes you! If you will give me your vote, I will give what you have not worked for. If you will give me your vote, I will meet the needs in your life." In exchange for freedom, government is promising to meet our needs. Before we accept that offer, maybe we need to remember who made it first, in the garden!

God is infinitely wiser than man. He has more experience in every area than man does. He is the Creator; we are the creation. We are like the pot that attempts to instruct the potter. God gave us the wisdom we needed to maintain economic, civil and social order. Our country, although not perfect, has thrived as a civilization by yielding, to some degree, to that wisdom. Although many things were done wrong, although there have been corrupt people hiding behind the biblical principles, it has worked better than anything in any society has ever worked.

The Church Was Responsible

Why would man move away from something that God says would work? After all, time has proven it would work and everything man has tried has not worked. Simple! Man still wants to be god of his own world. Since man does not trust God, and since the church has persuaded the world that God is the source of all their pain, we have a modern-day tower of Babel. We have a society seeking self-rule, seeking freedom from the imagined tyranny of God, and an economic system that binds us together independent of God! But we unwittingly fail to realize that those who offer this new "freedom" will take control. They (government) will become the god of this new world order. They will give and take our freedoms; they will decide good and evil.

Let me emphasize, I hold the church largely responsible for this turning away that has taken place in the world. The message of judgment and wrath has embittered the world against God. First, it created a concept of God that was unlovable. Then it created a concept of God that could not be trusted. Finally, it contrived a character of God that rejected man. The god of the religious church is an immoral, unfaithful, inconsistent murderer.

> MAN STILL WANTS TO BE GOD OF HIS OWN WORLD.

Historians tell us that Nimrod's message to the world revolved around these same New World Order ideas. First he convinced man that the reason God wanted them to spread throughout the earth was so they would be alone and could be killed. He made people afraid to trust God. So he bound men together in a community. He then convinced man that the prosperity they enjoyed had nothing to do with God and how He created the world. It was by their own ingenuity. Nimrod became a *hunter of men*. The Bible calls Nimrod a *"hunter before the Lord,"* but the majority of Hebrew scholars and historians translate that as a "hunter of men before the Lord." Those who would not comply were forced to comply or die. In other words, he made laws requiring compliance to anti-God ideologies. Then he led the people into open defiance.

Once the church unintentionally, unscripturally and ignorantly turned the world against God, man now had the opportunity to create a world after his own image. That is the world system in which we now live. One of the Greek words translated as world is *aion*. This particular word speaks of an age or era.[1] It is more than an age in the sense of time; it is like an era of beliefs. We have entered into the era of man that will climax with the rise of 666, the totality of man. Man's era will be total chaos and anarchy, resulting from policy that doesn't work. His ideas will reach the ultimate in failure and destruction. Apart from God and His wisdom, man's social order will fail at every point.

Codependency Is the Default Choice

So there is a system at work in the world and it is based on codependency. It is the process of getting men to depend on anything and anyone other than God. Regardless of the conspiracies that may exist, people do not have to conspire for this to happen. All they have to do is stop believing the truth and stop trusting God. Stop depending on Him and you have a codependent society that epitomizes this world's system.

> IF SOCIETY STOPS DEPENDING ON GOD, YOU HAVE A CODEPENDENT SOCIETY THAT EPITOMIZES THIS WORLD'S SYSTEM.

The Bible says in Romans 12:2, *"And do not be conformed to this world, but be transformed by the renewing of your mind, that you may prove what is that good and acceptable and perfect will of God."* Man must renew his mind to be consistent with the Bible or else he will find himself conforming to a system doomed for collapse. The world's system is a codependent system. Even Christians who have not renewed their minds are a part of this system. They are saved, their sins are forgiven, but they are still in the world system.

The will of God is not hard and difficult, contrary to what the church has proclaimed. It's just the opposite. Jesus said, *"Come to Me, all you who labor and are heavy laden, and I will give you rest. Take My yoke upon you and learn from Me, for I am gentle and lowly in heart, and you will find rest for your souls. For My yoke is easy and My burden is light"* (Matthew 11:28-30). There is no place in the Bible that describes the will of God as hard. A renewed mind realizes that God's will is good, acceptable and perfect. It is a good thing.

The goodness of God is a reality that exists in the minds of people who have rejected their personal religious opinions and accepted God as Jesus presented Him. The fearful, unbelieving mind continues to draw back from God, leaving no choice but codependency. This person must look to some source other than God to meet his or her deepest needs.

Because the world has accepted the religious view of God, they have determined that they want God out of every area of their life. They don't want their kids to pray to Him in school. They don't want their government to mention His name. They don't want His name on their currency. They want to stamp His memory from the face of the earth. To this day, people are censored, imprisoned and sometimes killed for sharing the gospel.

But can you blame the world for taking this view? After all, they only know the concept of God that has been presented by a church that models codependent control. For the most part, they have never heard the good news (gospel); all they have heard is bad news. I would not want to trust the god who was blamed for famine and draught. I would not want to know the god who was responsible for killing my children. I would not be friends with a god who always found fault with my every action. Neither does the world! They don't want the god the church has preached. He can't be trusted!

> EVERYONE NEEDS TO BELIEVE IN SOMETHING.

In light of the misinformation that has been proclaimed to the world, they have attempted to build a new Babylon, a society that exists without God. But everyone needs to believe in something. There is something in the very fabric of man that wants some type of "higher power." So man has created a god for man to depend on. He has built a system that calls for people to trust the government, trust the professionals, trust the educators or trust in your riches. Pick the god of your choice; just don't trust the Living God!

Through advertising, education and politics, we are led away from a simple trust in God. We choose to trust in the ideas of man. When a society turns away from God, there is no alternative but codependency. Man must have his deep emotional needs met in order to live. He must depend on someone to meet the needs that only God can meet.

Thus we have an entire system, a way of life and a society that reject God. In His place, we have created the world's system, which does not work. It is not meeting the needs of society, but without God, what else is there?

So the truth is, there is a conspiracy. It may not be deliberate. It may not be the product of people getting together in a dark room to plan the destruction of the world. But it is a conspiracy that says, "The enemy of my enemy is my friend." They say, "Because you want a world without God and I want a world without God, we will serve one another's cause. Because no matter how much we hate one another, we hate the idea of trusting God more."

Endnote

1. *Theological Dictionary of the New Testament*, abridged edition (Grand Rapids, MI: William B. Eerdmans Publishing Company, 1985), NT:165.

17

THE GOD OF GOVERNMENT

The progression toward codependency is not the fault of the church alone, however. The church, in its carnal quest for power, simply validated man's excuse not to trust God. From there the world insidiously justified its insatiable appetite for control. Every world leader has beliefs and agendas, cloaked in the guise of social justice or humanitarian good, which are imposed upon the unsuspecting citizens. It is essential, therefore, that governments brainwash the people through systematic programming via education, news programs and other media in order for them to work their agenda with a minimum amount of resistance.

One of the most fundamental differences in presenting ideas to the masses lies in understanding the difference between propaganda and promotion. In the promotion of an idea, the end goal is presented up front. People are allowed to evaluate the goal and the process. Openness allows the people to become a part of the process. Based on its merit, it is either supported or rejected by the people. Through propaganda people's sense of lack, through fear or guilt, is exploited. Polished politically correct motivational statements, illusionary enemies and created crisis move people to action without actually knowing the true end goal. Thereby the ultimate manipulation occurs. Once the imaginary problem is created, the people give the government the power to "fix the problem." The problem is always fixed by passing laws that take away some of our freedoms. In the end the politician says, we only gave you what you wanted.

The farther a nation departs from the wisdom of God, the more that nation will plunge into irrational codependency. This is why leftist ideologies have always had as their goal the abolishment of all religion. The communist, socialist, progressive and leftist leaders were shrewd enough to realize you cannot create a totalitarian government in a God-honoring society. They knew man had a need to yield himself to a higher power. Only after God was removed or minimized from the consciousness of society, would man look to the government as that higher power.

The Government Wants to Be Your Source

Codependent governments function no differently than drug addicts. Drug addicts keep people around them from identifying their problems by continually creating chaos. Chaos keeps everyone off balance. People's attention is directed away from the real problem and projected onto a synthesized crisis. It's called creating a straw man, i.e., an imaginary enemy. While we're putting out the fire that is burning our house, they are stealing our possessions through the back door.

THE FARTHER A NATION DEPARTS FROM THE WISDOM OF GOD, THE MORE THAT NATION WILL PLUNGE INTO IRRATIONAL CODEPENDENCY.

It has been amazing to see the atrocities committed against people in the former Soviet Union, China, Germany and dozens of other nations. Who could imagine that masses of people would stand idly by and allow the slaughter of other human beings. But they could not rise up against their source of security...the state. It is never long, however, before that which controls us by offering security, begins to control us through fear. Sadly, when governments do act in the name of humanitarian relief or social justice, it is little more than a mask to work some corrupt agenda.

While the state is rejecting God and blaming Christianity for cruel oppression, they are organizing another diabolical form of oppression. It seems that codependent controllers in government always attempt to create a society that empowers their group, their party and themselves personally. This can only be done when the masses are disempowered and codependent. There need not be a formal conspiracy for this to happen; this is the world's system.

Seldom does anyone sit around and say, "How can we make the people codependent?" Instead, they say, "What do these people want?" Government leaders determine what it will take to buy your vote. They can count on the greed, insecurity and fear of the people to blind them when offered an "easy way out." If there are not legitimate needs, the party seeking your vote will create a need. As the government meets needs, people begin to become more and more dependent on government. Thus you have a codependent society. As people depend on the government they become less and less independent and less capable of trusting God.

> ONCE ENOUGH PEOPLE BECOME DEPENDENT ON THE GOVERNMENT, THE MOB RULES!

Entitlement programs in America have never been about meeting the needs of the people. It has been about buying the vote. Imagine, they have convinced generations of people that they cannot make it on their own. Like an overprotective parent who emotionally cripples the child, the government has blinded the eyes of the poor masses to true opportunity. Big government can count on the fact that selfish people will revolt when faced with the threat of losing their *free* ride! Once enough people become dependent on the government, the mob rules! Manipulation is as easy as any threat to take away the free money! In every country where socialism or communism has taken over, they have always done so by creating class warfare. Class warfare is virtually impossible without the promise of entitlement programs! The people who work to pay bills do not have time to protest and riot. The people, however, who are being supported by the government have plenty of time to create chaos. In First Thessalonians 4:12, Paul told believers to work and earn their own living *"so that you will not be dependent on anybody"* (NIV).

It has been said that men will quickly trade freedom for security. The United States has slowly proven that to be a reality. Every year, new laws are passed to protect the people—laws that ultimately take more freedoms from the beneficiaries of the law as well as the rest of the population. The government that once existed to protect our freedom and our rights under the Constitution has now taken the role of meeting our needs. In the spirit of the Constitution no law should ever be passed to benefit one person at the expense of another.

Caretakers and Saviors

One of the roles of the codependent controller is the "caretaker." The caretaker justifies violating your freedom in order to protect you from harm. But the more one person tries to protect another, the more he or she must violate the other's freedom of choice. The caretaker often assumes the superiority role and says, "These people are too ignorant to make the right choices; we must make the choices for them." Caretakers feel that their superiority gives them the right to make your choices for you and take away the rights of others to accomplish their "humanitarian goals."

Then there is the "savior mentality," which goes a few steps beyond the caretaker. The codependent savior not only wants to save people from their mistakes, but the savior also wants to save them from themselves, i.e., from the consequences of their mistakes. This mentality will keep a person from ever growing or maturing. Fools only learn by paying the price for their actions. This is what the Bible means when it talks about beatings being for the back of the fool (Proverbs 19:29). Remove personal consequences from choices, and there is never personal growth. Even more sinister, there is no independence, which is the goal of the controller. If I undermine your confidence, if I cripple you through overprotection, blind you through deceitful education, then become your source through entitlements, you have no other options! You will give me complete power!

God is not trying to get us to inflict punishment upon the fool, but He by no means wants us to help the fool escape the results of his or her actions. This is what is called enablement. When we do for others what they should do for themselves, we enable their destructive behavior. When we offer them support, training and opportunity, this is called empowerment. Entitlement assures that he or she will continue in the same destructive behavior. It reinforces his or her already faulty belief that there are no consequences for his or her actions. This is why most people who are released from prison go back again. They have seldom been made to bear the true consequences of their actions, nor have they been empowered through biblically based personal development programs. Empowerment breaks the cycle. But it also frees people from the controller.

Every day, millions of dollars are awarded to people who are considered to be victims. On the one hand, companies pay millions of dollars in damages for making their coffee too hot. There is never any mention that an individual should use some precautions and assume some responsibility. Never mind responsibility; the person is a victim. At the same time, a murderer is acquitted because he (or she) is not considered to be responsible for his actions. Society is blamed for the actions of the individual. Think of the irony: a murderer goes free without so much as paying restitution, while a company that makes its coffee too hot pays millions. It has long been the detailed plan of communism and socialism to frustrate Americans by corrupting our court systems through socialist philosophy. To make the laws complicated, in opposition to the wisdom of our founding fathers. To make society, not the individual, responsible. In time the entire country is corrupt, angry and crying out for a savior.

The codependent savior is willing to violate the rights of the true victim in order to save the criminal from his or her consequences. The codependent savior has no real help for the true victims, the hurting individuals. He or she can only be perceived as savior by someone who needs a savior. Thus you have the criminal justice system designed for the criminal. Rejection of God's wisdom about dealing with crime has led to an epidemic of crime in this country, unparalleled by any other generation.

Upside-Down Thinking

A person who has succeeded in life is somehow made to feel that he or she is the reason someone else is living in poverty. A man who works hard to provide a living for his family is penalized (taxed). Part of his earnings are forcibly taken and given to a man who is healthy, yet refuses to work. The citizens of our nation

TAKE CONTROL OF YOUR LIFE

who cannot afford their own health care are made to pay for the health care of illegal aliens. There is more motivation for people with low income to become dependent on the state than there is to earn a living. People who know how to work the system would be foolish to work a job.

There is a message that rings loud and clear in this nation: "If you are in lack, it is not your fault. If you've committed a crime, it is not your fault. If you are emotionally unstable, it is not your fault. Someone else is responsible to meet your needs." Therefore, our country, as a whole, has become a codependent nation. There is too much motivation to be irresponsible. But only irresponsible, codependent people need a codependent government.

> OUR COUNTRY, AS A WHOLE, HAS BECOME A CODEPENDENT NATION.

Politicians run on a platform that says, "If you'll vote for me, I'll meet your needs." Every special interest group in America is promising to meet somebody's needs, but it will cost you some more of your freedoms. The most important freedom it will cost you is the freedom to trust God and experience His great goodness and provision. It will cost you your self-worth. After the government supports you, you lose confidence in your ability to survive apart from the government. You slowly become a slave to the world's system.

God's Way Brings Freedom

True freedom is only found in trusting God. True self-worth is only known in a meaningful relationship with God. Awareness of significance is only experienced through living a life of significance. Unless God is our source, we will become the slaves of the world's system. The degree to which we assume personal responsibility is the degree to which we can experience real freedom!

God's economic structure, as presented in the Old Testament, provided for the poor. They were allowed to go into the fields and *glean* what was left behind. But never did the farmer pick it and take it to them. And it was never forcibly taken by the government. When the government takes money from the worker and gives it to the slacker, the slacker thanks the government. He (or she) never thanks the person who worked and earned the money. In fact, because of deep psychological factors, the slacker always ends up despising the hand that feeds him. So, the government plays on these emotional factors and creates a class war. If the slacker got the food from your hand, his appreciation would be to you, his fellow citizen, not the government who stole it from you. His accountability would be to someone in his community, not a bureaucrat hundreds of miles away in Washington. He might learn that your values contributed to his well-being. He would then be influenced by those values. He would be compelled to live in harmony with his community.

In the Old Testament, all debts were cancelled every 50 years. This would reset the economy. It would prevent the greedy wealthy from owning all the land. The poor were allowed to work the fields they did not own. There were many provisions for the poor, but not one of them made someone else responsible. God established a social order that would protect the innocent and deal with the guilty, yet man has become the god of his own world. He now calls evil good and good evil. *"Woe unto them that call evil good, and good evil; that put darkness for light, and light for darkness; that put bitter for sweet, and sweet for bitter"* (Isaiah 5:20 KJV)!

> CONTROL IS THE BOTTOM LINE FOR THE CODEPENDENT.

God is not punishing us or our country for this perversion of justice; we are simply living in the fruit of this mentality. Our "punishment" is the fruit of our doings. God did not want us to live in the results of this kind of thinking; that's why He warned us. Yet, we chose to reject His wisdom and depend on our own. This gives us an opportunity to be in control. We can get our needs met without trusting God and His wisdom.

Remember, control is the bottom line for the codependent. What greater way to control you than to make you dependent on me? So a political party offers to meet this need for you and that need for you and, ultimately, you will need the party. You will not trust God. You will not even trust yourself. You will trust the party. You will vote for and give your loyalty to the source that meets your needs.

Our nation is suffering from a self-worth crisis. In this environment of low self-worth, people are looking to someone to meet their needs and give them security. In exchange, they will surrender their freedom, their dignity and their confidence in God.

The only solution is a God who loves (has value, holds in high regard and considers precious) His creation. The message that Jesus came to die for our sins so we would never have to pay that price is the heart of the gospel, the proof of the love of God and the hope of those who live in despair. Responsible believers do not vote along party lines or special interests. They vote for biblical and constitutional integrity. They do not stay in churches that control and destroy. They find places that build up and promote God and His love for mankind! Those who vote the party line and support controlling churches are the real problem. These are the people who have the power to turn it all around. But instead of being disciples who follow the teaching and principles of the Lord Jesus, we have millions of "Christians." They enjoy the culture of Christianity but have no sense of the conviction. They want to go to heaven when they die but they do not want to manage their life, time and resources around God's wisdom for today. The codependent Christian says if the government will change, everything will be better. A disciple would say, "I am in a free country, I will live by God's values and I will vote God's values. I will be the change I hope to see in my nation."

18

THE POWER OF PARENTING

There is little in this life that affects us as much as the influence of our parents. Some experts say our life paradigm is established before we are five years old. In fact, new studies reveal that through cellular memories we are actually affected by previous generations, by the thoughts, feelings and belief of our parents while we were in the womb, all before we are ever born! Before we are old enough to reason it all out, someone else has determined the way we will see the world. Our view of the world is filtered through our sense of self. What we believe about "us" alters the way we see and interpret everything around us.

With new scientific understanding about energy, we now know that every thought, word and emotion has its own unique frequency. These frequencies bombard the baby even while in the mother's womb. Long before a child can speak or understand what is being said, his (or her) deepest interpretation of the world is created by the stress in the home: whether or not the mother and father both want the baby, the fears the mother experiences and every other thought, word and emotion in his environment. The child's view of the world is shaped by something that cannot even be put into words. But then, as the child starts learning to communicate, things are modeled and taught that reinforce his already imprinted subconscious.

Because of a departure from godly, Bible-based principles of child-raising, coupled with gravitation toward negative religious concepts, many well-meaning parents have rooted their children in a dysfunctional lifestyle that leads to codependency. Between the misunderstanding of biblical principles and the humanistic philosophies of the world, the average parent has been hard-pressed to find the answers to raise emotionally healthy children. Now, as the government becomes more anti-God, some basic values are even illegal.

> WHEN WE DON'T KNOW WHAT ELSE WILL WORK, WE SHOULD KNOW THAT LOVE WILL ALWAYS WORK.

The extremely negative, dominating concepts of child-raising presented by the religious legalist don't appeal to loving, gentle parents. They want to do what the Word of God says, but the punitive approach just doesn't "sit right." These extreme interpretations of the Word of God force people to look to other sources to find principles for child-raising. The humanistic approach was gentler and more "loving," yet it still left children just as dysfunctional as the legalistic, religious approach. This, however, has seemed to be the only two options available to many Christians: legalism or permissiveness.

Because so many parents felt they were unqualified to read, understand and apply the Bible, they failed to find the simple solutions offered in the Word of God. They failed to understand that *agape* love has to be the guiding factor in all relationships, including the relationships with our children. According to one interpretation, First Corinthians 13:8 could read, *"Love never ceases to be effective."*

Love Should Be the Guiding Force

When we don't know what else will work, we should know that love will always be effective. This is what God does for us…He keeps on loving us. He keeps on being good to us, and the *"goodness of God leads* [us] *to repentance"* (Romans 2:4). Most people are afraid of walking in love. Because of a liberal, unscriptural concept of love, they are afraid that walking in love will make them vulnerable. When applying love to child discipline, they have no functional concept of what that really means.

Love, however, is the only way to *keep* from being taken advantage of. If I accept God's definition of love, I will not accept yours; therefore, you cannot control me with guilt. You can ask me to love you, but only God can define how that love is to operate. Although I love you, I will probably not do everything that you want. Jesus didn't do everything people wanted. He was not a pushover. No one took advantage of Him, yet all that He did, He did in love. He got tough. He drove the money changers out of the temple with a whip. He confronted the Pharisees and the religious leaders about their destruction of God's people. But He never departed from *agape* (God's love).

All the actions Jesus took were motivated by His love for God and His love for people. He was never motivated by anger. The Bible says, *"Be ye angry, and sin not: let not the sun go down upon your wrath"* (Ephesians 4:26 KJV). When love drives us, even our anger will motivate us to do something healthy. Our problem is that we don't realize we can be angry and resist sin at the same time. When we walk in love, all that we do is for the benefit of the person we love. Yet, it does not violate our own boundaries and choices. Ultimately, all that we do in love has its basis in the Word of God. The moment we surrender one of these three guiding posts, we are no longer walking in love. Ask yourself, "Am I doing this for the benefit of the person? Is this consistent with the Word of God? Have I violated my choices?"

> AS CHRISTIANS, WE TEND TO BECOME LIKE THE GOD WE BELIEVE IN.

Many well-meaning parents have done things for the good of their child, but their interpretation of the Word of God caused it to be ineffective. As Christians, we tend to become like the God we believe in. If we believe God is quick to punish, we will be quick to punish. If we believe God is longsuffering, we will be longsuffering. If we think God is angry at those who sin, we will be angry at those who sin.

Because we have accepted the concept of an angry God, we have become angry Christians. We are quick to judge and slow to forgive. We are anxious to discover and reveal the faults of others. Where this does the most damage is with our children. We fill them with rejection and insecurity. They are often unsure of our love and God's love. Because of the God we depict, our children are anxious to leave the church and leave our beliefs.

Our concept of Christianity places the highest emphasis on being right, so we try to make our kids do right. In this process, worth starts being determined by how right one is. If one is not right, then he or she has no value. In our attempt to make our children do right, we often dominate, control, reject or overprotect. Thus, the dysfunction begins. Keep in mind, *agape* love is first and foremost about value. Children are either made to feel valuable because they are our children or because of their performance. The former builds up; the latter destroys.

> REGARDLESS OF WHAT WE TELL OUR CHILDREN, IT IS HOW WE TREAT THEM THAT LEAVES THE LASTING IMPRESSION!

Make Your Children Feel Loved

As parents, our first priority should be to make our children feel loved. I am not talking about spoiling them or giving in to their every whim, but we should make it our goal to cause our children to experience our love, i.e., feel valuable and precious. If children do not become confident in the love of their parents, they will seldom become confident in the love of God. Parents are the model of God that children perceive. Regardless of what we tell them, it is how we treat them that leaves the lasting impression!

As parents, we would do well to remember that our children *belong* to God, not to us. We are not preparing them to please us in life; we are preparing them to have a relationship with the Lord and please Him. We "cast the die" concerning our children's ability to relate to the Lord. They tend to transfer the experiences with us, their parents, onto their understanding of God.

We are not raising them to be successful in business as much as we are raising them to be successful in life and relationships. Our children need the relationship skills that come very naturally from a strong sense of love and self-worth. The ability to have meaningful relationships is the most important capacity we can ever pass on to our children. It will determine their happiness more than any other single factor. How much money they make will not affect their happiness as much as their ability to relate to others.

When children do not feel a sense of love and worth from their parents, they will develop the need to look to others to meet this need. They will not be capable of objective, healthy friendships. They will become codependent takers. When they are confident in our love, however, it will be an easy thing to convince them of the love God has for them. They will ultimately turn to the one unfailing source of love and worth: God the Father. They will relate to their heavenly Father much like they have related to us and they will relate to others from that positive, healthy emotional base as well.

> THE ABILITY TO HAVE MEANINGFUL RELATIONSHIPS IS THE MOST IMPORTANT CAPACITY WE CAN EVER PASS ON TO OUR CHILDREN.

Without realizing it, we can quickly put our children into a lifetime struggle with "works-righteousness." It is as simple as giving and withholding love based on their performance. In the mind of a child, this translates into what makes them valuable. Rewards should be earned but love and affection should never be the reward or punishment. After a while, they will develop an association that says love and acceptance is earned. Then in their relationship with God, they never feel like sons; they always feel like hired help. They feel they must be right to earn God's love.

Subtle Rejection

We have failed to develop the ability to express displeasure without expressing rejection. This falls into that paradoxical concept of being angry without sin. Most of us have never developed the skill to do either. If we are angry, we handle it in a destructive way. When we have displeasure with someone, we tend to convey personal rejection. When the person brings us pleasure, we tend to express love. We have failed to understand how to withhold privileges without withholding affection. We don't know how to say no and still portray love. Most people have to be angry to say "no!" In fact, we seem to only say no for the purpose of punishment. We should be saying yes or no with an awareness of what will develop personal responsibility and integrity in the child!

The overprotecting and controlling parent creates just as much dysfunction as the abusive parent—sometimes more. Abused children are exposed to open, obvious rejection. Because it is overt, they understand why they struggle with self-worth. It is sometimes easier for them to accept their parent's dysfunction and disassociate themselves from their parent's problems.

A controlling, overprotective parent, however, conveys a total lack of confidence in the child. Because the parent makes all of the decisions, the child assumes that he or she is too dumb to make decisions. This can be done in such a subtle way that the child cannot identify the dysfunction of the parent. The child cannot see that the parent is a codependent controller. The child does not understand his or her feelings of inadequacy or anger at the parent.

The child of a controller lacks confidence to such a degree that he or she feels guilty for even questioning the parent. The parent has proven the child wrong at nearly every decision. How could it be the parent? He or she is always right. This child is much less likely to ever be free than the child who was abused or openly rejected.

Controlling parents are much like abusive parents. They convince the child that love is the motivation behind their actions. Just like abused children will never feel loved unless they are abused, controlled children will subconsciously seek out other controllers to whom they will continually give their life and choices, or they too will become controllers.

One of the things that most children are cheated out of is the opportunity to experience failure and still feel good about themselves. So much emphasis is placed on the need to be right that the child feels shame and disgrace when he or she fails. This can easily bring about all sorts of extreme reactions and can position the child to spend a lifetime trying to prove him or herself right. The child is set to be a codependent controller who needs for people to think he or she is right. Then there are the ridiculous concepts of social justice that don't believe kids should be graded or scored. There are no winners and there are no losers. Sadly, this child is less prepared for the "real world" than the child of the controller or abuser.

Parenting in a Nutshell

The two main goals of parenting should be making our children feel loved and teaching them responsibility. These two will balance one another. Responsibility without love can be hard and mean. Love without responsibility can be liberal and undermining. But, love and responsibility will bring a child to maturity while planting the seeds for healthy self-worth. The capacity to feel loved and the ability to accept personal responsibility address the two areas of greatest struggle. The primary theme woven through the majority of the parables was personal responsibility. This is key to Kingdom living!

> ONE OF THE THINGS THAT MOST CHILDREN ARE CHEATED OUT OF IS THE OPPORTUNITY TO EXPERIENCE FAILURE AND STILL FEEL GOOD ABOUT THEMSELVES.

Most of the church's ministry to children is attempting to reach the children the previous generation of Christians lost. Then after we reach them, we spend a lifetime trying to heal them from the hurts that the last generation of confused Christian parents inflicted upon them.

After all of his children were grown, an elderly man in Canada shared his insight into child raising with me. He said, "I think child-raising should be 90 percent affirmation and 10 percent confrontation." I think he's right! If we, as parents, can affirm our love for our children and build a healthy self-worth through our love and the love of God, I think they will be able to face and win the game of life. If children are not dealing with the issues of self-worth and rejection, they will be free to place their attention on the task at hand.

A child with a healthy self-worth is not subject to peer pressure. This child doesn't need the acceptance of the group to such a degree that he or she falls into the traps of adolescence. Because we have missed the objectives of parenting, our children spend their adult years trying to find what is easiest found as a child: self-worth!

LOVE AND RESPONSIBILITY WILL BRING A CHILD TO MATURITY WHILE PLANTING THE SEEDS FOR HEALTHY SELF-WORTH.

One of the ultimate misconceptions emerges from confusion about disciplining and punishment. Discipline is about teaching, developing and nurturing. Discipline seizes the failure of a child as an opportunity to help him or her grow. Discipline allows children to face the organic consequences of their choices. It then helps them cultivate better choices as a way to emerge triumphant. It builds confidence. It develops the ability to make good decisions in the future.

Punishment, on the other hand, is the infliction of pain beyond the natural consequences. It focuses on the failure. Rather than inspire the desire to make good choices, it creates the fear of being wrong. Punishment makes the parent the source of pain instead of the "bad decision."

The absence of love is the problem. The Bible tells us what to do, but love tells us how to do it. Love must be the guiding force behind all actions. No matter what we do, we should always ask, "Does this convey value? Does this make the child feel precious and held in high regard? Will it leave his or her dignity and worth intact?" Only when we can act from these guiding principles are we ready to act!

19

MENTAL HEALTH

Mental health is a broad field comprised of many differing opinions. Although the truths involved in obtaining mental health are the same for everyone, the journey to mental health can differ due to the variety of backgrounds and influences. Our mental condition is never developed from one source. It is more of a combination of influences that come together to create our life paradigms. Therefore, good mental health, from a biblical point of view, can never be obtained unless there is some resolving of heart issues!

Scientists now understand that through cellular memory we have a record of every bit of information we were ever exposed to, as well as a record of every emotional experience. Contrary to early psychological theories, mental health is neither a product of simple thoughts nor the end result of a chemical in the brain; rather, it is the way we have been programmed. It is a combination of conscious and unconscious thought, cellular memory and biological reactions. However, this country has been lulled into a false hope of mental health that feeds the codependent mindset.

There seems to be at least three streams of conflicting thought among those who search for ways to establish emotional stability in man. There are those who see man's need to accept responsibility for his actions. These professionals are very close to the biblical approach to mental health. Then there is another stream of thought that focuses on society as the cause for emotional pain and stability. This group seems to be more concerned with placing blame than placing responsibility. Then there is the third group who see emotions as mere chemical reactions occurring with the body independent of our thoughts. This group never calls for personal responsibility; they simply medicate the symptoms.

The Blame Game

In the world at large, there seems to be a prevailing ideology that says, "If you can find someone to blame, then you don't have to feel guilty about your problems. If you don't feel guilty about your problems, you will get better." This model says that society has imposed standards upon you. When you reject these false standards, you will be relieved of false guilt and you will be cured. This group is very anti-God, very anti-morality and very anti-responsibility. In their mind, if they could eradicate the idea of God and morality, there would be no social ills.

> MENTAL HEALTH IS NOT A PRODUCT OF SIMPLE THOUGHTS; RATHER, IT IS THE WAY WE HAVE BEEN PROGRAMMED.

The sad thing is that the groups that focus on the damaging effects of guilt are right. Guilt is a problem. Guilt causes stress. Stress causes the body to malfunction. The majority of all mental and physical disease comes from stress. Where these groups go wrong is blaming society or simply seeking to alter the chemical reaction. After a person is freed from guilt, he or she must still assume responsibility. Knowing who to blame has never set anyone free.

Some of the greatest breakthroughs in mental health have occurred in the past 20 years. Some researchers are finally realizing that the mechanical model of man was totally incorrect. In some areas of behavioral psychology, people are moving closer to a biblical concept of man, although most of them don't realize it.

Society has been duped by the mental health "experts" in the past. Stop and think about it. We have people who believe only in the physical world specializing in the area of thoughts. This is the very realm of existence they deny, the non-physical! If that is not breeding ground for contradiction, I don't know what is. By starting with a mechanical model of man, the problem can never be addressed internally. It must be addressed externally by the professional.

Since we cannot see the spirit or soul of a man and can only observe the reactions, no one can measure thought, worry, fear, happiness, peace, love or any other emotion. All we can do is measure some of the body's responses to those emotions. Therefore, there is always a certain amount of speculation concerning any conclusions pertaining to thoughts, feelings and emotions.

This dilemma makes it easy for researchers to begin their research with all sorts of unproven theories. These theories determine in advance how we will interpret all of our data. Thus, our research is tainted from the beginning. Every experiment must begin with certain absolutes; therefore, those who study the mind begin with some concepts they consider to be absolute. But what if their predetermined concepts are wrong? Then the way they interpret all of their data will be wrong!

The liberal believes that religion is the cause of man's problems. He (or she) has had religious values imposed upon him; therefore, he has a false sense of guilt about his actions. He falsely asserts that if he had no religious beliefs or moral standards, he would have no sense of guilt. After all, he surmises, there is no right or wrong. The liberal's cure for man is to cast off all restraints and fulfill his every passion.[1] Society has sought this path of recovery only to find itself sinking deeper into the trap of instability and codependency.

It is this logic that drives the extreme left's view of capitalism. If we could remove capitalism and make everyone equal, there would be no envy. If we could remove these unjust economic outcomes, man would give up his need for religion. Therefore, socialism is the cure for all of man's ills. There are those in the extreme left who actually believe Christians, Muslims, Jews, Hindus and all religions will actually abandon their convictions once capitalism is destroyed. The carnal, worldly model starts with an anti-God motive and extrapolates the data to a conclusion that is beyond bizarre. Yet, it is taught in various forms in our schools, universities and, sadly, in many pulpits. The unsuspecting public naively accepts it as the scientific work of the qualified professional, not realizing that the path to a Godless society is paved with codependency!

The Destruction of the Soul

When I first read the Bible, I remember coming to this phrase, *"The soul who sins shall die"* (Ezekiel 18:4,20). When I asked my pastor what the Bible meant when it talked about a soul, he said, *"Soul* is just another word for person." It made sense, for Acts 2 speaks of 3,000 souls being saved. It seemed like it was talking about people. Yet, as I looked at the various passages that mentioned the soul, I realized it was more than a synonym for a person. It was speaking of a specific aspect of a person. It was talking about the mind and emotions.

> *SOUL* SPEAKS OF A SPECIFIC ASPECT OF A PERSON. IT IS TALKING ABOUT THE MIND AND EMOTIONS.

Then I began to see that sin destroys the soul, i.e., the mind and emotions. People did not fall over dead when they committed a particular sin, but they did experience a degree of death in their soul. Proverbs 8:36 says, *"He who sins against me wrongs his own soul; all those who hate me love death."* When we violate the wisdom of our Creator, there are negative effects in the soul. This caused me to take another look at our "religious" concepts of sin to determine if they were really rooted in sound biblical thought!

The destruction that works in our soul is not the work of an angry, vengeful God. Rather, it is like trying to make your engine run on watered-down fuel. It is destructive. It doesn't work. Many times I have heard people say, "If only we had gotten an operator's manual for life…." Well, we did. We just don't like what it says. God created us; He knows what will bring us life and what will bring us death. He gave us the information we need. We simply don't trust Him enough to live by His truth!

The most common Greek word translated as "sin" is a word that is normally understood as "to miss the mark." From that simple translation all the emphasis is on the fact that we did something wrong. But upon closer examination you see that is only a partial definition painted by religious legalism. *Strong's Concordance* defines sin as "to miss the mark (and so not share in the prize)."[2] The problem with "sin" is not so much that we have done wrong. The problem with sin is that it is a belief or action that keeps us from being who we could be, having what we could have and enjoying life at its best, including healthy positive emotions!

The world says it is the lack of fulfilling your desire that is destroying you. "Go for it! Do what you want. Then you'll be happy." Wrong! Then you'll be emotionally unstable. Proverbs 6:32 says, *"Whoever commits adultery with a woman lacks understanding."* The world says, "If you want her, that's the only way you'll ever be fulfilled."

The world has encouraged us to close our eyes and run down the path to destruction. A loving God is saying, "Please don't do those things. They will kill you. I have something better for you." But we have stopped our ears and said, "I don't trust You. You don't want me to be happy. That's why You won't let me do what I want to do."

We have this concept that sin is the list of fun things God will not let us do. It is as if He made all of the fun things to be sin so He could somehow test us. Wrong! Sin is a list of all those things that will kill you. Sin will rob you of emotional and eventually physical health. Mainly, sin will keep you from ever living up to who you were created to be! On the negative side, it will bring death to your soul—your thoughts and emotions.

> THE PROBLEM WITH SIN IS THAT IT KEEPS US FROM BEING WHO WE COULD BE AND HAVING THE HEALTHY POSITIVE EMOTIONS WE COULD HAVE!

The church has failed miserably at presenting the issue of sin to the world. We have made it a matter of right and wrong, good and bad. This will never be enough motivation for a person to leave sin. Once the world believes that sin will cause them pain, they will leave it alone. Once they see that godliness will produce joy, they will want it. We have simply not presented it to them in a wise manner.

The second basic flaw of our mental health system is its desire to find someone to blame. This is food for the codependent mind. There is a difference between peace and relief. Peace comes from God because all things are as they should be. Relief can come from many sources. I used to get relief by doing drugs. I would get relief by committing adultery. I got relief from a lot of destructive sources. Finding someone to blame gives relief, not peace. But relief never lasts. Relief is like the high a person experiences on drugs: it never lasts, we need larger quantities each time and it perpetuates destructive behavior, which makes us need more relief.

The Professional Counselor

Why do people spend a lifetime in therapy? Simple! They need to keep getting temporary doses of relief. When people experience the peace of God, they don't need relief anymore. They don't need someone to blame. It doesn't matter who caused the problem. In the book *The Healing Code*,[3] Drs. Alex Loyd and Ben Johnson point to research that indicates that rehashing our problems creates stress and adds to the problem. In fact, anything that makes us "cope" adds to our problem. Coping isn't curing; it is simply finding a way to live with the problem.

> SIN IS A LIST OF ALL THOSE THINGS THAT WILL KILL YOU.

I am constantly amazed at the rationale of some counselors, including Christian counselors. A dysfunctional person will sit in a counseling session and give his or her version of the problem. The counselee could be lying or simply viewing the circumstances through a faulty paradigm. Nonetheless, it is treated as true. The counselor doesn't check any of the facts for accuracy. Instead, he or she gathers all the information about who did what to the poor victim and creates a treatment strategy based on flawed information!

I have seen parents of problem children assassinated by mental health counselors. It was as if the entire family was crazy and this person, who is now in the mental ward, is the only sane one in the group. What's wrong with this picture? This approach has grown out of the predetermined attitude that society is responsible.

A counselor never knows if the patient is truthful or not. Many emotionally unstable people are very effective liars. They have spent a lifetime making the irrational and untrue seem rational and true. The one and only thing a counselor can deal with is whether or not the patient is responding to the people around him or her in a responsible way.

Sadly, these "professionals" have now become the heart and soul of the criminal justice system. They have taken their bizarre form of interpretation into our courtrooms and made the criminal to be the victim. His (or her) past somehow frees him from the consequences of his actions.

The criminal justice system does not exist to rehabilitate the criminal. I think there should be tremendous attempts made to rehabilitate criminals, but not in the courtroom. The justice system is there to protect the rights of the innocent. Criminals are not put in jail to punish them as much as they are put in jail to protect society. Rehabilitation is another issue altogether.

Our mental health system in this country has invaded the classroom, the courtroom and the living room. People who operate from unproven theories are controlling the way we perceive the treatment and prevention of the emotionally unstable, yet, their very philosophies ensure that mental disorders will grow out of control. Codependency will be nurtured and society will be crippled. If these new theories were sound, the use of antidepressants and other psychiatric drugs would not be skyrocketing!

Our approach to mental health has failed miserably. Some research has shown that the same percentage of people will improve whether they do or do not receive treatment from a mental health expert.[4] That means our system is not working. It seems that no one is noticing that the more these unproven theories are implemented, the worse our society spins out of control.

By rejecting God's method of mental health, which the church has poorly represented, we have given ourselves over to those whose own methods have failed…the experts! The socialist, progressive ideas are driven by two categories of people: the people ignorant enough to think they are true, and those seeking to promote chaos and anarchy as a means of destroying our society! The biased liberal is convinced that once every shred of belief in God is eradicated, the world will become a humanitarian utopia. Rather than deal with the facts, they blindly blame the Bible for keeping their ideas from working. This is why communists believe they must either kill or imprison all people over 30 in order to create their utopian society They need to build on the young minds that have not been corrupted by religion and capitalism.

Despite the vain attempts of the world's system, the Bible offers the only complete resolution to our struggles: a continual cleansing of the conscious (awareness of self) that comes as a result of living in fellowship with the Lord Jesus. The Apostle John tells us that if we will walk in the light, truth, integrity and honesty, we will have fellowship with Jesus. In other words, we will share in the life He has and He will impart that life to us. John goes on to say that in the intimate relationship that has fled the darkness, His blood will continually cleanse us from all that would keep us from sharing in the prize!

Endnotes

1. Jay Adams, *The Christian Counselor's Manual* (Grand Rapids, MI: Zondervan, 1973).
2. *Biblesoft's New Exhaustive Strong's Numbers and Concordance with Expanded Greek-Hebrew Dictionary* (Biblesoft, Inc. and International Bible Translators, Inc., 1994, 2003, 2006), NT:264.
3. Dr. Alex Loyd and Dr. Ben Johnson, *The Healing Code* (Peoria, AZ: Intermedia Publishing Group, 2010).
4. Adams, *The Christian Counselor's Manual.*

20

EDUCATION

America once had the greatest education system in the world, but today we are falling behind other nations in both quality and content of education. The problem with U.S. education, however, is not because we do not have the right information to teach our children. It is because of the beliefs and agendas of those who control the education system. High on the list of anti-God agendas was the goal of controlling the classrooms.

Our founding fathers believed that education was essential to sustaining a strong country. In fact, they believed without education...specific education... our country would never be able to sustain its freedoms. The founders wanted all Americans to read, write and know math, but they also wanted them to know the Bible and the Constitution. In the book *The 5000 Year Leap*, Daniel Webster is quoted as saying, "It is not to be doubted, that to the free and universal reading of the Bible, in that age, men were much indebted for right views of civil liberties."[1]

Our founders never believed America could survive apart from what they called religion, i.e., Christianity. They built our Constitution on the principle of unalienable rights. These are the rights that are granted to men by God and understood through nature. Since God gave them, no man had the right to take them away. The idea of separation of church and state never existed in the manner it is understood today. In fact, one of the main goals of government was to protect our religious freedoms.

The Fundamental Factors

The removal of God from the classroom and from public view is not a movement to preserve the freedom of some who do not believe. It is designed to take away the freedom given to man by God. Once the idea of God is destroyed, the idea of unalienable rights is no longer defensible. It then becomes the government that gives and takes rights. The education system has long been the target of communist, socialist, progressive and other leftist ideologies aimed at the subversion of our government, the erosion of our Constitution and the abandoning of our Bible-based values.

CODEPENDENCY IS THE GOAL OF THOSE WHO SHAPE OUR EDUCATIONAL SYSTEM.

It was not enough that the educators removed the mention of God from the classroom; they also removed all principles of development and tutoring that were consistent with biblical principles of training children. Everything that the Bible teaches that will make one responsible, stable and have good self-worth, has been replaced by mere theories that are not working and never will work.

Make no mistake, the removal of these proven approaches is not accidental. It is strategic by those who must indoctrinate our children and render them incapable of responsible living. Control is the goal and codependency is the process of those who shape our educational system.

The effort to return prayer to the classroom is valiant and I agree with it, but it will not come close to dealing with the real problem. What we need is godly teachers in the classroom, on the board of education, on the city council, in the courtrooms and in the White House. We need the unions' control over teachers

156

broken. In the 1950s the communists stated that the infiltration of unions would be essential to accomplishing their long-term goal of destroying capitalism. There are no simple solutions. Prayer, without a practical return to biblical principles, will never make a noticeable difference.

Self-worth, self-respect and self-control are among the most fundamental factors for success. In a system that rewards failure, has no power to punish misbehaving students and no way to fire nonproductive teachers, these qualities can never be developed. Children cannot build a sense of self-worth if they cannot identify with God as their Creator. For a child to think he or she is the offspring of some amoeba that swam up out of a swamp is not the breeding ground for good self-worth—or for the respect of human life in general.

> SELF-WORTH, SELF-RESPECT AND SELF-CONTROL ARE AMONG THE MOST FUNDAMENTAL FACTORS FOR SUCCESS.

If children are not made to be responsible for their actions, they cannot be taught. The courts have disempowered teachers by taking away authority and giving more responsibility. The concept of education as a right instead of a privilege has taken all power away from the teacher and the school system to protect those who are willing to obey and learn. Education, however, is a privilege that belongs to parents and children who will yield themselves to the process.

When I visited a first grade classroom in our city to discuss some education problems that were affecting my daughter, the teacher openly confessed, "I don't have time to teach; I simply try to keep the class under control." The hands of the teacher have been tied by the legal issues, the political system, the unions and the special interest groups. These groups have no value for the child or education; they simply have an interest in having things their way. As the NEA has openly stated for years, their goal is not education. It is control.

What About the Teachers?

Only the successful have earned the right to teach and hold influence over our children. The Bible says, *"Imitate those who through faith and patience inherit the promises"* (Hebrews 6:12). We should only follow those who have succeeded by observing biblical principles, yet we have people with no success in life dictating how the education process should work. We have those whose children are in trouble telling us how our children should be handled. Textbooks are written by rebellious "rejects" with anti-God and anti-American agendas. This doesn't just happen at the primary level. It continues all the way through college.

I once needed some people to work in one of my businesses. I knew part-time people could do the job, so I went to one of the local universities. I met with the head of the business department to discuss my desire to hire students. I felt it would be good for the students to have an opportunity at real business while they were still in school.

The more I talked with this man, the more frustrated I became. As he described his philosophies of business, I determined that I didn't want to hire anyone who had his mentality. As I talked further with him, I found that he had never started or managed a business. In fact, he had never had a job other than teaching. He didn't have a clue about the real world.

Think of it: the government that regulates the laws for business does not create one dollar of profit for the country. Many of the people in political offices never had a real job. They are professional politicians. They have wrecked our economy, yet they tell us how to run our businesses and educate our children. After they shipwrecked the economy in 2008, they insisted that giving them more control would solve the problems. We are asking the fox to guard the henhouse. Then we wonder why we have no chickens. I think this qualifies for "the blind leading the blind."

Our educational system spends 12 years steeping our children in living out of control, proving that there are no serious consequences for actions. By graduation every student believes that one can get by with little or no effort. They have been steeped in socialism. They have read books that are anti-American. History is nothing more than propaganda. Schools do all this while providing one of the most inferior educations of the industrialized world. The facts bear this out; our education system has failed. To add insult to injury, there are laws that require us to have our children educated by these failures and, in some states, we can't even select our school of choice.

Much of the material that is taught in school is inaccurate. God is mocked. People of faith are ridiculed. Even those who hold conservative political beliefs are treated unfairly by instructors. Communism is hailed as the savior of the world. The Constitution is never taught. History has been rewritten to leave out any mention of God or godliness. It has made our heroes into villains and has undermined all confidence in our country, our values and our God. Some textbooks would lead you to believe that communism has worked around the world. It takes only a casual observation to see education in America has little to do with teaching children academically and much more to do with forming their political opinions and values.

> IT TAKES ONLY A CASUAL OBSERVATION TO SEE EDUCATION IN AMERICA HAS LITTLE TO DO WITH TEACHING CHILDREN ACADEMICALLY AND MUCH MORE TO DO WITH FORMING THEIR POLITICAL OPINIONS AND VALUES.

There is a subtle and even sometimes overt message sent forth to the students that their parents are not the final authority. The child is made to believe that the state is the ultimate parent. All of the devaluing of the family becomes another important factor in undermining identity and self-worth, all of which creates a deep need to find a source of identity and worth. The humanistic educator is more than glad to facilitate this need. It may actually be his or her goal.

It's the Codependent Progression

Although these have been the stated goals of communists, socialists and progressives for generations, it is more than a diabolical conspiracy. This is just the world system. This is man depending on himself and others for that which he should only depend on God. These are people who truly want to make the world a better place to live and raise children. These are the children of parents who departed from God. The world leaders of today are the codependent children of yesterday's faithless society.

As far as these people have drifted from God, that still does not mean they are a deliberate, willing part of a sinister plot. Most teachers want to do their jobs. Their hands are tied by union rules, school board policies and governmental mandates. The more the church attacks them, the farther they withdraw from God and His wisdom. We need to demonstrate the effects of godliness. They need to see our godliness affect our cities and schools. They need to see us have peace and success within the body of Christ. We need to be involved as peacemakers who know the Bible, know the Constitution and know how to work the system. We need to be there to support good teachers and principals. We need to reclaim our schools and our children.

> THE WORLD LEADERS OF TODAY ARE THE CODEPENDENT CHILDREN OF YESTERDAY'S FAITHLESS SOCIETY.

The farther the educators move from God, the farther they move from an understanding of His entire creation. Planet Earth has become a trash heap of toxic waste. Governments are corrupt. People are needlessly starving. Disease is running out of control. All of this is the product of insecure people departing from God's wisdom and seeking self-worth through greed, power and control.

God created man and placed him in an environment that is conducive to his needs. The first rebellion in the garden brought about the first environmental changes in planet Earth. It brought the introduction of pain, sickness and suffering. As man has lost touch with God, he has lost touch with his need to function in a healthy social and physical environment. This loss of the big picture has given rise to the era of the specialists.

The "Specialist"

Specialists focus on one part to such an extent that they lose touch with the whole. The specialist makes phenomenal inventions, but the by-product of those inventions create toxic waste. While they heal one part of the world, they destroy another. The pharmaceutical specialist creates a medication that kills one sickness while causing five others. The economic specialists keep the market strong while creating financial disaster for the economy as a whole. The human rights specialists help the poor at the cost of the middle class. The religious specialists get people to heaven, but don't have a clue about how to live effectively in this life. The education specialists can teach a particular subject with no understanding of the values that must undergird the learning process.

In 1979, a group of academic specialists admitted to *The Washington Post* that they did not know how to solve global problems. We have had so many years of focusing in on the individual details that we have lost sight of the whole picture. When people do not understand God's plan for man, they desperately grasp for the meaning of life. Everyone desperately hopes that his or her little bit of knowledge will be the key that changes it all. Desperation, greed and ignorance lead us to a specialized, idealistic society. We offer people false hope if they will just trust our plan or our idea. The truth is, there is no freedom for neither the saint nor the sinner apart from knowing, trusting and experiencing God.

> THERE IS NO FREEDOM FOR NEITHER THE SAINT NOR THE SINNER APART FROM KNOWING, TRUSTING AND EXPERIENCING GOD.

There is a battle waging for the minds of our children. So far, the church has lost. We have inexperienced, codependent controllers forming the paradigms of the youth. In the name of education, they are being led down the primrose path of codependency. Like the youth of Nazi Germany or the young communists, they are being offered a utopia that only exists in the minds of emotionally unstable, ungodly, dishonest leaders who seek to validate their life through vain philosophies and unproven idealism. Their lives and ideas are being forged by the idealistic, codependent controllers who hate God, hate America and hate capitalism.

Abraham Lincoln said something like this: "What is taught in the classroom today is the law of the land tomorrow." If you want to know why the youth of today are so irresponsible, lazy, disrespectful, dishonest and immature, look at who spends the most time with them and what those people are teaching them.

Those who hate God and hate America must have your children so codependent that they one day willfully surrender themselves to the god of government. They must see the government as their source. They must be weak and fearful.

Endnote

1. W. Cleon Skousen, *The 5000 Year Leap: A Miracle That Changed the World* (National Center For Constitutional Studies, USA, 1991), 255.

21

CHRISTIAN MENTAL HEALTH

Positive mental health is a goal and a benefit of believing and experiencing the realities of the gospel. The Apostle John said it like this: *"...that you may prosper in all things and be in health, just as your soul prospers"* (3 John 2). He understood that man's ability to be physically healthy and enjoy a prosperous life required that his soul, i.e., mind and emotions, be healthy. Jesus said, *"Peace I leave with you, My peace I give to you; not as the world gives do I give to you. Let not your heart be troubled, neither let it be afraid"* (John 14:27). *"These things I have spoken to you, that in Me you may have peace. In the world you will have tribulation; but be of good cheer, I have overcome the world"* (John 16:33). Peace, love and safety are essential elements of emotional stability. They are all ours in a real, intimate relationship with Him!

Because man has not trusted God, he has looked to every other source in the world to find the answers to emotional health. But the more theories man comes up with, the more mental and emotional sickness emerges in our society. Year by year, as we have cast away God's standards, we dove deeper and deeper into a crisis that is giving rise to every imaginable horror. The arrogant unbeliever insists that if we will just reject more of God's standards, we will ultimately find the man-made utopia. It is incumbent upon us to remember that the world insists that it is the acceptance of God and moral standards that causes all of life's stress. In the end, it is the rejection of God that all worldly systems seek to accomplish that brings the pain and destruction.

Since there is not a single scientist who can explain all the processes of the brain, much less the mind, I feel that I should reconsider the source of my opinions about mental and emotional health. The only theories of man that have worked are the ones that have been consistent with the Word of God. Therefore, I must look to the Word of God for absolute information about the mind and emotions. That which is in conflict with the Word of God is in conflict with how God created man and therefore will not work!

> MAN EXPERIENCES AND INTERPRETS BOTH SPIRITUAL AND PHYSICAL LIFE IN THE REALM OF THE SOUL.

We must be careful to separate the teaching of the church and the teaching of the Bible. Unfortunately, many theories of the church are as inconsistent with the Word of God as the theories of the world. It has been these unscriptural, unworkable concepts of the church that have caused serious-minded people to look to another source for authoritative answers. Religion, because of its "vaccination-like effect," is actually more deadly than corrupt worldly philosophies. One of my favorite preachers, John Osteen, used to say something like this: "Religion is like a vaccination. It gives you just enough of the real thing to keep you from actually catching it."

The Realm of the Soul

In Genesis, God created man's body from the dust of the earth. He then breathed into man something of Himself, some of His own Spirit. When these two elements came together, man did not become a living body, as the medical world would have us to believe. Nor did he become a living spirit, as the religious world would have us to believe. God's Word says that man became a living soul!

"And the Lord God formed man of the dust of the ground, and breathed into his nostrils the breath of life; and man became a living soul" (Genesis 2:7).

Man's body is what keeps him alive to this world. The body makes it possible to interact, feel and sense things in the physical world. That physical input is turned into thoughts and emotions in the soul. Likewise, the spirit of a man gives him awareness of the spiritual world. That information also becomes feelings and emotions in the soul. Man experiences and interprets both spiritual and physical life in the realm of the soul.

Since God created man, He is the only one who fully understands how real mental health should work. Everything we need to know about mental health would be found in the Bible and supported by scientific experimentation—if either of the two sides could give up their prejudices and work together. Regardless of scientific validation, time has proven that the principles of the Word of God work consistently to bring about a healthy mind!

> KNOWING GOD IS THE PRODUCT OF A RELATIONSHIP, NOT JUST A SINGULAR EXPERIENCE.

Zoe Life

"And this is eternal life, that they may know You, the only true God, and Jesus Christ whom You have sent" (John 17:3). When the Bible talks about eternal life, it is referring to a particular quality of life found only in God. The Greek word is *zoe*. *Zoe* life is the quality of life as possessed by the one who gives it.[1] In this case, we are speaking of the quality of life God has that is given to us freely through the Lord Jesus.

Jesus said this quality of life would be the product of knowing God. Knowing God is the product of a relationship, not just a singular experience. Although it is absolutely essential that we have a "born again" experience, that experience alone will not produce *zoe*. If we do not develop a relationship with God and find fullness of life, that experience can be frustrating and cause us to disbelieve the promise of zoe!

In the Old Testament, there were people who believed in God, but they never had the opportunity to experience this quality of life. This can only be found in the finished work of Jesus. Through Jesus' propitiation (the satisfying of wrath), we have the opportunity to experience God's love in a way that is different than anything the world has ever known. This quality of love leads to the quality of life. But the quality of life (*zoe*) is only experienced when we *experience* the quality of love! By accepting the love of God as expressed through the Lord Jesus' finished work, we can be brought into a realm where we experience *zoe*.

> KNOWLEDGE OF WHAT REALLY IS CONSTITUTES THE SUPREME POSSIBILITY IN LIFE.

Jesus said it is "knowing" God that brings us into this life. The word *know* comes from the Greek *gnosis*. This word for knowledge is beyond mere academic study. Here is a definition of this incredible concept of knowing: "this act embraces every organ and mode of knowledge, e.g., by seeing, hearing, investigating or experiencing. This is related to the Greek view of reality. The truly real is a timeless reality that is constant in every change. Those who see or know this possess and control it. Hence knowledge of what really is constitutes the supreme possibility in life. Those who know participate in the eternal."[2] To know God with every aspect of our being is to participate in an aspect of reality that is to enter into the realm of the eternal! This can only be known through the person and work of the Lord Jesus!

Righteousness Is the Key

Through Jesus, we have complete peace with God. *"Therefore, having been justified by faith, we have peace with God through our Lord Jesus Christ"* (Romans 5:1). True mental health is only found when man is at peace with God in his own heart. That peace only comes when one trusts the reality that Jesus has not only died to become his or her Savior, but He also has risen again to become his or her righteousness.

This meets the deepest need that man has. This is the basis for all emotional health. This is the stabilizing factor that brings all of life together. However, this is also the reality that the church and the world have rejected. Both groups have rejected the truth, neither one realizing the implications. Both groups have robbed man of the one and only thing that would bring him absolute stability and peace, the qualification for the total love and acceptance of God: righteousness!

Romans 9 talks about Jesus being the stumbling stone. But, it really doesn't say that Jesus was *personally* the stumbling stone. It explains that faith-righteousness that is found in Jesus is the stumbling stone. *"What shall we say then? That Gentiles, who did not pursue righteousness, have attained to righteousness, even the righteousness of faith; but Israel, pursuing the law of righteousness, has not attained to the law of righteousness. Why? Because they did not seek it by faith, but as it were, by the works of the law. For they stumbled at that stumbling stone. As it is written: 'Behold, I lay in Zion a stumbling stone and rock of offense, and whoever believes on Him will not be put to shame'"* (Romans 9:30-33).

JESUS AS OUR RIGHTEOUSNESS IS THE STUMBLING STONE.

The Gentiles were not looking for righteousness, but they found it. Why? They were willing to accept it as a free gift. Israel, on the other hand, was trying desperately to find righteousness so they could be accepted by God. They could not find it. Why? They refused to believe it could be received as a free gift. They stumbled at the stumbling stone. Jesus as Savior is not the stumbling stone; Jesus as our righteousness is the stumbling stone. In fact, the Judaizers were a group of Jews who vainly attempted to mix the Old and New Covenants. They taught that Jesus was Savior but your works kept you righteous. This was the first great heresy to undermine the early church. The Apostle Paul said this belief neutralized the grace (power, ability, capacity) of God in our lives.

One of the great doctrinal errors of the church lies in its inability to believe that Jesus could become our sin and deliver us from sin and its power; that

He could become the curse and thereby deliver us from the curse; and that He could become our righteousness, thereby obtaining our righteousness. The refusal to accept this foundation of the death, burial and resurrection has been the rationale behind many Christian cults, the doctrine of Islam and the limiting beliefs of many orthodox Christians. But this is the root of the gospel! Believing and experiencing this as our reality is what actually gives us the peace promised in Jesus! If Jesus is not our righteousness, He cannot be our peace.

> THE HUMAN MIND CAN ONLY FUNCTION OPTIMALLY WHEN IT IS AT PEACE.

Faith-righteousness is the best kept secret in the church. Preachers preach day and night trying to get people to work harder to become more righteous so they can be accepted of God. This was a load that the Jews could not carry. And now the bar is raised even higher. In the New Covenant we are called upon to do what we do from a heart of love! This is why Jesus came. We didn't just need a way to get to heaven; we needed freedom from the power and guilt of sin, a conscience cleansed from the burden of righteousness. By making us righteous, we now have complete peace with God.

It is this burden of responsibility that has made the world turn its back on God. The world was smart enough to know that no one could ever be righteous enough to please a perfect God. Laboring under that load has driven many people completely crazy. So the world said, "Nobody can do this, so why try? Let's erase the mention of God from our memory so we can be free from trying to please Him. Then maybe we can get on with life." The church and the world have both stumbled over the stumbling stone: Jesus Christ as our righteousness.

The human mind can only function optimally when it is at peace. The absence of peace is destructive to both body and soul. Peace is only found in a meaningful, loving relationship with God through the Lord Jesus. It is found in a place where we accept the finished work of Jesus. We have received Him as Lord and Savior but we must be sure to believe on Him as our righteousness. Nothing else brings absolute peace.

Many Christians have lost emotional stability believing that Jesus was Lord but not knowing if God would accept them. Trying to qualify is the torment of the Christian. Trying to qualify destroys self-worth. Trying to qualify makes a statement to the heart that says, "I am not qualified." This is the cause of condemnation, the root of "Christian insanity."

Condemnation is the expectation of judgment.[3] If one is not fully convinced that Jesus paid the full price for our sin and met all of our qualifications for righteousness, he or she will only have one other source of comfort and peace: his or her performance. This means one must become a totally deceived, self-righteous legalist or ride the roller coaster of performance. When we perform well, we are self-righteous; when we do not perform well, we feel guilty. Guilt has to do with punishment. When we feel guilty, we expect things to go wrong. It is this fear that becomes the breeding ground for physical and emotional instability.

Neither the totally false concepts of the world nor the warped religious concepts of the church have been able to provide man with the peace and stability offered in the Word of God. Both systems are failing and neither one wants to admit it. The world may ignore God, but the need that every man has to know and feel the love of God will not go away. The incidence of addiction, immorality, violence, insanity and other social ills will continue to grow as the world moves farther from the God who loves them.

The religious church will continue to be an impotent force in the world. It will hold out promises that are not fulfilled in this life. It will only experience small degrees of victory. Fortunately, though the church may fail a person in this life, it will not fail in eternity. At least the majority of the church world preaches salvation through faith in the Lord Jesus. The world system may bring some relief in this life, but it will fail in eternity. Either of these extremes, however, will prevent a person from knowing God and finding *zoe*, a quality of emotional and physical life that can only be found in God in this life on earth.

It is this love and peace that comes from knowing God through Jesus that meets the deep need man has to feel the acceptance of his Creator. When God is our source, people are no longer able to control and manipulate us. The love of God is the root of self-worth that establishes us in dignity and worth. Dignity and worth is the only antidote to a codependent life! The free gift of righteousness in Jesus is what makes us feel, safe, at peace…and emotionally stable!

Endnotes

1. Hermann Cremer, *Biblico-Theological Lexicon of New Testament Greek* (Edinburgh: T & T Clark, 1977), 272.
2. *Theological Dictionary of the New Testament*, abridged edition (Grand Rapids, MI: William B. Eerdmans Publishing Company, 1985).
3. *Thayer's Greek-English Lexicon of the New Testament* (Grand Rapids, MI: Baker Book House, n.d.).

22

THE CODEPENDENT CHURCH

Let me begin by saying I love the church. With all its flaws and failures, the church is my family. It is not my desire to cast stones; nor is it my intention to undermine your confidence in the church. Yet, it is essential that the church examine itself to see if it is *"in the faith"* (2 Corinthians 13:5). Even more important, it is essential for believers to understand if they have replaced a relationship with Jesus with a relationship with an organization. You can only be a blessing to a local church if you remain strong in the Lord. When you begin to expect from the church what can only come from God, you will damage the church.

Even that which is ordained by Scripture becomes destructive when it becomes a substitute for intimate relationship and heartfelt trust in the finished work of the Lord Jesus. There is an ancient proverb that says, "The path is not the mountain. We don't stop and live on the path. We travel the path to reach the top of the mountain." Many of the wonderful tools God has given—the local church, the fivefold ministry and even the Word of God itself—are often used as a substitute for intimacy instead of a pathway to intimacy.

The defense of the leader or organization that has become unhealthy is often the fact that its existence can be justified through the Scripture. Regardless of where we find it in the Scripture, when we relate to anything in such a codependent manner that it becomes a substitute for what can only be found in an intimate, faith-filled connection with God, we have elevated it to a place that is near to idolatry. It is essential that you realize no leader can cause you to make such a shift in your loyalties. If your relationship with a church or leader is codependent, it was your choice.

The church is scriptural, but not everything about "how we do" church is ordained of God. The roles of the ministers (servants), like the existence of organizations, should never abandon their biblical basis, but rather should be flexible and adaptable to facilitate the goals defined by New Testament Scripture.

The church has lost its identity in the world's system. What was to be fivefold ministry designed to serve and equip became a hierarchy of political power. Although Jesus directly spoke against it, carnal leaders have not found a way to lead God's people without ruling over them. And God's people have been more than accommodating in exchanging the inconvenience of a personal relationship with Jesus for the domination of leaders.

Please understand, not all churches are bad and not all leaders are bad. It is foolish to lump all churches and leaders into one lot and blame them for your life's problems. Spiritual leaders, like political leaders, only have the power we have given them. This is not a focus on who we will blame; this is a pathway to identifying and solving the problem! Controlling leaders produce codependent followers. Codependent followers can never and will never fulfill the great commission, nor will they experience God for themselves to any great measure! Therefore the individuals never become who they were really "called out" to be and the church never becomes what it is destined to be! Conversely, codependent followers facilitate controlling codependent leaders. Leaders desperate to fulfill their destiny and reach the world succumb to the temptation to force people to do what they should do out of personal relationship with Jesus.

What Happened to the Church?

The first 300 years after the resurrection were possibly the most spiritually dynamic and numerical growth period in church history. Yet, there were no buildings and very few professional clergy. Organization was more organic; it was more about the individual than the organization. Spiritual activity was more the fruit of men's own conviction than an organizational edict. As people followed Christ in their own hearts, they were led into something that was world-changing. As the church grew as an organization, it tended to die as an organism. In our attempt to hold on to what the organization has become, we have spent the past 1700 years attempting to fabricate that which once happened organically. But the organized church has never matched the spiritual dynamics nor the numeric growth of the inspired church! Once the church copied the model of the world, the spiritual dynamic was lost. It was much like the time Israel desired a king so it could be like other nations. They did not want the responsibility of knowing, hearing and following God for themselves. They wanted the codependent system of a king who would be responsible to hear from God and make their choices. God explained the root problem to the prophet when He said, *"They have not rejected you, but they have rejected Me, that I should not reign over them"* (1 Samuel 8:7).

> AS THE CHURCH GREW AS AN ORGANIZATION, IT TENDED TO DIE AS AN ORGANISM.

It is impossible for anything organized in this world to not eventually give way to the world's system. Whether it's a business or a local congregation, one becomes a corporation and the other becomes a denomination. In time they both lose their original life and uniqueness. Each new movement that is full of life, following God today, will tomorrow be the movement that resists what God is doing in the earth. All things organized in the world go the way of the world. Tradition overtakes truth. Leaders replace servants. Carnal men find their way into power because they are the ones who most naturally seek power. Thus, like the children of Israel, we cycle through times in history of spiritual life and vibrancy and times of decadence.

The church went into the Dark Ages by departing from the teaching and lifestyle of the Lord Jesus. The battle for power and control overtook the commission to make disciple who know and follow Jesus from the heart. Following the Spirit gave way to following the rules. Rules gave way to legalism, and legalism gave way to death. The Reformation did not really bring us out of the Dark Ages; it simply turned on a few lights. Many of the very beliefs that took the church into darkness still abound today in a milder form. It is essential that we recognize and understand what is at work in the church so we can avoid its pitfalls. This is not a call to criticize the church. But this is a call to be personally responsible no matter what the "church" says!

The early church eventually organized around carnal concepts of carnal men. Christianity became the excuse for greedy, power-hungry men to conquer the world. Constantine believed that he would conquer the world if he would go to war under the sign of the cross. Carnal, corrupt leaders always wanted to conquer the world, only now they had a just cause to rationalize their lust for power. The agenda for organization was not one of godliness; it was one of power and control. To this day, one of the great struggles within the church is control.

Let me be the first to say not all organizations are bad. They will in time become bad. They may at times recover themselves. We are in the world and we are imperfect people seeking to do the best we can given all the factors. Many churches are organized around New Testament goals as much as they know how. Many times it is not the leaders who make an organization go bad. It is very often the people. As the people start looking to the leaders to meet needs that should be met in their own heart, they set up the basis for codependency. As we look to the organization to do for us what we should do for one another through relationships, we destroy the fabric of the relationships.

> TO THIS DAY, ONE OF THE GREAT STRUGGLES WITHIN THE CHURCH IS CONTROL.

Controlling Leaders

I truly believe that many of the leaders who disempower God's people do so with the greatest of intentions. I do not believe the problem is wicked, evil leaders as much as it is ignorant, unbelieving leaders. Every leader is, to some degree, the product of what he has been taught. He is simply continuing in what has been passed down from generation to generation with little thought about the effects.

In my years of preaching grace, peace, the love of God, dignity and worth and other empowering realities, I have only had extreme, negative reactions from two groups: those who fear the loss of control and those who think freedom will contribute to people living irresponsible lives. In either case the reactionary solution is always control. There is so little trust for God that pastors don't even trust God to take care of His own children. We have become like the teenage babysitter who thinks she knows more than the parents.

Keep in mind, control can look different in any given situation. Most leaders control because they believe that is what they have to do for the "good of the people." One leader controls by sheer force of character. He (or she) is the strong dynamic leader. This person controls with the vision. He has a vision from God and everyone "who loves God" must follow. Weak, indecisive people love to give control of their life to the strong leader.

> THERE IS SO LITTLE TRUST FOR GOD THAT PASTORS DON'T EVEN TRUST GOD TO TAKE CARE OF HIS OWN CHILDREN.

Then there is the leader who controls by rules. He is getting everyone right. He thinks that getting people right is the same as getting people righteous. He believes this to be the true purpose of ministry. He tends to make people feel guilty. He creates a sin-consciousness in the hope that people will become so aware of sin they will recognize and reject it at every turn. Self-righteous and guilt-ridden people love to follow this leader. Because they do not trust Jesus as the gift of righteousness, they must find it through their works.

There is also the safe, non-confrontational leader. This leader seldom has a clear-cut plan and everyone is welcome to do his or her thing. He may talk a lot and say nothing. Those who are working their own agendas love this leader. He is easily manipulated and needs you to succeed to make him appear successful.

Of course, we can't forget the inspirational, exciting, high energy, charismatic leader. We just like this guy. And we feel like he likes us. He creates a very social environment. He is able to build a church that substitutes real social interaction with the community. It's popular and exciting to go to his church!

None of these types are bad, necessarily. But when we look to them for things that we should be discovering in Christ, when we seek a church that feeds our dysfunction more than it facilitates our heart, we make it something destructive regardless of the leader's intention.

Leaders are so afraid that if they lose control of the people, the people will run wildly into sin. Yet, we never face the reality that they are already struggling with sin. Our attempts may have been noble and valiant, but they still are not really working. We have fallen into the codependent world system. We trust our vain attempts at control that have failed more than we trust God. Before long we think that just keeping them active in our organization will be the litmus test for their spiritual growth.

> WHEN WE SEEK A CHURCH THAT FEEDS OUR DYSFUNCTION MORE THAN IT FACILITATES OUR HEART, WE MAKE IT SOMETHING DESTRUCTIVE.

Followers cannot blame leaders for where the church is. Leaders cannot blame followers. We all have walked this path together. In silent agreement we have shared in the unspoken conspiracy of fear and unbelief.

Get Ready for the Next Section!

These next chapters will challenge all of us. They will make us question everything that we have trusted, other than God Himself. They will call for us to bring things into perspective. They will remove the blinders that have kept us from the life and power of God. For some of you, they may be the first time since your conversion that you will once again have the opportunity to truly trust God.

My greatest concern in writing these chapters is how the codependent thinker may twist this. The codependent is great at placing blame. Some may use this as an opportunity to blame the church or pastor for their failures. If this is your temptation, let that be the greatest proof that this is talking about you. No one in the church or anywhere else has ever used you or taken advantage of you without your cooperation.[1] As much as it may anger you to hear this, any church that has ever taken advantage of you has done so because you sought something from it that you should have sought in Jesus!

There is also the person who will feel the spotlight is on him or her. If this is you, because the opportunity to assume responsibility and bring about change seems like placing blame, you may respond in anger. Please accept this as a codependent tendency that will keep you trapped where you are. I am not interested in placing blame. I am, however, interested in exposing the workings of codependency in the church so that we can escape the subtle trap and move on to the life we so deeply desire.

THE CHURCH IS THE FAMILY OF BELIEVERS.

The church can only be a powerful, positive force in the world when the people who make up the church are whole. The church can continue in its codependent quest for control and false security, or it can set people free to experience God. When the church leaves the codependent principles upon which it has operated, it will experience true restoration within and real organic evangelism without.

The church is not the organization. The Greek word for "church" means "called out" by God.[2] We are the church; the place where we worship is the building. The structure that the pastor has chosen to fulfill his or her ministry is the organization. It is essential that you know the difference between each of these entities lest you too strongly intertwine their meaning and place in your life.

The church is the family of believers. It is something we belong to by birth, not by denomination. It is only as alive as it is connected to and nourished by the head...the Lord Jesus. A church disconnected from its head is like a comatose body kept alive by machines but unable to function as it should.

The church is not Jesus and Jesus cannot be held responsible for what the church has done. It is the most bizarre and codependent expression to throw away God for what the church has done. If your life is in Jesus, you can survive without the organization. If your life is in Jesus, it can have healthy expression through the organization. But if your heart is not alive through Jesus, it will always expect of the organization what can never be delivered.

We have only known church as an organization for so long we have lost the ability to know what church is as an organism. Our fellowship has been reduced to organized meetings by the "church." We have lost our ability to "be" the church. In this cultural dilemma every individual will have to search to find a way to *attend* a church while finding the deeper meaning of being the church.

Endnotes

1. Dr. James B. Richards, *My Church My Family* (Huntsville, AL: Impact Ministries, 1995), 64-65.
2. *Biblesoft's New Exhaustive Strong's Numbers and Concordance with Expanded Greek-Hebrew Dictionary* (Biblesoft, Inc. and International Bible Translators, Inc., 1994, 2003, 2006), NT:1577.

THE CODEPENDENT CHURCH

23

SWAPPING ADDICTIONS

It is nearly impossible to escape the codependent trap in our society. Codependency has become the norm in every corner of our world. Everything in the world's system is designed to seduce people into giving their power and freedom to others. As the world is lulled into the feelings of lack and incapability, we are rejecting our God-created identity in exchange for false security.

People's ability to have meaningful relationships is at an all-time low. As the social agenda of both predominant political parties permeates our society, the total control of government is becoming the world's norm. Church leadership seems to have followed the way of the world and sees submission to authority, which is the politically correct way to say "total control," as the solution to all problems. Divorce, child abuse, violent crime and the tremendous increase in substance abuse all attest to the fact that social problems are getting worse, not better. All of this is the product of a faithless society that has engineered monumental emotional lack in its people as a way to seduce them into giving up their freedoms.

The Codependent Finds a Church

As I have mentioned before, all experienced counselors know that "codependency is the mother of all addictions." I agree, codependency does give rise to every kind of addiction and abuse. At the heart of every substance abuse problem you will find a socially inept person using his or her addiction of choice as a means of coping with or compensating for his or her feelings of lack. The absence of experiencing the love of God leaves a person desperately in need. It is like having a thirst that can't be quenched…that's why the alcoholic drinks. It is having a longing unfulfilled…that's why the drug addict craves. It is an inescapable loneliness…that's why the sex addict lusts. It is a deep feeling of smallness…that's why the control freak dominates. It's a great emptiness we try to fill with everything imaginable, but none of these substitutes ever meet the need.

Then we hear about Jesus. We see something in the life of a Christian; we hear hope in the sermon of a preacher; we hear life in the words of a believer and we allow ourselves to hope one more time. Something about all of it rings true! We know inside that this is what we have longed for. So, we surrender our life to Jesus. We run to the one place that should establish us in our God-given identity and empower us to be responsible followers of the Lord Jesus: the church!

Far too many times, however, instead of entering a meaningful relationship with God, we simply exchange one codependent lifestyle for another. Most people are never set free from their addictions; they simply exchange them for a new type of addiction that is more socially acceptable. It may not be as socially destructive, but it is still an addiction. Once again we accept the offer of false security in exchange for a living relationship.

Often the codependent will go into a good church that is not trying to create codependency, but because of his own tendencies, he creates a codependent situation. He forms an unhealthy dependency on the pastor, counselors or a particular person. Going to church, talking the talk and playing the game becomes his new way to find approval. He is often doing all the right things for all the wrong reasons and he is once again left empty.

Unfortunately, many churches unknowingly play into the game of the codependent. In fact, many churches unknowingly and unintentionally are set up to reward and nurture codependency. Rather than developing disciples who follow God in their heart, for themselves, they call the person to follow the leader. Although serving in church is important if we are to minister to one another, serving in church is not synonymous with becoming a disciple of Jesus.

Serving in church is where we become a blessing to others. Becoming a disciple is how we manage our life and beliefs.

The church has become so ingrained with the philosophies of the world system that the codependent comes in, unconsciously identifies the system and immediately continues in the same routine that he worked in the world. All he has to do is change his terminology and he's in. We don't say, "I will earn your approval." We say, "I'm committed, brother."
We no longer call it bondage; now we call it submitted. We no longer say, "I want to run your life." Now it's, "I have a word from the Lord." Same system, different lingo.

> MANY CHURCHES UNKNOWINGLY PLAY INTO THE GAME OF THE CODEPENDENT.

I was recently ministering to someone from China. She had not been in America very long. She was horrified at what she found in the American church. She said, "This is just like communism. We had meetings that you were obligated to attend. We sang songs that motivated us. The speaker had a little book that he spoke from. You were to follow the leader without question. If you questioned the leader, you were considered a trouble maker. The American church is just like communism."

It is not the mere similarity of how the two groups functioned that was so unnerving for this and other former communists to whom I have ministered; it is the similarity in attitude. It is the similarity in the way the system works. There are the same dogmas, the same controls and the same quests for power in both systems. In the church, we think our quest for control is just; after all, we are right! But control is destructive no matter what the justification.

Religion: Simply Another Codependent Addiction

For more than 20 years I have seen people come to Jesus only to become totally disillusioned by the carnality of the church. These people realized that it was not much different in the church than it was in the world. No doubt this is not always the church's fault, but far too often the church is set up to thrive on codependency, just like the world system.

Without a doubt, a religious person has more potential to be mean and hard than almost any other kind of person. Religion has started and sustained wars. People are murdered every day somewhere in the world based on religious beliefs. Religion, however, is not the same as Christianity. Religion is the world's system using God's terminology. Religion is man's attempt to reach God on his own terms. Religion sees the church as an army instead of a family. Religion believes we are to attack the world and stamp out unrighteousness. The Bible presents the concept of adopting these orphaned people into the family of God and making the people whole. Christianity is a response of trust to the terms that God has presented to man through the New Covenant. Religion is man-centered. Christianity is God-centered. Religion works from the basis of disempowerment and control. Christianity works from the basis of empowerment, freedom and responsibility.

> RELIGION IS THE WORLD'S SYSTEM USING GOD'S TERMINOLOGY.

One of the biggest differences between religion and Christianity is faith. Faith is trust for God and His integrity. Faith produces a healthy dependency on God. A healthy dependence on God stimulates a healthy interdependence on others. Religion is codependent. It is built around a lack of trust for God through the finished work of Jesus. Religion produces a fear of God that discourages a healthy relationship. It encourages dependence on man, ceremonies and rituals to provide a sense of security that should come from God.

Before people can become mean, angry and religious legalists, they must first be codependent. Religion has nothing to do with trusting God. It has to do with finding security apart from God. It has to do with controlling people and circumstances to meet needs that should be met through God.

For the codependent, religion is a natural, comfortable move from one addiction to another. He (or she) accepts forgiveness of sins, but he never enters into a meaningful relationship with God. He is on his way to heaven, yet dysfunctional in this life. He is susceptible to all the religious extremes that offer security. He chases every man, tries every formula, feels victimized and in the end blames God. As the writer of Proverbs warned, *"People ruin their lives by their own foolishness and then are angry at the Lord"* (Proverbs 19:3 NLT).

Religious codependency can be as destructive in this life as any other addiction, maybe even more destructive. The religious addict can become an extremist father who alienates his children because of his idealistic expectations. She can be the wife who drives her husband away because he is not spiritual enough. He can be the controlling husband who twists Scripture to justify his control. She can be the woman who goes into depression because she feels she can never live up to what she believes to be God's requirements. He can be the David Koresh or Jim Jones who justifies murder for religious reasons. They can be the parents who neglect their family in an attempt to be committed to the local church.

> RELIGION PRESENTS AN IMAGE OF GOD TO THE WORLD THAT IS UNATTRACTIVE AND UNDESIRABLE.

Religious codependency, however, has the power to do something that no other addiction can do. It has the power to turn people away from God. It has the power to cause people to run from the gospel. It makes people ashamed of the church. It can cost people their eternal salvation. It presents an image of God to the world that is unattractive and undesirable.

For the codependent, it ensures that he (or she) will never experience freedom. He will never have intimacy with God. He will spend his life attempting to find security in his doctrines, rules, ceremonies and the approval of men.

The codependent places his confidence and security in the most deadly religious addictions: legalism or ritualism. If he doesn't find his security in these, he would have to find it in a real relationship with God. A relationship is the most threatening of all things to the codependent. It is what he wants more than anything, but what he will never let himself experience. His self-centered attempts to protect himself and get his needs met will keep him from freedom. He merely gives up his worldly addiction in exchange for religious addictions. When we come to Jesus, we are to die to self. Dying to self means I give up every dimension of life to my Lord. But it also means I give up my every idea about how to function in life. I give up my attempt to control the process to happiness. Instead, I follow Jesus with all my heart. It means I give up all of the life that has originated in "self" and put on a new life that originated in Jesus. I determine every aspect of my identity, my life and my pathway to happiness in light of the teaching and personal leading of the Lord Jesus. To be a Christian without giving up my idea of how life works and how happiness comes is simply swapping addictions!

24

WORLDLY SUCCESS

One of the first things that must happen in the life of any believer is the renewal of the mind. Why? It will be your mind that gets you into trouble. It is in the soul, i.e., the thoughts and emotions, where every battle will rage (1 Peter 2:11). It will be the way you think and feel that will keep the power of God from working in your life (Romans 8:7). It will be the way you think and feel that leads you into life's struggles. When you were born again, your heart and mind were made new. But you have control over your thoughts. You choose what you will think. Unless you renew your mind to see yourself as you are in Christ, your thoughts will drift back to how you have always seen things. Then your mind and emotions will tend to be in opposition to the voice of God in your heart!

If you still think the way you previously thought, you will simply "Christianize" your methods and terminology and plod ahead with the same strategies you used in the world. This has been the pattern of the church for most of its existence. We have struggled with the simple truths of serving, yielding, trusting and surrendering as taught by the Lord Jesus. We could not see how these things would lead us into victory. Because we could not reason these things out, we rejected them. We leaned on our own understanding. We depended on our wisdom and rejected the wisdom of God.

After all, we have spent a lifetime working a particular system. Why change now? Now that we're "straight and sober," we can work this system. We erroneously think the only thing wrong with the old system was us. Now that we're not a mess, the old plan we had should work. We fail to realize it wasn't just us that was a mess before Jesus—it was also the plan we were working.

Work God's System Instead

We have spent a lifetime working the world's system. It's the only system we have known. But, now we are *"in the world but not of the world."* We are aliens on planet Earth. We have our citizenship in heaven. We are citizens of the Kingdom of God (Ephesians 4:17). We must learn to live in that "system." We must learn the principles that operate in the Kingdom of God...principles like giving of self, serving, trusting God, walking in love, overlooking offense and placing others before ourselves. But we don't trust this system. So we do what we have always done, expecting different results! It never happens!

We should have received a warning sticker when we got saved that said, "WARNING: THE TRUTH ONLY WORKS IN THE KINGDOM OF GOD!" It's like buying the best appliance in the world, but having an electrical current that is incompatible. It just doesn't work. This does not mean that the principles of God do not work in this life; it simply means they only work when motivated by Kingdom principles: love, based on the Word, thereby empowered by grace.

The church desires to succeed, and we should. We have a call to succeed. We are to *"occupy* [do business and gain ground] *till* [He] *comes"* (Luke 19:13 KJV). The first command God gave man was to subdue the earth. We should be winning the world. We should be making disciples unto the Lord Jesus. We should be the thriving force in the world. But we should not abandon the wisdom of God to accomplish these goals. We should know how to empty ourselves and walk in God's power. But we don't.

We use the right words, but when it comes down to it, we're just working our plan in our strength and asking God to bless it. We don't know His plan or how to walk in His strength. This is foreign to the unrenewed mind. We are trying to do all we can *for* God, instead of being all we can with God. We are willing to praise Him for what happens in our strength because we don't really trust His strength.

The Promise Bible says, *"From the time of John the Baptist until now violent people have been trying to take over the Kingdom of Heaven by force"* (Matthew 11:12).[1] The church rejected Jesus' teaching and has tried to take the Kingdom of God by force. We have turned everything into a carnal attempt to do the things of God. It's not that the church is not trying to fulfill the commission of Jesus. The problem is, we are using the world's methods and principles.

We are like the sons of thunder who wanted to call down fire on the cities that rejected their message. *"And when His disciples James and John saw this, they said, 'Lord, do You want us to command fire to come down from heaven and consume them, just as Elijah did?' But He turned and rebuked them, and said, 'You do not know what manner of spirit you are of. For the Son of Man did not come to destroy men's lives but to save them'"* (Luke 9:54-56a).

> WE'RE JUST WORKING OUR PLAN IN OUR STRENGTH AND ASKING GOD TO BLESS IT.

These disciples wanted to use force to turn people to Jesus. They were willing to abandon all the attributes of love to get the success they desired. I guess they thought the end would justify the means. This is too much like the church today. "We will win the world if we have to stay in the flesh every day and kill everyone to do it!" So the church turns to the same tactics as the world. There is little difference; only the terminology has been changed to disguise the truth.

Leadership Does Not Mean Authority Over Others

Before Jesus left planet Earth, the disciples were arguing over who would be in charge. They were already planning how they would rule the Kingdom of God. Jesus' answer is never found in a leadership class. It is contrary to almost all modern teaching concerning church leadership. *"But Jesus called them to Himself and said to them, 'You know that those who are considered rulers over the Gentiles lord it over them, and their great ones exercise authority over them. Yet it shall not be so among you; but whoever desires to become great among you shall be your servant. And whoever of you desires to be first shall be slave of all'"* (Mark 10:42-44).

Jesus said we could not exercise authority over one another! But the church makes a major doctrine of submitting to authority. We should, no doubt, show respect to those who serve in offices of the church. Leaders must have authority in how they manage their organizations. But we are denied authority over one another. We do, however, have one authority over us: Jesus. His authority is expressed through the written Word. The Lordship of Jesus is the only authority that should reign in our life. To the degree that we share God's Word, people have to make the individual decision to submit to the Lordship of Jesus in response to what they hear, but never to our authority! Every time we hear a sermon, read a book or read the Bible, we must decide if we will yield to the truth presented therein. We must honestly ask God how this would be applied in our own life. That is submission to authority!

> THE LORDSHIP OF JESUS IS THE ONLY AUTHORITY THAT SHOULD REIGN IN OUR LIFE.

The codependent leader sees authority as a central issue. He (or she) must continually have his authority validated. Therefore, serving is no longer the goal; rather, being in control becomes the goal. The head of a ministry has the right (authority) to make all the decisions he feels necessary concerning how he will conduct business, do the work of the ministry, etc., but he has no authority over another person.[2] The codependent leader, however, has no concept of authority in the ministry without authority over people.

People can choose to follow my leadership or not follow my leadership. That is their choice. I only have the right (authority) to do what I do. I must live with their reactions and consequences. They have the right (authority) to do what they will do and they must live with the consequences. I can compel, motivate, inspire and correct, but I never have the right (authority) to use force!

In the codependent church, control is a major issue. Few churches split over any other issue. When different groups start wanting control, there will usually be a split. The codependent leader tries to justify his control by his intentions. He intends to help the people. He intends to minister to them. If he would look a little deeper, he may find a deeper, more sinister need. The codependent leader needs to be needed. Therefore, he needs the people to be codependent. This would rarely ever be a conscious need. It would be cloaked under a lifetime of self-justification and codependence.

Circumstance Theology

Circumstance theology is a theology that people create in order to justify their circumstances.[3] Out of a need to have control, the codependent leader begins to create theological concepts to justify his (or her) position. At this point, I must say, when the major issues of a church are not centered around reaching the lost, making people whole, bringing people into a meaningful relationship with God and equipping (mending) God's people for the work of the ministry, it's starting to get a little far out. There are a lot of other issues, but these are central to the mission of the church.[4] It seems, however, that churches seldom split over the passion to do what we are called to do. It is usually over a control issue.

To manage the masses, the circumstance theology of covering appeared. The doctrine of "covering," submission and authority is completely contrary to Jesus' statement about authority. It is diametrically opposed to Paul's teaching that says, *"For there is one God and one Mediator between God and men, the Man Christ Jesus"* (1 Timothy 2:5). These doctrines emerged from the concept of control-oriented ministry. When we, as leaders, do not trust the Holy Spirit's ability to work in the hearts of God's people, we feel the need to control. This probably did not come from evil men; it probably came from compassionate, Christian leaders who did not believe Jesus' teaching about authority and control.

This whole concept says, "If you will submit to me (who is more spiritual), I will ensure that you can stay in God's will. After all, you're not nearly spiritual enough to hear and know God's will." This immediately removes people from personal responsibility to hear and obey God. This destroys their confidence in God's desire to commune personally with them. This places a leader in the position of mediator between God and man. If we couple this with the Gnostic heresy of special anointings, we have people looking to leaders to do for them what can only be done by the Lord Jesus working in their own heart.

Even if a man could find the "will of God" for you, he could not empower you with the grace of God to walk it out. You would still be left to your own strength.

> THE REALITY IS THAT NO MAN CAN CONSISTENTLY HEAR GOD FOR ANOTHER.

But the reality is that no man can consistently hear God for another. There may be the rare times that God will speak to someone else on your behalf, but your personal direction should come from the Word of God and the Spirit of God, both working in your own heart.

This doctrine removed the possibility of a healthy relationship of trust and real leadership. It is one thing for people to follow our leadership because we have earned their trust; it is quite another for them to follow our direction because they think we have the ability to affect God's blessings for them. This concept is a mixture of Old Testament, Gnosticism, Catholicism, socialism and other carnal philosophies. The terminology has been adjusted for the Protestants and spiritualized for the Charismatics. But every group and denomination has their own unique way of controlling. Some use prophecies. Some use titles and office. Others use fear and force. No matter what method is employed, the end result is a fearful, codependent, spiritually impotent church!

This is a control-motivated, fear-based approach to ministry. When fear is the basis of our actions and decisions, it is not a godly thing. The Bible presents the concept of seed bearing after its kind. This means that the emotions driving the action always produce more of the same kind. It is impossible for decisions made from fear to produce anything but more fear. Fear destroys the ability to experience the love of God. The love of God that we experience directly affects the level of fear in our life. *"There is no fear in love; but perfect love casts out fear, because fear involves torment. But he who fears has not been made perfect in love"* (1 John 4:18).

The Problem With a Church Run on the World's System

The new believer walks into the codependent church and very quickly realizes that this is the same system that works in the world. In order to function here, he or she must remain carnal-minded. This is the "good ol' boy" system among Christians.

There are many good churches in America and around the world, but there are also many control-oriented churches, led by codependent leaders, that nurture codependent attitudes in people as a way of control.

In my work in other countries, evangelists tell me that tens of thousands of people are being won to the Lord regularly. However, controlling preachers are running the new converts out of the church as fast as the evangelists can win them.

When the church functions on the same system as the world, it is stealing the life away from God's people. It becomes the barrier instead of the provider for people to have a meaningful relationship with God.

Every minister must determine if he (or she) will use his gift and the church as a way to help God's people or whether he will use God's people as a way to help himself.[5] How he answers this question will determine if he creates an unhealthy codependency on the system or a healthy dependency on God.

Because we view success the way the world does, we seek success the way the world does. We feel that our mission is so important that we can use and abuse the people for our own accomplishment. We have forgotten that *the people* are the mission. Our churches and ministries exist for the people, not for us. They are tools that should help us accomplish God's goals.

Real success is helping God's people to become whole through a meaningful relationship with God so they can do the work of the ministry. Whole people serve God. Whole people live godly lives. Whole people have integrity. On the other hand, whole people can rarely be controlled or manipulated. So you can't have both!

A successful leader serves God's people. He (or she) resists the temptation to use God's people to meet the needs that should be met in his relationship with the Lord. The successful leader understands what Jesus said when He stated, "I have food to eat of which you do not know." Jesus said to His disciples, *"My food* [My success] *is to do the will of Him who sent Me, and to finish His work"* (John 4:32,34).

Our success is found in the quality of ministry we provide for our people. Our feeling of success is found in our relationship with the Lord. Our numerical success is the fruit of these two. Our food, or fulfillment, is not from success as the world defines it. It is from following God as He defines it! If we accept the world's definition of success, we will destroy and not build...we will hurt and not help.

The ultimate test for following God's process is whether or not I am doing what I do because I love (value) God's people. If I have God's love for people I will always strive to minister to them in a way that sustains their feeling of being valuable and precious to God!

.

Endnotes

1. Douglas Rumford, Ronald Beers and Gilbert Beers, *The Promise Bible* (Carol Stream, IL: Tyndale House Publishers, 2001).
2. Dr. James B. Richards, *Leadership That Builds People*, Vol. I (Huntsville, AL: Impact Ministries, 1993), 91.
3. Dr. James B. Richards, *Taking the Limits Off God* Huntsville, AL: Impact Ministries, 1989), 33.
4. Dr. James B. Richards, *Leadership That Builds People*, Vol. II (Huntsville, AL: Impact Ministries, 1990), 103.
5. Dr. Richards, *Leadership That Builds*, Vol. I, 11.

25

THE MAN-CENTERED GOSPEL

The codependent church has developed a man-centered gospel. There are many versions of this gospel. The one factor they all have in common is a skewed logic that places man at its center. All things depend more on man than on God. Instead of looking to the finished work of Jesus, it looks to the current works of man. In one version of the man-centered gospel, while using all the New Testament terminology, they have pushed man back under the law. Man attempts to relate to God on the basis of personal performance, i.e., works-righteousness. We believe that Jesus came to save us; we know He is Lord; we know He died for us; but, we still attempt to earn righteousness on the basis of personal performance. This is no more than the doctrine of the Judaizers, which Paul strongly condemned in the epistle to the Galatians.

In this version of a man-centered gospel, all the burden is placed upon man. This is a burden that man can never handle. The early church struggled with this very problem. The converted Jews did not want to turn loose of the false security of the law. It had been their basis of security all their life. In order to maintain this false sense of security, they attempted to require the Gentile converts to be circumcised and obey the law.

When the problem was presented to the elders at Jerusalem, Peter gave the most astute answer. *"Why do you test God by putting a yoke on the neck of the disciples which neither our fathers nor we were able to bear?"* (Acts 15:10). The patriarchs of the Old Covenant could not bear this load. It didn't work. That's why we needed a new covenant. Why attempt to rebuild what has been torn down in order to find the security that should only be found in God? Fear produces a resistance to trusting God, which then creates the need to put man back at the center of the equation. A works-oriented gospel creates the illusion of being in control, something essential to the carnal codependent mind.

> WE STILL ATTEMPT TO EARN RIGHTEOUSNESS ON THE BASIS OF PERSONAL PERFORMANCE.

The Law's Weakness

The law had one prevalent weakness: it depended on the performance of people to make them righteous. *"For what the law could not do in that it was weak through the flesh, God did by sending His own Son in the likeness of sinful flesh, on account of sin: He condemned sin in the flesh"* (Romans 8:3). Jesus came to deliver man from the power of sin and to give us the gift of righteousness because we could not earn it. Our inability to earn or maintain it was the weakness of the law. So the law did not work because it depended on us!

For the codependent, peace with God is based on performance. For the man of faith, peace with God is based on the finished work of Jesus (Romans 5:1). The codependent puts man at the center of salvation; faith puts Jesus and His finished work at the center of salvation. The codependent attempts to find security in trusting his or her own efforts; the man of faith finds security in trusting the death, burial and resurrection of Jesus.

With man at the center of salvation and our hearts established in law and not grace, we have our paradigm of walking with God set to take us into complete *codependent Christianity*.[1] With this paradigm, every decision that the new believer makes will take him or her deeper into the man-centered gospel of performance, insecurity and more codependency.

What About Anointings?

The issue of anointing brings us to another area of extreme codependence. In the Old Testament, individuals received an anointing. The anointing was something that came and left. The people were not born again. They were not righteous before God. The anointing could not remain on them. Additionally, they had to sanctify themselves to prepare for the anointing. In other words, they had to make themselves holy enough for God to temporarily place His anointing upon them.

In the New Covenant, Jesus has sanctified us. He has made us holy and blameless before God (Colossians 1:22). The work that He has done prepares us to receive the anointing. Unlike the anointing of the Old Covenant, this anointing is for everyone who is born again. Likewise, it does not come and go; it abides on us. Nowhere does the New Testament present the concept of special anointings or individual anointings. Conversely, the Bible openly states, *"Now He who establishes us with you in Christ and has anointed us is God"* (2 Corinthians 1:21). *"These things I have written to you concerning those who try to deceive you. But the anointing which you have received from Him abides in you, and you do not need that anyone teach you;*

> OUR INABILITY TO EARN OR MAINTAIN RIGHTEOUSNESS WAS THE WEAKNESS OF THE LAW.

but as the same anointing teaches you concerning all things, and is true, and is not a lie, and just as it has taught you, you will abide in Him" (1 John 2:26-27). The only anointing we have is His anointing. We share that with Him because we are in Him. The delusional quest for personal anointing lends itself to a self-righteous quest to have more of God than someone else!

The New Testament speaks of the Anointed One...Jesus. The word *Christ* means anointed. He is anointed, and we are in Him. What anointing we have is something that we received freely at salvation. What happens through our ministry happens as a result of His anointing. Once again, the Bible places Jesus at the center of our attention. The prevalent teaching about anointing places man at the center. The codependent gains confidence to trust God's power based on performance and subjective feelings. The man of faith has confidence because of the finished work of Jesus and the Word of God.

The whole concept of anointing as it is presently taught places one man above another. It seems to say, "You need me because I have more of God than you have. I have something special, something that you don't have. Come to me and get it." It places man in a position to look to another man to receive something that he should receive from God. It places man at the center. This was the doctrine of the Gnostics, a cult whose doctrines undermined the faith of the early church and continues until this day

THE ONLY ANOINTING WE HAVE IS HIS ANOINTING.

Yes, God works through man. God's power is demonstrated through man. But, this can happen in a way that causes man to look at how great Jesus is instead of how great the man is. It can cause us to leave a meeting realizing that God is in us the same way He is in the "man of God."

We can feel more confident in God or we can feel less confident. We can feel more equipped or less equipped. We can yield to the anointing or not yield to it, but the anointing never changes since it is His and not ours.

Another aspect of the personal anointing message is that in the end it usually says, "If you'll do what I did, as good as I did it, God will anoint you like He anointed me," or "If you'll let me disciple you, you'll learn the secrets I know." In this generation it even goes to a more corrupt place: "If you'll give to my ministry, you will benefit from my anointing." Somehow, man always seem to be at the center, getting the glory. The codependent looks at this and is immediately drawn into a codependent relationship with the man of God instead of into a meaningful relationship with the God of the man.

The Way of Balaam

Much of so-called "ministry" does to the Christian what advertising does to the unsuspecting viewer: it creates a sense of lack. It points to what we don't have instead of what we do have. It creates a feeling that we are somehow not where we ought to be. When the Apostle John wrote to the believers, he said, *"I have not written to you because you do not know the truth, but because you know it, and that no lie is of the truth"* (1 John 2:21). He didn't attempt to make them feel they were in lack. He wanted them to feel complete and confident in Jesus.

Like the advertiser, the codependent minister creates the sense of need or lack and then offers the solution, which somehow always places the codependent Christian in an obligatory position. Millions of dollars have been given to ministers with a "special anointing" to get your prayers answered, get your loved ones saved and get you more anointing. When that doesn't work, there is always one more thing you must do, one more sacrifice you must make...one more thing turns into an unending list of things that steal your life and confidence in God!

> MUCH OF SO-CALLED "MINISTRY" DOES TO THE CHRISTIAN WHAT ADVERTISING DOES TO THE UNSUSPECTING VIEWER: IT CREATES A SENSE OF LACK.

The Bible calls this the way of Balaam. Balaam used his ministry to profit instead of to serve the people. The way of Balaam is actually pretty easily identified by those who have their eyes open. Any time a person/ministry makes you feel that giving to his or her ministry will give you access to something Jesus died to give you, he or she is in error. Support a ministry because it helps you. Support a ministry because it helps others. But the moment you support a ministry because you think it will give you some special favor with God, you have rejected the finished work of Jesus as your qualification.

Jesus Did It All

The Bible teaching that says, *"You are complete in Him,"* was written to the Colossians because they were being made to feel that they somehow needed something more to protect them from the devil.[2] They thought Jesus just wasn't enough. From the time of the garden until now, Satan has always used the strategy of creating a sense of lack as a way to lull the unwitting, ignorant believer into the snare of destruction.

Adam had no lack in the garden, yet Satan falsely convinced him that he did. Once he stopped focusing on what he had in God, he felt lack and was led into temptation and destruction. To this very day, Satan continually attempts to refute the simple reality that *"you are complete in Him."* When you stop looking to Him, you will look to someone else. When you look to someone else, the grace of God can no longer empower you to live in victory. When you entertain the idea that you are not complete, you begin to feel lack. When you begin to feel lack, you look for that which cannot be found.

FROM THE TIME OF THE GARDEN UNTIL NOW, SATAN HAS ALWAYS USED THE STRATEGY OF CREATING A SENSE OF LACK.

The new believer walks into church expecting it to be different. He (or she) really expects to experience God. He expects to be empowered and have his life changed. Instead, he is almost immediately robbed of the confidence of what God has done for him. Instead of walking in a simple trust for Jesus and His completed, perfect work, he is given a list of things he must do to get God to do what He promised in Jesus. He is made to feel that he must look to a mediator instead of a personal Savior. Living in victory is made very difficult and mystical. The new believer who thought he would be offered a new life of power and victory is instead disempowered and offered the opportunity to exchange his past addiction for some new religious addiction that will offer him only a mere substitute of the security that could be found in trusting the finished work of Jesus.

The man-centered gospel places man at the center. It moves us to look to a man instead of God. In the end, however, man will always fail and disappoint us. Unfortunately, once we have "bought into" the man-centered gospel, we think God has failed us. We blame Him for the shortcomings in those we have idolized. Our ability to trust God is further diminished, pushing us deeper into codependency.

Jesus and His finished work must be the center of our faith, the core of our existence and the foundation of our hope. Anything or anyone that we allow to breach that intimacy will alienate us from the life of God that is in us. It will make that which we have inaccessible.

Endnotes

1. I realize this is a contradiction in terms. I use this to describe the Christian caught in the trap of religious codependency..
2. *The Expositor's Bible Commentary*, Vol. II (Grand Rapids, MI: Zondervan Publishing House, 1984), Colossians 2:10.

26

ANGRY GOD

Of all the things that create codependent tendencies in a believer, there may be nothing more destructive than the "angry God" doctrines. The "angry God" doctrines focus on God's wrath. They make Him appear to be hard to please, hard to understand, difficult to know, reluctant to communicate and virtually impossible to appease!

Most of the "angry God" doctrines come out of the Old Covenant.[1] Under the Old Covenant, sin had not been dealt with; the penalty for sin had not been paid; and man had not been given the free gift of righteousness. Was God angry? Certainly! Definitely! Without question! But, the angry God doctrines have a total disregard for the finished work of Jesus. It represents a lack of belief in the New Covenant established in the blood (death, burial and resurrection) of Jesus!

Did God change from the Old to the New Covenant? *No! "For I am the Lord, I do not change; therefore you are not consumed..."* (Malachi 3:6). God has never, and will never, change. The question then becomes, how do you reconcile the wrath of God in the Old Covenant with the mercy and love of the New Covenant?

God Has Not Changed

Simple! God is a holy God. His holiness and righteousness require that sin be paid for in the body of the sinner. Yet, He is a loving Father who has never wanted to punish man. He has always wanted fellowship and communion with man. But righteousness required that sin be punished. God did that by allowing Jesus to become a man. Man brought sin into the world; only a man could take sin out of the world.

> WE LOVE GOD IN RESPONSE TO THE LOVE HE HAS SHOWN US.

Jesus lived a sinless life. Had He not done so, He would not have qualified to be our sacrifice. He did not die for His sins, but for ours! When He went to the cross, God made Him to become our sin (2 Corinthians 5:21). The prophet Isaiah says, *"But He was wounded for our transgressions, He was bruised for our iniquities; the chastisement for our peace was upon Him…"* (Isaiah 53:5). He wasn't punished for His sins, but for ours. Because the penalty for our sins has been paid, all the wrath of God against sin was appeased, satisfied completely in Jesus. The Apostle John said, *"He Himself is the propitiation for our sins, and not for ours only but also for the whole world"* (1 John 2:2). Thayer's defines *propitiation* as "the means of appeasing."[2] God's wrath was appeased or satisfied in His punishment upon Jesus…the punishment we deserved.

In fact, John goes even further to say that it is in this propitiation that the love of God is revealed. *"In this is love, not that we loved God, but that He loved us and sent His Son to be the propitiation for our sins"* (1 John 4:10). So mankind didn't love God. We love Him in response to the love He has shown us. His love is shown in the fact that Jesus satisfied all His wrath against our sin. If we don't believe in the propitiation, we will not love God; rather, we will be afraid of Him. Thus, those who do not believe in the completed work, the full sacrifice of the Lord Jesus, will never grasp the value (love) of God that delivers us from the fear and the subsequent belief in a wrathful God!

We are called to live by faith, i.e., trust! We cannot trust the one we fear. Trust is the automatic response of being loved. Mistrust is the natural response to fear. Our options with God are love or fear. Love comes when we believe that He loved us first and that His wrath has been satisfied. Fear comes when we are afraid that

He will harm us. In his deep wisdom and understanding of the dynamics of love and fear, the Apostle John explained this dichotomy. *"Such love has no fear, because perfect love expels all fear. If we are afraid, it is for fear of punishment, and this shows that we have not fully experienced his perfect love"* (1 John 4:18 NLT).

The codependent controller keeps you in bondage by making you feel unqualified for the love of God. He (or she) sees his job as "getting you right." A true servant of the New Covenant declares the good news (gospel) that God offers you righteousness as a free gift. Just as Christ became sin and paid the price we should have paid, He also satisfies all the requirements of righteousness. *"Christ is the end of the law for righteousness to everyone who believes"* (Romans 10:4). Thus Paul declares, *"Therefore, since we have been made right in God's sight by faith, we have peace with God because of what Jesus Christ our Lord has done for us"* (Romans 5:1 NLT).

> THE WORK OF JESUS CLEARLY EXPRESSES AND DECLARES GOD'S EXTREME LOVE FOR MAN.

God did not change from the Old to the New Covenant. Because of the finished work of Jesus, all of the love that God desired to express to man could be legally given without violating truth, justice or righteousness. This work of Jesus clearly expresses and declares God's extreme love for man. This is the place where peace was made between God and man, once and for all.

Religion Is the Next Best Option

This work is consummated in the life of the believer who receives Jesus as Lord, Savior and righteousness. Unfortunately, very few people are told that Jesus is their righteousness. As a matter of fact, it is almost as if it has been deliberately hidden. Those who don't believe in the power of righteousness are afraid you won't live right if you find out about the gift of righteousness in Jesus. So, instead, they cut you off from the power to live and walk in the righteousness that God has freely given: faith-righteousness.

The "angry God" message denies everything that Jesus accomplished at the cross. *"Much more then, having now been justified by His blood, we shall be saved from wrath through Him. For if when we were enemies we were reconciled to God through the death of His Son, much more, having been reconciled, we shall be saved by His life"* (Romans 5:9-10). The "angry God" message puts enmity between God and man. It makes God appear to be the angry God who must be appeased by our sacrifices. God didn't need the sacrifices of the Old Covenant, and neither does He need our sacrifices today. The price has been paid. There is no more sacrifice for sin. When we do not accept and trust in the finished work of Jesus, we live in the paranoid fear of wrath and judgment that shall devour the adversary. This is what the Bible calls condemnation. Because we assume ourselves to be adversaries, we feel like adversaries, alone and afraid.

MAN WANTS GOD.

The concept of an angry God puts man into the throes of codependent thinking. Since he doesn't believe he qualifies for God's promises, he cannot get his needs met from God; therefore, he must look elsewhere. But he wants God. The next best alternative is religion. Religion looks enough like the real thing, it sounds enough like the real thing and it has enough components of the real thing that if we close our heart…it can almost pass as the real thing. Thus, you have the makings of an environment of control.

Basically, the different denominations and religions are people who have come together and made lists of what they think it will take to make a person righteous and acceptable to God. Every group has its list of requirements. The ignorant and unlearned look over the list to see which one makes sense to them. They want to know which one will make them feel the most secure, and that's the one they choose.

Now that they have found the doctrine that makes them secure, they must protect that doctrine. It's sort of like building an idol and calling it your god. Even though you call it your god, you have to protect it so no one can steal it and use it for firewood. Some god, huh?

The reason people become so dogmatic and argumentative about their doctrine is because it is their security. When you cause them to question their doctrine, you are actually causing them to question the security of their salvation. It is no wonder people become so closed and defensive. They are afraid, and you are undermining their only sense of confidence.

206

Experiencing Truth Sets You Free

The man of faith believes and then experiences the truth. He accepts Jesus on His terms. He believes and trusts God more than he trusts his own logic and reason. Because he is not trusting a myth, he has the opportunity to experience the Person behind the truth. His experience goes far beyond the intellectual concept that must be argued and protected. It is in a Person, Jesus. There is a constant inner witness that we are the sons of God, that we are loved and accepted in the Beloved.

Truth is not the reality; it only represents and expresses the reality. Truth is information about the reality! It is a portrait of God. The Word of God is truth, and it expresses many realities. However, until we leave the realm of truth (information) and enter the realm of experiencing that truth (relationship), we are not dealing with Jesus; we are simply embracing the information, gazing upon the portrait...the portrait the Word presents of Him. The man of faith is not content to live in the realm of information. Even if the information is correct, it is still merely information. The person of faith wants to experience the reality behind the truth, the Person behind the portrait!

> TRUTH IS INFORMATION ABOUT THE REALITY!

Jesus never said that merely knowing the truth would set you free. The word know as used in the New Testament means to experience with all of our senses, all that we are. This knowing continues to express itself in the experience of application. Thus He said, if you continue in it, or put it into practice, then you will know it experientially. Only then, when you experience it, will it set you free. *"Then Jesus said to those Jews who believed Him, 'If you abide in My word, you are My disciples indeed. And you shall know the truth, and the truth shall make you free'"* (John 8:31-32).

The man of faith allows that truth to draw him into a relationship with God through Jesus, a relationship based on truth. His trust for the incredible wisdom and goodness of God compels him to put the Word into practice. The codependent, on the other hand, who is too fearful to have a meaningful relationship with another human much less with God, draws back and embraces the information, never entering into the realm of experience and freedom. The concept of an angry God presents a picture of fear and rejection that is too overwhelming for the codependent to face.

If you are not righteous through Jesus, you must earn your righteousness. Based on the level of righteousness that you earn, you will feel acceptable to God. That is the subtle, unspoken message behind the codependent gospel, which is no gospel (good news) at all. This news puts man in the most extreme emotional stress he could ever encounter. You are not; therefore, you must become.

Every religion in the world tries to get you to become by doing. Christianity, however, says you can do because you have become. You can live righteous because you are righteous. You can be happy because you have joy. You can be at ease because you have peace. You can enter into rest because you are accepted; you are not laboring to become. There are more than 200 scriptures in the New Testament that tell us who we are and what we have in Jesus.[3] These must become more than information. They must become our experiential reality! They must become our identity, our total sense of self!

The codependent leader who desperately needs to be needed, tells us who we are not. He (or she) tells us how much we lack. He tells us what we do not have. The man of faith tells us who we are, what we can do and what we have because of the finished work of Jesus. He doesn't make us feel like needy beggars. He makes us feel like priests and kings.

Endnotes

1. It must be noted that nearly all of the prophecies of wrath in the Old Testament were to nations that embraced some form of Luciferian doctrine designed to alienate men from God. All of these nations would eventually become the nations of the last days anti-christ nations. God's wrath and judgment toward those nations was for the protection of the world, then and now.
2. *Thayer's Greek Lexicon*, electronic database (Biblesoft, Inc., 2000, 2003, 2006).
3. Dr. James B. Richards, *The Prayer Organizer* (Huntsville, AL: Impact Ministries, n.d.), 25-53.

27

THE MESSAGE OF FAITH

One message that has been restored to the church that has presented the greatest potential for growth in years has been the message of faith. Like anything with great potential for good, there is also great potential for harm. When this wonderful message falls into the domain of the codependent leader, it can easily be twisted to dead works. No matter how great the truth, the codependent will always manipulate the message for personal validation or control.

When I first began to hear the faith message, it was as pure as the driven snow. It was like someone opened a window and filled the room with fresh air. For the first time, I heard people preach many of the things I had believed and preached. It was such a confirmation. In the beginning, there was much emphasis on the finished work of Jesus, faith-righteousness and the goodness of God.

Like every movement, though, the followers didn't have the heart of the leaders. Codependency crept in, and in less than a decade a message that had so much potential to heal began to bring forth its potential for harm. Like every good thing, the potential for detraction (for diminishing, lessening, reducing), was present at its conception.

What Happened to the Message?

The first trouble sign was the apparent lack of emphasis on a relationship with Jesus. Obviously, many of the original leaders had strong, meaningful relationships with the Lord that empowered their faith. True to form, however, as the codependent followers assimilated the message of faith, they left out the relationship with God and kept the formulas. Before long, the emphasis on God and His faithfulness had been pushed aside for the message of how much man had to do to get God to respond. It had become man-centered and legalistic.

> FAITH IS A RESPONSE OF TRUST.

The message of faith has very subtly changed from our response of trust to what God has done, to how we can get God to respond to us by what we do. The man-centered message of works crept in, perverted the original faith message and robbed it of its power. What once glorified God, now glorified the faith of man.

The very first biblical foundation of the faith is *"repentance from dead works"* (Hebrews 6:1). The dead works the writer mentioned are not all of the sinful things that a person did before he or she got saved. It was all of the religious things he or she did to earn God's approval. Under the law, man did things to try to get God to respond. Under the New Covenant, God did everything in Jesus. He now gives us the opportunity to respond to what He has done. Faith is a response of trust to the persona and character of God and the covenant He made with Jesus.

Unbelief responds by de-emphasizing what God has done and placing the burden to perform back on man. It places man at the center of the equation. Otherwise, the codependent would have to trust God and His integrity. Instead, he (or she) trusts in his performance, or what he feels is his faith. The codependent is capable of turning any truth or any relationship into something self-serving and destructive.

By the message of faith being twisted to what we must do to get God to respond, we come up with all manner of wrong questions. How much faith does it take to get God to move? How can I make my faith stronger? How long do I have to believe? Why isn't God doing anything? Is sin blocking my faith?

In all of Jesus' teaching about faith, He never emphasized how much it took to make something happen. Instead, He emphasized how little it took. Our problem with God is rarely a lack of faith as much as it is the abundance of unbelief. Every man has a measure of faith. We believed God for the greatest miracle that would ever happen with infantile faith: we got born again. God changed our very nature. There is no miracle any greater. Why should anything else require more faith? It should also be noted that the word *saved* comes from the Greek word *sozo*, which means saved, healed, delivered, blessed, prospered, protected, set apart and every other aspect of the New Covenant. It is impossible to have enough faith for one and not have faith for all.

> OUR PROBLEM WITH GOD IS RARELY A LACK OF FAITH AS MUCH AS IT IS THE ABUNDANCE OF UNBELIEF.

In some circles, the proof that you had faith became defined by the amount of "stuff" you had. If you had a lot of stuff, you must obviously have a lot of faith. Getting the stuff so you could prove you had faith became more important than knowing and serving God. For many, what had originally been presented as trusting and walking with God became an attempt to get a lot of "stuff" so they wouldn't need God. Security came when a person was convinced he or she had enough faith to get all the "stuff" he or she wanted.

Once again, codependent people twisted truth and de-emphasized a meaningful relationship with God. Security was found in the amount of faith one could prove that one had. The codependent heart will pervert and twist any message away from God and to a place of dependency on other things.

With this twist, the standard answer for every problem simply became, "You don't have enough faith." Once again, the emphasis was placed on what you don't have in Jesus, instead of what you do have. Man was once again made to feel incomplete and inadequate.

Remember, one of the basic goals of the codependent is control.[1] When he (or she) is in control, he feels secure. There is also the codependent who wants to be controlled to avoid personal responsibility. These are two sides of the same coin. They seek each other out! The codependent leader always seeks to disempower others. If others can somehow be convinced of their lack, then they will need the codependent leader. He will be in control and he will be secure. All of this will be justified by the legitimate needs that exist in the people. The codependent passive is always ready to give his power away. If someone else will assume his responsibilities, he has a false sense of security. Jesus is the missing factor in either of these extremes.

What It Should Be Like

The man of faith would approach those needs with an emphasis on your ability to handle and solve these problems because of Christ in you. While he would lovingly point out the problem, he would not tell you that you were not righteous. Like Paul, he would tell you to *"walk worthy of the calling"* (Ephesians 4:1) or *"yield your members…to righteousness"* (Romans 6:19 KJV). Or as Peter said, "Since all these things will be dissolved, what manner of persons ought you to be in holy conduct and godliness" (2 Peter 3:11). Even when Paul wrote to the Corinthian church and rebuked them for their apparent carnality, he reminded them of their righteousness. *"But of Him you are in Christ Jesus, who became for us wisdom from God—and righteousness and sanctification and redemption"* (1 Corinthians 1:30). *"For He made Him who knew no sin to be sin for us, that we might become the righteousness of God in Him"* (2 Corinthians 5:21).

The true preacher of faith would never move you to take your eyes off Jesus and His finished work. He or she would desire that you trust in and depend on the power of God. The codependent would always have you take your eyes off Jesus and look, instead, to your need, and ultimately to him as the one who will help you meet your need.

Codependency Is Pervasive

I have found that it does not matter what the message is. The codependent will pervert it into something that drives him or her to look everywhere to find the solutions except in his or her own heart. In the early 1960s and '70s, as people were baptized in the Holy Spirit and leaving the denominational churches, there was the realization that people needed to be discipled. This is a truth. The Bible tells us to make disciples of all men.

But regardless of the sincerity of those early leaders, this movement ended up totally revolving around control. What started out as people being discipled unto Jesus, became people being disciples of other people. The grace of God working in our heart gave way to the influence of men working on our mind. For the carnal, insecure leader, this became the justification to control. One man would make another man godly by discipling him. How utterly codependent!

The same thing has happened with the prophecy movement. What started out as an attempt to restore a precious gift to the body of Christ became a method to control and dominate the lives of the people. When a church member does anything that displeases leadership, that displeasure can always be expressed as a "word from the Lord." The New Testament believer then begins to consult the prophet instead of consulting God.

> IT DOES NOT MATTER WHAT THE MESSAGE IS; THE CODEPENDENT WILL PERVERT IT INTO SOMETHING THAT GIVES HIM OR HER CONTROL.

The codependent instinctively turns every great phenomenon into something that every person "should" do. If you are not involved in what I am involved in, you're going to miss the last great move of God. Or, if you don't do what I'm doing, you are in rebellion to God. The codependent insists that everyone have all of the same experiences that he (or she) has. This validates him and his experience. Think of it: Jesus never had a movement. He ministered to every person differently. It rarely happened the same way twice. There wasn't a "spit in the mud and rub on your sickness" movement. There wasn't a "wash in the pool" movement.

Jesus ministered to every person individually. He yielded to the Holy Spirit as He led Him to minister in specific ways. Jesus was not committed to a method;

He was committed to God and to people. He didn't need for everyone to approve of His method. His validation came from His relationship with the Father, not from the approval of man or the size of the crowd.

Love Is the Foundation

"Faith works by love!" The real man of faith is established in the love of God. His roots go deep into the soil of love. His confidence is not in how much faith he has, but in how much love God has. He knows that God is good and He is faithful. He knows that trusting God's love is the key. As Paul prayed in Ephesians, *"I pray that from his glorious, unlimited resources he will empower you with inner strength through his Spirit. Then Christ will make his home in your hearts as you trust in him. Your roots will grow down into God's love and keep you strong. And may you have the power to understand, as all God's people should, how wide, how long, how high, and how deep his love is. May you experience the love of Christ, though it is too great to understand fully. Then you will be made complete with all the fullness of life and power that comes from God"* (Ephesians 3:16-19 NLT).

> IT'S NOT A MATTER OF HOW MUCH FAITH YOU HAVE, BUT WHAT YOU HAVE FAITH IN.

Being filled with the fullness of God is a matter of faith. It's not a matter of how much faith one has, but a matter of where he or she places faith. Faith in the love of God causes us to be filled with the fullness of God. In First Corinthians 13, Paul instructs the overly "spiritual" on the value of love. He concludes his explanation of love by saying, *"And now abide faith, hope, love, these three; but the greatest of these is love"* (verse 13).

Paul did not say faith was the greatest. He said love was the greatest. As the greatest it should be valued and pursued more than any of the other attributes. But that is not the message of the church today, and it is no longer the emphasis of the faith movement. In what was probably the last message taught before the death of Kenneth Hagin, Sr, one of the fathers of the faith movement, he exalted the message of love as the gospel. It seems that although many misunderstood and misrepresented the faith message, he held it in clear priority all the way to the end. Every group has something it pursues with a greater fervor than the love walk. For some it is faith, for some it is prophecy, and for some it is soul winning. Although all of these and the thousands of other ideologies are true and must not be neglected, they are not truth when they are taken beyond importance and exalted to the perversion of God's priorities.

Love will produce all the lesser things. Love will compel the believer to soul winning. It will create a hunger for the gifts of the Holy Spirit. But just as Paul points out in First Corinthians, hope and faith cannot produce love, but love can produce hope and faith. People who believe in God's incredible love for mankind expressed through the cross of Christ have no problem trusting God (operating faith)! People who walk in love never violate the rights, freedom and responsibilities of others!

Endnotes

1. There is passive control, aggressive control and passive-aggressive control. The codependent seeks the illusion of control regardless of how it is expressed. This is not intended to give the codependent ammunition to accuse the aggressive, overt controller. Avoiding responsibility is also a form a control.

BREAKING FREE FROM CODEPENDENCY

28

FINDING THE CURE

Without a cure this book would simply be another "you ought to" book that makes you feel inadequate and less than capable. In fact, without a cure, this book would feed right into the type of teaching that has encouraged codependency! Anything that makes you feel inadequate and does not offer a solution feeds codependency.

But, I offer you a cure that is simple. It is so simple that it has been overlooked, doubted and rejected for hundreds of years. It is the heart and purpose of the gospel: Have a relationship with God through the Lord Jesus! I know that sounds too easy. But like all relationships, it actually requires more than anything else.

Jesus said this in John 17:3: *"This is eternal life, that they may know You, the only true God, and Jesus Christ whom You have sent."* He came so we could know God, have the righteousness to approach God without fear and have the power to live a quality of life the Greek called "zoe." Zoe, if you remember, is the Greek word used for life. But this isn't just any kind of life. This is the quality of life possessed by the One who gives it. In other words, it is the quality of life possessed by God Himself! Or, as Jesus said, *"I have come that they may have life [zoe], and have it to the full"* (John 10:10 NIV).

Remember, according to our definition, the ultimate codependency is when we look outside of ourselves to meet any need that should be met in our own heart by God. Every time we use anything as a substitute for fulfillment, acceptance, approval or happiness, we are functioning in codependency. Even when the substitute is a good thing, in the final analysis it is still destructive if it is a replacement for intimate fulfillment in God.

A New Relationship

In Christian circles too many of the things God gave us to become a bridge to Him have become walls that separate us from Him. The Bible was given so we could know about God. But it is no substitute for knowing God! To read the Bible without opening our hearts to the Great Teacher (the Holy Spirit) for personal application is to turn the blessing into the curse. Nearly every codependent religious tendency we have mentioned in this book is based on something that could be good if it were used properly. It is just like Paul said of the law: *"But we know that the law is good if one uses it lawfully"* (1 Timothy 1:8).

WITH GOD AS OUR SOURCE, THE WORLD AROUND US STAYS IN PROPORTION.

God is the source of life! But as a whole it seems that few people, even many who invoke His name, really know Him as their source. With God as our source, the world around us stays in proportion. For example, if God is the source of our happiness, others may contribute but they cannot be our source. This means no one or no thing could take our happiness from us. They could momentarily affect it in some negative way, they could contribute to it, but they cannot give or take it away!

In the New Covenant, we have the most wonderful yet potentially threatening promise imaginable. Under the Old Covenant, believers were not born again. Although the Spirit came upon someone from time to time to empower him or her to some great feat, the person was never regenerated, given a new nature and indwelt by the Holy Spirit. This is exclusive to the terms of the New Covenant.

Under the Old Covenant you could read the Torah and gather information. But you still could not know God personally or intimately. The law was eventually expanded into hundreds of commands that must be observed every day in the hopes of living up to what they "thought" God wanted. Only the high priest could meet with God personally, and that only happened one time per year as he entered the holy of holies with the blood of sacrifice and stood before the mercy seat. So, laws and rules were handed down from person to person and changed to meet the different schools of thought, but no one really knew God for him or herself except for those few rare individuals like King David, who was said to be *"a man after God's own heart"* (Acts 13:22). Rules had so replaced God that the Apostle Paul recounted the words of the Psalmist, *"There is none who understands; there is none who seeks after God"* (Romans 3:11).

> # IT IS UP TO YOU TO KNOW GOD PERSONALLY.

In the New Covenant we have a new arrangement. Every person becomes individually responsible to know God for him or herself! *"...I will put My laws in their mind and write them on their hearts; and I will be their God, and they shall be My people. None of them shall teach his neighbor, and none his brother, saying, 'Know the Lord,' for all shall know Me, from the least of them to the greatest of them. For I will be merciful to their unrighteousness, and their sins and their lawless deeds I will remember no more"* (Hebrews 8:10-12).

Now the holy of holies is in our own heart. It is there that we meet God on the mercy seat and the throne of grace. We have mercy because He has forgiven our sins and we have grace as the power to overcome temptation and live above sin. He is with us and in us to lead, guide, comfort and empower us.

On to the Challenge

None of this is the challenging part. The challenging part is this: *"None of them shall teach his neighbor, and none his brother, saying, 'Know the Lord'...."* No one else can bring you what you need. It is up to you to know God personally. There are no special anointed people who can bring any aspect of God to you.

You seek Him because you want Him. You have confidence and trust because you choose to believe His covenant made in Jesus. But there can be no mediators between you and God other than the man Christ Jesus. *"For there is one God and one Mediator between God and men, the Man Christ Jesus"* (1 Timothy 2:5). Teachers can share information. They can give you examples, but in the end, that is merely information that should inspire you to seek God for yourself!

Ministers are like painters. They capture a scene that has inspired them. They then translate that scene onto a canvas in the form of a lovely picture. But no matter how closely they interpret what they have seen, it is still not real. It is only a replica. If you saw a breathtaking depiction of the Grand Canyon, you could still not say you had been there. In fact, the replica only serves two possibilities. First, it adds a bit of beauty to the life of the person who will never make the journey. Or, second, it inspires the observer to make the journey and see it for him or herself! Preaching and teaching that do not inspire us to make the journey for ourselves is lacking in either its motive or persuasion, or there is something in us that is out of harmony with God's purpose and call to our heart!

> INFORMATION IS NO SUBSTITUTE FOR PERSONAL INTIMATE EXPERIENCE.

Information is no substitute for personal intimate experience. Information is deceitful. It appeals to the ego. As the Apostle Paul so aptly stated, *"Knowledge puffs up, but love builds up"* (1 Corinthians 8:1). Encountering knowledge about God will puff up your ego. Allowing that knowledge to inspire you to intimate involvement with God will build you up…in every way!

Run the risk. Meet God on His own terms. Put aside all of your fears and doubts and enter into a place that few people choose to go. Enter into the place that people sing about, pray about, write poems about and preach sermons about, but seldom enter into for themselves. Enter into the love of the Father. Abide in Him! Do whatever it takes to know and experience Him with your whole heart!

Should you choose to make this journey, you will spend a lifetime incorporating the following chapters into your life. Not because it will be hard or difficult, but because it will involve a lifetime of walking with God. It is a never-ending process of believing, experiencing and growing in your confidence of the love of God. His love never ends! Every day His mercies are renewed. There is no end to knowing God!

A relationship is not a destination; it is a process. Thus, it must be continually updated, renewed and allowed to undergo change and growth. You will spend all of this life and eternity growing in your relationship with God. Begin now; make Him the center of your life. Read the following chapters carefully and prayerfully. Ponder them! As you read, ask God to help you discover the reality behind the words and to know the God behind all reality!

29

DIGNITY AND WORTH

The level of a person's self-worth will control everything he or she attempts. Self-worth is the basis for interpreting all information. It will affect the amount and quality of effort put into any endeavor. Self-worth is one of the deepest needs of a human being. Our sense of dignity and worth determines if we will steal or work for the things we desire. It determines if we will lie or tell the truth to gain favor. Man always seeks to fulfill his desires in a way that is consistent with his self-perception; therefore, self-worth becomes the moral compass for all self-expression. The worldwide epidemic in codependency is no doubt closely linked to an epidemic in low self-worth!

In Hebrews 2:7 it says that God originally crowned man with *"glory and honor."* These words *glory* and *honor* include the concept of dignity and worth. In the beginning, man walked and ruled planet Earth from a deep sense of dignity and worth that came from knowing who he was in relation to his Creator! His sense of identity and worth came from the safety and security of that relationship. He knew who he was in relation to God…and it was good! There was absolutely no fear.

After the fall, man lost his sense of dignity on many levels. But the most pervasive was his newfound fear of God. He hid in shame from the One who previously met his every need. Fear choked out love as his ruling "feeling." Shame replaced honor. Cowardice drove out confidence. Unbelief consumed faith. Fear and unbelief led to sinful, self-destructive actions, which further confirmed these negative emotions. Thus, you have the destructive cycle of low self-worth. Negative feelings and low evaluation of self lead to actions consistent with that low evaluation. Then those actions bring about more negative feelings, which bring about more negative actions, and it goes on and on.

When man emerged a sinner (with a sin nature) the primary sense that changed in him was motivation. Instead of being motivated by love, he became motivated by fear. He no longer had that sense of glory and honor, i.e., dignity and worth! When God called out in the garden for reconciliation, man judged that He was calling out for wrath. The sin nature is manifest first in fear. Fear causes us to judge with negative expectations. The Bible calls this condemnation! Judgment was the primary new capacity man had as a result of being god of his own world.

SELF-WORTH IS THE MORAL COMPASS FOR ALL SELF-EXPRESSION.

Fear is inherently untrusting; therefore, it always leads to unbelief. Fear cannot believe in the unconditional love of God. Fear expects punishment! But fear is also incapable of believing the promises. The promises are just too good to be congruent with man's sense of self. Therefore, fear creates unbelief, which leads to disobedience. Disobedience is the result of doubt. Unbelief is when a person does not believe. Doubt is when one believes something else more than the promise of God! Trusting other things (doubt) leads to actions contrary to the Word of God. Disobedience leads to a destructive lifestyle that makes us less than who we really are and reduces what is really ours through our Father. Thus you have sin...missing the mark of the reward. At its heart, sin is failing to be who we have the potential to be!

In the vacuum created by the absence of glory and honor man has a need that can only be filled by an intimate relationship with his God. If man is driven by fear and unbelief, he will not look with trust to God to meet every need and fulfill every desire. Fear and unbelief will drive him to look to other external sources to give what can only be found internally through the love of God our Creator. Thus we have the ultimate codependency.

The Key to Transformation

Being born again does not automatically break this cycle. Sadly, there are actually churches that nurture low self-worth as if it had some spiritual value. What will change this cycle is the renewing of the mind. Paul exhorted the Ephesians to *"no longer walk as the rest of the Gentiles walk, in the futility of their mind"* (Ephesians 4:17). He told the Roman believers, *"Do not be conformed to this world, but be transformed by the renewing of your mind"* (Romans 12:2a). He told the Corinthians to *"[cast] down* **imaginations**, *and every high thing that exalteth itself against the knowledge of God, and bringing into captivity every* **thought** *to the obedience of Christ"* (2 Corinthians 10:5 KJV). The real warfare that the New Testament presents for the believer is bringing his or her thoughts and beliefs in line with the finished work of Jesus. To be born again and continue to think the same will bring little change. There is no place where this is more important than in our beliefs about being loved and accepted by God through the Lord Jesus!

> JUDGMENT WAS THE PRIMARY NEW CAPACITY MAN HAD AS A RESULT OF BEING GOD OF HIS OWN WORLD.

Man's sense of dignity and worth is only restored when he fully accepts the terms and conditions of the New Covenant. Dignity and worth are restored because our loving, peaceful relationship with God is restored. As we experience acceptance from God as our Father, we have a restoration of identity. As we experience God's love and value for us, we establish our sense of self-worth. As we realize the true image of God, our Father and Creator, we develop a new image of ourselves.

We were created from the very essence of God. He breathed us into existence. *"We are members of His body, of His flesh and of His bones"* (Ephesians 5:30). He did not create us by His spoken word; we are part of Him! Through

Jesus, we have been adopted into the family of God. We have been given a new nature and a new identity. We are made completely righteous before God, in Christ. Because we are in Jesus, we are as righteous as He is at this moment (1 John 4:17). Through the cross we are delivered from wrath. If we believe and experience this love, we are delivered from fear. In the absence of fear, love can flourish and dignity and worth can return! These are the terms of the New Covenant. This is the covenant that Jesus established for us through His (blood) death, burial and resurrection. To believe that God raised Jesus from the dead is to believe in this finished work.

> AS WE REALIZE THE TRUE IMAGE OF GOD, OUR FATHER AND CREATOR, WE DEVELOP A NEW IMAGE OF OURSELVES.

Unbelief causes us to look back to the performance mentality of the Old Covenant and we attempt to mix the Old and New Covenants. We are simply afraid to believe that God is so good and so loving that He would have made us such an offer. That unbelief is exactly the source of our problem.

Even when someone comes to believe that God is good, he or she may still reject the idea that he or she is qualified to be the recipient of that goodness apart from works. Paul said that *"the Father…has qualified us to be partakers of the inheritance"* (Colossians 1:12). We can't qualify ourselves. To attempt to qualify ourselves by our performance is to reject the finished work of Jesus. We are no longer seeking the promise by faith, but by work, which means it is no longer a promise but a payment! All we need to function in this New Covenant is freely given in Jesus! And we are qualified in Jesus! There is nothing left to do but believe and receive.

We are no longer the same person we were, but we must renew our minds to see ourselves and think of ourselves in this finished work. We should not allow one thought or imagination about ourselves to emerge that is inconsistent with who we are in Jesus. When those thoughts or imaginations do emerge, we should not entertain them. It is the belief in the finished work of Jesus that transforms us!

As the realization of righteousness becomes the foundation of our self-perception, our self-worth will be restored to the New Testament reality. When we see ourselves the way God sees us, we will experience the power to live life the way God says we can. When we believe we are righteous, the power of righteousness will flow out of our spirit into every aspect of our being.

Changing Your Mind

Many resources tell us it only takes a few weeks to establish a habit and a few more weeks for that habit to become second nature. If people simply invested a few minutes each day persuading their heart of their new identity, the rest of their life would change. A few weeks of meditating[1] on the new you based on the realities of the New Covenant would transform your self-worth. You would no longer see yourself as the sum total of your life's actions; rather, you would see yourself as righteous, sanctified, anointed and qualified in Jesus.

> IT IS THE BELIEF IN THE FINISHED WORK OF JESUS THAT TRANSFORMS US!

It is not what you stop that will change your life...it is what you start. An attempt to stop thinking the wrong thoughts would be tormenting and self-defeating. The key is thinking the true thoughts. There are a few basic things you can do to transform your thought life. You must decide which method will work for you.

When I first began the process of establishing my thoughts in the finished work of Jesus, I developed what I now call *The Prayer Organizer*.[2] The Prayer Organizer is a system where I organized hundreds of identity scriptures into topics that related to the promises and nature of God. I would spend time daily acknowledging and worshipping God from these scriptures. I would engage every aspect of my heart, mind and being into seeing and experiencing my new identity as a present tense reality! It was an incredible time of transformation.

The first 30 minutes of the morning and the last 30 minutes of the evening are the times that the subconscious mind is the most receptive to input. Therefore,

I would use those times to renew my mind. In the morning, I would spend time verbally acknowledging Scripture. In the evening, I would spend time meditating on Scripture.

I never turned this into a legalistic ritual. I knew I was not trying to become what the Scripture said nor was I trying to get God to do something. I was simply renewing my mind. The wrong motivation could make this or any other scriptural endeavor a legalistic nightmare.

During the day, if I found myself thinking thoughts that were not consistent with who God said I was, I would simply interrupt the destructive thought (put off) and replace it with a scriptural promise of identity in Christ (put on). I would bring those thoughts captive to the obedience of Christ. I always went back to what Jesus had accomplished by His finished work. I refused to see myself in any way other than how God has made me, in Him.

> IT IS NOT WHAT YOU STOP THAT WILL CHANGE YOUR LIFE...IT IS WHAT YOU START.

Over the years I have developed an entire system designed to help renew the mind and establish the beliefs of the heart in God's realities, in Christ. It is called Heart Physics®. You can find out more about Heart Physics® at www.heartphysics.com. When we believe the truth about anything in our heart, it becomes effortless to live and walk in that truth. The gospel benefits us little when we have an intellectual grasp of the information but do not actually believe it in our heart. Transformation comes by changing the beliefs of our heart!

As the years have gone by, I have found myself spending less and less time doing any of these things. I no longer have the need. My new identity is written on my heart and my mind. I seldom act in a way anymore that is contrary to my new nature. I no longer have negative feelings about myself. I no longer wonder if I am qualified for God's promises. I have a sense of identity, self-image and self-worth that is based on the finished work of Jesus. My actions and emotions are empowered by believing the truth.

I am not who you say I am. I am not who my circumstances say I am. I am not even who my actions say I am. I **am** who God says I am. He says I am a righteous son because of the finished work of Jesus.

Out of this new identity in Jesus flows a new sense of dignity and worth. Dignity and worth guide my emotions and my decisions. They provide me with consistent emotional stability.

It is my opinion that dignity and worth are the essential foundations for a healthy emotional life and for meaningful relationships with God and man.

> TRANSFORMATION COMES BY CHANGING THE BELIEFS OF OUR HEART!

Endnotes

1. Look at www.heartphysics.com for information about biblical meditation and how to write God's truth on your heart.
2. Dr. James B. Richards, *The Prayer Organizer* (Huntsville, AL: Impact Ministries, n.d.).

30

PEACE WITH GOD

Romans 5:1-2 gives us what I call the continuum of the gospel. It is here we find the line that connects all the major dots of how to live a powerful life. *"Therefore, having been justified by faith, we have peace with God through our Lord Jesus Christ, through whom also we have access by faith into this grace in which we stand, and rejoice in hope of the glory of God."*

The word *justified* means "to render righteous or such as he ought to be."[1] It is the fact that we have been made and declared righteous by faith that gives us peace. The fact that it is a gift received by faith removes us from the constant struggle of "dead works," i.e., our religious efforts to be approved by God! Having reached the place of peace, we now have access by this faith to the grace of God. Grace is an incredibly comprehensive word. But as far as practical application goes, grace can be understood as a divine influence upon the heart[2] that makes one able[3] and is received by unmerited favor. So, the key thing is that grace makes us able to stand. It is our source of strength. But it is also the basis for our hope of the glory of God as a reality in our lives.

What starts with faith-righteousness leads us to peace, which facilitates the operation of faith (trust), which give us access into the strength and power of God that makes us able to stand in this new life. Accepting righteousness as a free gift in Jesus puts our heart at rest. We never have to wonder where we stand with God. *"If our heart condemns us, God is greater than our heart..."* (1 John 3:20). Knowing who we are and what we have become gives complete peace with God (Romans 5:1).

An Essential Root

Peace is far more essential to living than we think. It is the root emotional state that keeps us normal! The moment we move from peace, we lose our capacity for the life God has given! Our "works mentality" places all the emphasis on being right. Being right means proving I am right. Proving I am right means proving you are wrong. Proving you are wrong means conflict. Our entire approach to Christianity has been one that has robbed us of peace with God and man. Instead of giving us peace, it has placed us in the throes of insecurity and conflict. Without God's peace through faith-righteousness, we are striving in a field of antagonism.

> PEACE IS THE ROOT EMOTIONAL STATE THAT KEEPS US NORMAL!

Peace is only found in the absence of striving. Peace exists in a place of rest. In the New Covenant, Jesus is our Sabbath; i.e., the place in which we rest from all our religious performance. Few things rob us of peace like striving to become. Striving to become what I think God wants me to be demands that I reject who I am. Accepting that "I am" in Jesus establishes peace. *"Be anxious for nothing, but in everything by prayer and supplication, with thanksgiving, let your requests be made known to God; and the peace of God, which surpasses all understanding, will guard your hearts and minds through Christ Jesus"* (Philippians 4:6-7).

By trusting the finished work of Jesus, I am trusting that I am righteous before God. Because I am righteous, I am qualified for all my needs to be met. Therefore, I can present my needs to Him with absolute confidence. This confidence keeps me from striving. It keeps me from being anxious. In that place of trust and dependence on a faithful God, I will experience a peace that doesn't even make sense. Living in peace should become one of the top priorities in the life of a believer. It is the "normal" to which we are called!

What Is Peace?

When we think of peace, there are many concepts that come to mind. Let's see if we can bring all of these concepts together into a biblical understanding. The New Testament word for "peace" is a very inclusive word. It involves a tranquility of mind, but fortunately it does not stop there. The word for "peace" in the New Testament is very similar to the word *shalom* in the Old Testament. It speaks of tranquility in relationships and tranquility of mind. It speaks of completeness, wholeness and prosperity.[4] A person could have a tranquil state of mind simply because he or she was deceived into it. In others words, it was a false, circumstantial peace. People will often inform me of unbiblical decisions they have made. When I point out that their decision is inconsistent with Scripture, their defense is, "Well, I know it's of God because I have peace." Then I have to ask if they know the difference between relief and peace. Peace that is not based on truth is deceitful. It may give a measure of relief, but be assured, that relief will soon disappear and give way to destructive, negative emotions.

> LIVING IN PEACE SHOULD BECOME ONE OF THE TOP PRIORITIES IN THE LIFE OF A BELIEVER.

The peace of God, however, is a tranquility that is based on reality. It has substance. It is a tranquility that comes, first and foremost, from believing and experiencing peace between you and God through the Lord Jesus (Colossians 1:19-20). Often times, the first thought to attack us when things go wrong is, "What did I do to cause God to allow this?" That is what the Bible calls condemnation. Our first response to those kinds of vain imaginations must be, "There is peace between God and me because I am in Jesus." According to the Apostle Paul, the gospel of peace—the good news that there is peace between God and man—is the foundation that gives us footing in times of struggle.[5]

James says it this way: *"Let no man say when he is tempted* [tested, tried, scrutinized], *I am tempted* [tested, tried, scrutinized] *of God: for God cannot be tempted with evil, nor tempteth* [tests, tries, scrutinizes, that which causes me to strive] *he any man"* (James 1:13 KJV). When we think it is God testing us, we are not in faith (trust) and therefore cannot have peace. God teaches, guides, directs, empowers and comforts by the Holy Spirit. He is not the spirit of destruction; He is the Spirit of Life. The Apostle John said it like this: *"If we are afraid, it is for fear of punishment, and this shows that we have not fully experienced his perfect love"* (1 John 4:18b NLT).

> PEACE THAT IS NOT BASED ON TRUTH IS DECEITFUL.

In the Book of Colossians, Paul says, *"... having made peace through the blood of His cross. And you, who once were alienated and enemies in your mind by wicked works, yet now He has reconciled in the body of His flesh through death, to present you holy, and blameless, and above reproach in His sight"* (Colossians 1:20-22). Because God has made peace with us through Jesus, He presents us to Himself holy and blameless. He has no basis for reproving us.

If we are not holy enough for God, it is His problem. He made us holy. He made us righteous. Why would He make us righteous and then criticize us? He wouldn't. *"Who shall bring a charge against God's elect? God who justifies. Who is he who condemns? Christ who died, and furthermore is also risen, who is even at the right hand of God, who also makes intercession for us"* (Romans 8:34).[6] Paul is asking a simple question. Is the God who justified you going to bring a charge against you? No! Is the Savior who died and rose again for you going to condemn you? No!

God is not duplicitous or deceitful. He is either for us or against us. Religion has robbed us of a peaceful, fruitful life by seducing us into questioning the love and integrity of God. Paul settled this issue time and time again. That's why he started the previous passage with this statement: *"What then shall we say to these things? If God is for us, who can be against us? He who did not spare His own Son, but delivered Him up for us all, how shall He not with Him also freely give us all things?"* (Romans 8:31-32). Why would God give us His Son as the gift of righteousness and then find fault with us? Simple! He wouldn't!

God is not schizophrenic. If He criticizes your righteousness, He is criticizing His own handiwork. That would be like God criticizing the stars and blaming us. Why would He blame us? We didn't make them. Likewise, we didn't make ourselves righteous; we accepted it as a free gift. If our righteousness is not perfect, then neither is Jesus' righteousness, for the righteousness we have is His. If His righteousness is not good enough to bring us before God, then Jesus cannot come before God.

In Jesus

ALL THAT
JESUS HAS IS
ALREADY OURS.

This peace we have is also based on the fact that we have completeness in Jesus. We have *"all things that pertain unto life and godliness, through the knowledge of Him"* (2 Peter 1:3). I have more than mere tranquility; I have tranquility that is based on the fact that I have all I need for life and godliness. I need not be troubled or worried whether or not I have enough faith to get God to give me something, since there is nothing left for Him to give me! I have it all in Jesus. Because we are in Him, we are joint heirs. All that He has is already ours. We lose our peace because we think the inheritance is something that is sought outside of and independent of Jesus!

I may not be experiencing all that I need at this moment, but I need not be concerned that this indicates something is wrong between God and me. I need not be concerned that I am lacking enough faith or righteousness. There may be problems in my life that I must deal with and there may sin in my life that should be conquered through grace, but I can face that without fear of separation from God. As Paul asked in Romans 8:35-39, can any of these things separate us from the love of God that is in Jesus? No! None of these can separate us from His love. There is not one place in the New Testament that tells me my sin can separate me from God. Does this mean that it's all right to continue in sin? No! John warned that an unacceptable life will cause our heart to condemn us. In other words, we will feel separated from God. But God is greater than our heart. Just because we feel it doesn't mean God is doing it!

The thing that makes us acceptable to God is the fact that we have been made righteous in Jesus. This is the good news (gospel) of Jesus. The good news is not that you could go to heaven when you die. The Old Covenant believers looked confidently to eternity with God. The good news is not that there would be healings or miracles; they had seen healing and miracles in the Old Covenant. The good news is this: I will give you righteousness as a free gift; you can now be at peace. *"Are you tired? Worn out? Burned out on religion?"* (Matthew 11:28a The Message). Jesus is offering you rest for your soul.

> PEACE WILL KEEP ME STABLE IN A WAY THAT I DON'T EVEN UNDERSTAND.

"Therefore, if anyone is in Christ, he is a new creation; old things have passed away; behold, all things have become new" (2 Corinthians 5:17). We are not a cleaned-up version of who we were; we are a totally new creation, a perfectly righteous creation. We can stroll right into the holy of holies with no fear of falling over dead. We can stand before God unashamed. We can "come boldly to the throne of grace" because there is peace between us and God. Sin has been punished, wrath has been appeased and righteousness has been given.

I must cling to the reality that there is peace between God and me because of Jesus. I must have my feet shod with a readiness of mind that comes from a thorough preparation in the gospel of peace. I must cling to peace. Peace will keep my heart and my mind stable. Peace will keep me stable in a way that I don't even understand.

This peace with God keeps me at the place where I can experience all the good things of God. My faith is functional to the degree that I believe, i.e., experience, the gospel of peace[7] (Romans 10:13-17). I can experience tranquility based on the fact that there is peace with God and He has given me all I need for life and godliness.

God's name says He is the God of Peace, Jehovah-Shalom. Jesus is the Prince of Peace, the covenant we have with God is the covenant of peace and the message that should be preached to the world is the gospel of peace. Peace should be the fruit of the spirit that defines our emotional state. It should be the goal of the believer to live in peace and be a peacemaker. We should have complete confidence in the way of peace! And it is all ours if we believe and make our hearts steadfast in the covenant of peace.

Endnotes

1. *Thayer's Greek Lexicon*, electronic database (Biblesoft, Inc., 2000, 2003, 2006).
2. *Biblesoft's New Exhaustive Strong's Numbers and Concordance with Expanded Greek-Hebrew Dictionary* (Biblesoft, Inc. and International Bible Translators, Inc., 1994, 2003, 2006).
3. *Thayer's Greek Lexicon.*
4. Ibid.
5. Ephesians 6:15 talks of having your feet shod *"with the preparation of the gospel of peace."*
6. I removed the italicized words to add clarity. The words *it is* are not in the original text.
7. Dr. James B. Richards, *The Gospel of Peace* (New Kensington, PA: Whitaker House, 1990).

EXPERIENCING GOD

Nothing has any value in this life unless it is experienced in this life. Being saved will definitely benefit us in eternity, but if being saved does not benefit us in this life, then it is of no value now. Being righteous is a wonderful thing, but if I am not empowered to live righteous, my life will still be filled with dysfunction and destruction. We should experience God here and now so we will benefit in this life.

Through the years, faith has been interpreted and viewed in many different perspectives. Today faith is taught as a force that we release to get things to happen. But there was a time when we were taught that faith was when you believed in something that you could not prove or experience...you just took it by faith. Neither of those interpretations are scripturally correct. As such, both concepts lead to problems. However, it is the latter concept we shall look at.

Man has consistently developed circumstance theology throughout the years. When he is not experiencing what the Bible says he should experience, man develops a theology to justify what he is experiencing, thereby protecting his ego. It was not many years after the death of Jesus that the church backslid. A relationship with Jesus was replaced with a relationship with the church. The church no longer existed to serve God by serving people. People were used to serve the goals of the organization. People were no longer encouraged to know God personally, nor even to read the Bible for themselves. That was reserved for the clergy. The clergy would know God and read the Bible, then pass it all along to us. It was a throwback to the Old Covenant where God could not inhabit the individual believer by His Spirit!

We know the real goal of the church as it embarked on this dark phase was control. But that control would have never been possible if man had maintained a meaningful individual relationship with God. Many began to accept doctrine "by faith." They accepted that it was true, although they had no proof and never experienced any power from what they believed.

The Bible says that the gospel *"is the power of God to salvation"* (Romans 1:16). If what we are believing has no power in it, then it is not gospel. Or, if we are hearing the gospel and do not believe it, it will not have power in our life. But if we hear and believe the gospel, it will have the power to bring us into the experience of salvation.

THE GOSPEL HAS THE POWER TO BRING US INTO THE EXPERIENCE OF SALVATION.

The Greek word for "salvation" is *sozo*. *Sozo* means to be saved, healed, delivered, blessed, prospered, made whole, set apart and a lot more. *Thayer's Greek Lexicon* says it is the "sum of benefits and blessings."[1] It has to do with a salvation in this life...not so much a change in circumstances as a change in us. Our heart and emotions change. We now have the power to win over the circumstances, whether they change or not. We have the Spirit of God dwelling within us. The grace of God, the same grace that worked in Jesus' earthly life, works in ours.

The ability to prosper and be in good health is directly related to something happening to us in the realm of the soul. *"Beloved, I pray that you may prosper in all things and be in health, just as your soul prospers"* (3 John 2). Salvation should not only affect our spirit; it also must affect our soul, which is our mind, emotions and will.

All About Emotions

For years we have been afraid to deal with the issue of feelings and emotions. Because of the extremes of some groups who give themselves over to emotions, we have rejected the validity of emotions altogether. Regardless of whether you believe it or not, your emotions are a major factor in what is controlling your life. Ideally, we should not follow emotions. We should follow the Word and the Spirit. But there is a paradox in this truth. When we focus on the Word or the Spirit of God, our emotions will change. In the end it will be the change in our emotions that makes it comfortable and enjoyable for us to follow God.

> SALVATION SHOULD ALSO AFFECT OUR SOUL.

Emotions are short-term. They are based on our mental focus. Where we place our attention changes our emotions. Therefore, our emotions change with every changing thought. This is possibly why the emotions have always been connected to our will. Although we should not follow our emotions, it has long been known that we will. As someone has said, if there is a struggle between emotions and will power, emotions always win! Since the will and the emotions are from the soul, it may be that will power and emotions cannot be separated. The power of the will is the dominant emotion. Behavior tends to follow emotions and emotions tend to follow thoughts. But emotions are not wrong or evil. We simply choose our emotions when we choose our thoughts.

When God breathed His life into a physical body, He said man became a *"living soul"* (Genesis 2:7 KJV). Our capacity to experience life is in the soul. The soul is neither good nor evil; it is simply the place where we experience the emotional effects of good and evil. Every battle we fight, every bad thing that controls us, every good thing that brings joy, does so because it affects our soul. Like it or not, we live out of our feelings.

Man was created a living soul. His soul was dominated by life, the very life of God that was breathed out from His own being! But when man decided to alter his connection to God, something radically changed. In Genesis 6:3 God said that man had become flesh. It could be that, after the fall, man who had been alive to God was now alive to his flesh. Therefore the soul, which had previously been dominated by the Spirit of life, was now dominated by the flesh. Man now focused his attention on the emotions generated by his five senses more than what was generated by his inner man. Whatever the case, man changed. As such, what drove his thoughts and emotions changed!

Emotions follow thinking. It is universally agreed that the soul is the place of the mind, the emotions and the will. The mind is where we think. These thoughts produce emotions. These emotions influence our biological function. They affect our will…our ability to make decisions and see them through. The will determines our actions, which over a period of time affect the span of our life!

LIKE IT OR NOT, WE LIVE OUT OF OUR FEELINGS.

We should not be led by our emotions, but we should know how to lead our emotions. Unbiblical thinking produces unbiblical emotions. The feeling of low self-worth is the product of thinking and believing certain things about oneself. Hatred is an emotion that is based on thoughts and beliefs. Joy is an emotion based on thoughts and beliefs.

Our momentary thoughts produce momentary emotions that come and go. Our habitual thoughts produce beliefs that reside in our heart and direct our life without conscious thought. Thoughts that become beliefs produce long-term emotions, which are called feelings. These feelings dictate our every perception and decision.

Thinking biblical thoughts based on the finished work of Jesus produces corresponding emotions of love, peace and joy. If we don't think what the Bible says, we will never believe what the Bible says, and therefore we will never experience (feel) what the Bible says. Accepting the fact that God loves us, believing that we have been made righteous, and thereby having peace with God produce deep-rooted, abiding feelings of dignity and worth.

It is essential to understand the difference between the thoughts of the mind and the thoughts (beliefs) of the heart. The thoughts of the mind generate short-term emotions. These emotions change with our focus. They require effort. When we lose our focus, our emotions change. Beliefs of the heart, however, produce long-term feelings that are more abiding. We may lose touch with feelings when we are focused on something that is producing emotions. However, when we stop focusing, we effortlessly revert back to our feelings. Feelings express the thoughts and beliefs of the heart; emotions express the thoughts of the mind. The only way to find absolute victory is to change our beliefs, not just our thoughts. But changing our thoughts is the first step toward changing our beliefs.

OUR HABITUAL THOUGHTS PRODUCE BELIEFS THAT RESIDE IN OUR HEART AND DIRECT OUR LIFE WITHOUT CONSCIOUS THOUGHT.

Feeling God's Love

The Apostle John put it this way: *"And we have known and believed the love that God has for us. God is love…"* (1 John 4:16). First they believed the love of God. Then they knew! The Greek word for "known" is from *ginosko*, which means "this act embraces every organ and mode of knowledge, e.g., by seeing, hearing, investigation, or experience."[2] When they said they "knew" the love of God, they were not talking about some abstract theological information. They didn't merely accept the fact that God loved them…they believed (deeply felt) it. They wrapped every part of their capacity to experience this love around this reality. It became a part of their subconscious thinking and feeling. As this thought formed a belief, they ultimately began to effortlessly feel and abide in His love. Love began to drive not just their thoughts and actions, but it also became the basis for their continuous feelings.

One of the greatest changes in my life took place when I began to feel the love of God on a continual basis. Much of my life I felt anger. The earliest strong emotion I can remember was hatred. I wanted to kill my father. I would lie awake at night when I was only four or five years old and plan to kill him. I can remember thinking, "If I can stay awake until he goes to sleep, I can sneak into the kitchen, get a knife and kill him in his sleep." I hated him and intended to murder him, a feeling I had until I was 21 years old.

I carried the feeling of hatred and anger in me all of my childhood and teenage years. I expressed anger toward others because that is what I was experiencing in my own soul; it was how I felt. The way we relate to others is always a reflection of what we are currently experiencing. Christians who believe in works-righteousness always feel rejected. Therefore, they reject others. People who feel small express themselves through belittling others or by overcompensating, ego-driven behavior. If they feel that God looks for fault, they look for fault. Whatever we are presently experiencing is what we pour onto others.[3]

AS A BELIEVER YOU ARE ALWAYS OUTWARDLY REFLECTING YOUR CONCEPT OF GOD.

The Apostle John brought us this incredible psychological insight: *"Beloved, let us love one another, for love is of God; and everyone who loves is born of God and knows God. He who does not love does not know God, for God is love"* (1 John 4:7-8). These verses are not debating whether you have ever met God. They are talking about the fruit of currently experiencing God! Everyone who loves, knows (is experiencing) God. He or she who loves not, knows not (is not experiencing) God. As a believer you are always outwardly reflecting your inner feelings, which is actually your concept of God.

When we are willing to believe God's love for us, we will begin to feel God's love. At first it will simply be an emotion that abides no longer than your attention span. When we feel love, we express love. Nearly every morning when I awaken, I feel the love of God. It is a deep feeling that is based on a belief that is rooted in reality. It is confirmed by the Word of God and expressed by the Spirit of God. This is more than a feeling that is generated by a thought. It is a feeling based on experiencing God. As I focus on that love, my feelings begin to stir up emotions. When my feelings, thoughts and emotions are harmonious, my experience is undeniable and life-altering.

To experience God, one must enter into a personal relationship with Him. You will have to find comfortable ways to spend time together. You will have to learn of Him. It is a relationship. Having a relationship with God is not as

246

difficult or as mystical as we have been led to believe. He wants to commune with you. He is for you, not against you. He did all that He did in Jesus because of His love for you. He wants you to believe His love, but He also wants you to feel His love.

Bible reading, prayer and worship can be dry and legalistic or they can be full of life. Your intention is what makes the difference. If you are just doing your religious duties, it will have no life. If, on the other hand, you do all that you do with the intention of knowing, hearing and experiencing God, then that will be your outcome. Wrapping your life around Him with every aspect of your being will evolve into a personal, rewarding relationship that meets every need in your life. As such you will no longer find yourself looking to every outside source to meet your internal needs. It will be the end to codependent searching! You will never again feel alone or empty!

> YOUR INTENTION IS WHAT MAKES THE DIFFERENCE.

The scripture that says, *"Behold, I stand at the door and knock"* (Revelation 3:20), was not written to the lost; it was written to the church…to believers who had closed Him out of their heart. They had religion, but they were no longer experiencing God personally. Open the door to Him and your longing will be satisfied!

Endnotes

1. *Thayer's Greek Lexicon*, electronic database (Biblesoft, Inc., 2000, 2003, 2006).
2. *Theological Dictionary of the New Testament*, abridged edition (Grand Rapids, MI: William B. Eerdmans Publishing Company, 1985), NT:1097.
3. Dr. James B. Richards, "Knowing and Feeling the Love of God," audiotape series.

32

COMMITMENT TO LOVE

Even though I am righteous because of the finished work of Jesus, that righteousness will benefit me nothing if I do not walk in it. In all of Paul's writing, he would spend chapters pointing out who believers are in Jesus or teaching about their righteousness in Him. After being sure that his readers understood their relationship with God, he would then talk to them about the way they lived. Paul was attempting to help people grasp one of the most difficult paradoxes: righteousness is given, you are free from dead works, but your quality of life is determined by walking in righteousness, that is, good works.

If we truly intend to live in the benefits, it is essential that we live according to our new nature. This does not earn us anything with God, but it does affect our confidence in relating to Him. It also has a great effect on every other relationship as well as on our own self-perception. God's Word, even the law, was never meant to make us righteous. It was meant to show us how to live effectively in the earth

Getting Back What You Are Giving Out

Luke 6:38 says, *"Give, and it shall be given unto you; good measure, pressed down, and shaken together, and running over, shall men give into your bosom. For with the same measure that ye mete withal it shall be measured to you again"* (KJV). This verse has traditionally been used to teach about money. However, Jesus is talking about how we relate to others. He is saying that if we judge, people will give judgment back to us. If we are merciful, people will give mercy back to us. Whatever we give others is exactly what they will give back to us…with one addition: they are going to multiply it when they give it back.[1] It will be pressed down, shaken together and running over.

> MOST OF WHAT WE DEMONSTRATE TO OTHERS IS SIMPLY A REFLECTION OF WHAT WE ARE EXPERIENCING IN OUR OWN HEART.

God is able to love perfectly and continuously, but people are not. With people, you will reap what you sow…plus some! This is the principle of the seed. The seed can only yield after its kind. In the current codependent, victim-oriented world, people blame others for all of their reactions. We somehow miss the interpretation of "re-action." It is a response to our action! We think we should be able to violate the accepted standards of society and not have a reaction. We have been promised that if we would only reject the standards and accept a more socialist view of the world, we would find that utopia. There is not enough social legislation or political correctness to keep people from reacting. The socialist utopia doesn't exist. People will always be people. You will always reap what you sow with people. You will continue to experience pain and rejection in your relationships if you fail to sow seeds of love and acceptance. You will destroy any opportunity for a meaningful, loving relationship unless you sow the seeds to produce that type of harvest. You will create all of the scenarios that originally pushed you so far into codependency.

By entering into a relationship with the Lord that is personal and intimate, you will grow in the love of God. You will begin to experience His love and you will find the source of your emotional needs. As you experience God's love, you will become more equipped, more capable of walking in love toward others. As we previously discussed, most of what we demonstrate to others is simply a reflection of what we are experiencing in our own heart. The way you relate to people will have a great influence on how they react to you.

One of the most interesting things about our personal development is what I call "growth on parallel planes." What is happening in one area of our life is always reflected in and influencing other areas. Sometimes it is not only reflected *in* other areas, but sometimes it also is a reflection *of* other areas. In other words, what happens on one plane can be the mirror I use to see what is actually happening on another plane.

> IT SHOULD BE THROUGH US THAT THE WORLD SEES THE TRUE NATURE OF GOD.

For example, when people go through relationship problems, it is common for them to harden their heart against the other person. This is a means of protection, a way to keep from getting hurt. However, when we harden our heart against an individual, to some degree we also harden our heart against God. What we thought would only affect us on this plane, begins to affect us on the spiritual plane as well. Likewise, when people harden their heart to the Lord, it begins to affect the way they treat people. So, growth or destruction tends to happen on parallel planes. There is always a correlation between how we relate to people and how we are truly relating to God! One is a reflection of the other.

The Love of God in Us

First John 4:12 says, *"No one has seen God at any time. If we love one another, God abides in us, and His love has been perfected in us."* God's love is perfected in us as we walk in love one to another. The word perfect means to be brought to the goal or to reach completion.[2] First of all, if God's love doesn't move us into loving relationships with others, it has not accomplished its goal for us or through us. God has never intended that we would be mere recipients of His love simply for our personal pleasure or experience. It is not supposed to stop with us. It is supposed to be multiplied through us. It should be through us that the world sees the true nature of God! This is why Jesus said, *"By this all will know that you are My disciples, if you have love for one another"* (John 13:35).

We are to be the channel through which the world sees and experiences God until they can see and experience Him for themselves. The world can't see God, but they can see us. Many times other Christians are so hurt that they can't see God, but they can see us. As others experience the love of God through us, we can potentially multiply love and peace in the world the same way rejection and codependency has been multiplied.

Likewise, as we walk in love toward others, the love of God grows in us. We become able to experience His love in a more real and meaningful way. Loving others does not make Him love us more. We are not earning the right to experience His love. Rather, we are developing the capacity to experience love.

God has always loved us with a perfect love. He has always wanted us to experience His love. What has been lacking is our capacity to experience love. Even though He has always been giving, we have not always been receiving (taking hold). The problem has never been His capacity to give love; it has been in our capacity to receive and experience love.

As we receive the grace (ability) of God to walk in love toward others, that capacity to give love expands our capacity to receive love. Not only do we grow on parallel planes, but we also grow bi-dimensionally. The grace (capacity and ability) to give love always brings the grace (capacity and ability) to receive love. The Psalmist said, *"I will run the course of Your commandments, for You shall enlarge my heart"* (Psalm 119:32). He knew he must be enlarged in his heart to have the capacity to "run the course of the commandments." Likewise, we need our hearts enlarged to run the course of love!

A part of what has rendered us incapable of experiencing God's love is the way we have withheld love or misused love in the past. We have reaped what we have sown. Our own heart has been affected by the way we treat others. It is difficult to believe in unconditional love when we only give conditional love. It is hard to believe in mercy when we are unmerciful. What we refuse to give, we justify by refusing to receive.

As we love others, however, the love of God is perfected in us. The love of God that we pour out of our heart heals our own heart. In every way, our capacity for love is expanded as we expand our capacity to give love. We must therefore remove all guile from our expressions of love. We must not use kindness as a means to manipulate. We must commit ourselves to the love of God and keep our motives in check. Remember, if you give "love" with any ulterior motive, it is not love. Because of the dynamics of giving and receiving, it will also make you suspect the motives of others. You will never be able to receive freely what you will not give freely!

Give Up Control!

Among the first and most primary decisions is the release of control. Whether we are the aggressive controller or passive controller, we must give up control. We must honestly face the pain that is brought into the lives of others as well as our own lives through our attempts to control. We must recognize control as an attempt to be god of our own world. We must give up control of the outcome we think we must have to be happy. We must give up our control of the process to receive what God has promised. We must learn to follow God as our Shepherd. We must trust Him in the promise and the process!

There is often great value in having an honest discussion with those around us to make them aware of our intention to release them from our control. It also essential to ask their forgiveness.

> WHAT WE REFUSE TO GIVE, WE JUSTIFY BY REFUSING TO RECEIVE.

Once the people around us are aware that we really intend to release them from our control, we may have to face things that we've never been willing to face. But with confidence in the love of God, we can face and conquer all the areas of life. Fear of facing these things in our own life has been a great contributor to our need to control. As long as we controlled others, we appeared to be right. Giving up control makes us face our fear and insecurity!

Although all this may seem overwhelming, the fact is, this is the doorway to real relationships. In every relationship, we all have to change and grow. If we only stay in the relationships that are comfortable, we will never be challenged and so we will never grow. If we maintain control, we will not grow—and neither will the others in the relationship. Everyone remains stagnant to guard our fragile sense of self-worth. No one wants to upset the fragile codependent system we have developed to hold our dysfunctional relationships together.

Along with our release from control, we must release others from our expectations. There is probably nothing that creates more rejection than imposed expectations. Our expectations say to others that they are unacceptable the way they are. Not only can there be no relationship when expectations are imposed, but there also can be no appreciation or recognition of current strengths and abilities.

The Purpose to Relinquishing Control

All of this will simply leave us in a vacuum if we don't replace these tendencies with something. Indeed, all of these codependent tendencies arise out of a lack of depending on and trusting God. In Philippians, Paul said, *"Be anxious for nothing, but in everything by prayer and supplication, with thanksgiving, let your requests be made known to God"* (Philippians 4:6).

> GIVING UP CONTROL MAKES US FACE OUR FEAR AND INSECURITY!

Paul didn't tell you to ignore your problems; he said not to become anxious about them. Giving up control will make you feel anxious if that has been your way of staying at peace. Trusting God is frightening when you've only trusted your ability to control or manipulate. When we face any difficulties, we must manage the emotions that arise. We can try to ignore them. We can think about the problems. We can do many destructive, codependent things. Or, we can present them to God.

Paul said we should present our anxieties with thanksgiving. This is not a formula about how to trick God into answering our prayer. We can present our concerns with thanksgiving because we are confident that we already have everything that pertains to life and godliness. We are thankful because we already have what we need. What we need is not the power of God in our circumstances, but the power of God working in our heart. He will never fail to manifest Himself in our heart when we lean on Him instead of on our own understanding.

Freedom from codependency does not come when we quit doing all the wrong things. Freedom from codependency doesn't even come from simply doing the right things. Freedom from codependency comes when we trust God, and from that trust we behave differently.

We must trust God with the people we love. We must allow Him to do in their life what He wants, not what we want. We must trust God for our own personal joy and peace. We must make Him our source of security and stability. Then, and only then, are we truly free from codependency.

> FREEDOM FROM CODEPENDENCY COMES WHEN WE TRUST GOD.

By giving up our outward focus on others we can focus on our own character development and allow those around us to focus on theirs. We all can individually grow in God. It will be as those people around us grow in God that we actually discover the real joys of life and relationships. If I allow you to become who you want to be in Jesus, I have to grow in order to maintain our relationship. Likewise, my growth challenges you. We enter into a journey of love and growth that never ends, never becomes dull or boring and is always interesting!

It is easy to convince myself that I love God until that conviction is tested in the crucible of relationships. How I relate to people is exactly how I relate to God. It may seem different because I use different words or pretend to have lofty intentions. If I try to control people, I am trying to control God. If I have to be in charge with people, I am probably in charge of my "Christianity." But if I am yielding and patient with people, I am probably yielding and patient with God and myself. The only true reflection of our spirituality is our relationship with people. I can only receive what I am willing to give!

Endnotes

1. Dr. James B. Richards, *My Church My Family* (Huntsville, AL: Impact Ministries, 1995).
2. *Thayer's Greek Lexicon*, electronic database (Biblesoft, Inc., 2000, 2003, 2006), NT:5048.

33

Breaking the Cycle

Even after an individual musters the courage and grace to break out of his or her individual codependent patterns, there is another major hurdle. You see, our codependency always involves others. Every person in our life is a player in this epic production we call life. Everyone around us has found his or her "niche." Our capacity to relate to one another has been subconsciously crafted around our shared dysfunctions. Each person is playing the role that best fits his or her codependent issues.

We only know how to relate to one another in our codependent, manipulative ways. We don't know any other way. We would not know the other players if they removed their masks. Therefore, when we change, we throw everyone's life into chaos. Or rather, we actually come out of chaos into order. The problem is, we understand the chaos, but we don't understand the order. If it's not dysfunctional, we don't know how to live with it. All we have ever known is what we have had.

When we change, everyone around us is placed in unfamiliar territory. They've never tried to live in this arena. Now, they may have prayed for this to happen. They may have despised us the way we were. But when this change comes, they may resist it "tooth and nail." Just because we are ready does not mean they are ready.

The mind always resists the unknown.[1] Some studies have shown that people will stay in an abusive situation they know rather than leave to enter a safe situation they do not know. Unknowns are interpreted by the mind as threats. Threats produce fear and we resist what we fear.

> JUST BECAUSE WE ARE READY TO CHANGE DOES NOT MEAN OTHERS AROUND US ARE.

I remember a woman who desperately wanted her husband to get saved. He was verbally and emotionally abusive and had made her life miserable. For years she had prayed for him and trusted God that he would get saved and change. She came in repeatedly for counseling, seeking to understand how to reach him. I encouraged her to abandon the antagonistic "religious" approach she had taken and to walk in love instead. It worked! You would have thought this would have been the beginning of heaven on earth. But just the opposite happened!

When he finally gave his life to the Lord, it brought about a series of challenges that ultimately led to their divorce. When she got what she had been praying for, she "blew out." As illogical as that sounds, I have seen it happen many times. She had become comfortable with her dysfunctional lifestyle. She had found her way to use it to her advantage. She used guilt and nagging as a way to control her husband. She used sympathy as a way to control her friends. She understood the role of the suffering wife.

When he got saved and changed dramatically, it meant she had to get a life of her own. She could no longer use his dysfunction as her identity. It meant that her unacceptable, unscriptural way of using the situation was now exposed. She could not hide her sins in the shadow of his more extreme sins. So she divorced him. The years of verbal and emotional abuse had stopped. The one thing she had never expected, happened. He got saved and changed. But this exposed her dysfunction and brought her face to face with a fear that she didn't understand... how to deal with her own problems!

It's Hard to Let Go…

People rarely do these types of destructive moves consciously. They are driven by some subconscious force that they do not understand. We create an identity, i.e., a sense of who we are, by the role we play. We then define our identity by our circumstance instead of by our relationship to our Creator! Once any role is accepted as our identity, we will not surrender that role. To do so is to die emotionally. We don't understand why we feel so threatened by change, but this is it. It is death to self. Maybe this is why Jesus taught us to die to self…that is, the false sense of self we have created by our environment. We must die to the false self defined by our relationship with anyone other than God!

CHANGE IS DEATH TO SELF.

A dominating parent can attempt to break out of the control cycle that has been imposed upon the children. Although the children have criticized and complained for years, they will not allow that parent to break free of the cycle. After all, if the parent breaks free, who will the children have to blame for their problems? The dysfunctional lifestyle, as painful as it is, is a cycle the children know how to work.

A dysfunctional family usually has a "strong" member. The strong member is the one whom the family turns to in times of crisis. This part is not the dysfunction. After the crisis, the dysfunction arises. When the strong one of a family helps solve the problem, he or she is then accused of being a troublemaker, trying to control. The help or advice that was given is viewed as control once the crisis is over.

Sometimes the strong one is a full-blown codependent who has a savior mentality, a "fix-it complex." Sometimes the strong one really loves and cares for the family, but doesn't know the value of establishing boundaries and breaking destructive patterns. He or she thinks fixing others is his or her "love language."

Whatever the case, when the strong one attempts to break the pattern, the real dysfunction will be revealed. All of the family may criticize the strong one, yet they have no intention of letting that person out of the cycle. Who would they go to for help? Other people would not be drawn into their game. Who would they blame for their problems? If they have no one to blame, they may have to deal with some responsibility on their own. How would they manipulate the strong one? There are just too many unknowns. They will fight to preserve the system they criticize. It is some part of their identity as an individual and as a family.

I have often seen an increase in conflict in a family when one member attempts to break free from the cycle of codependency. If a dysfunctional family member breaks free from the cycle, the rest of the family will no longer know how to control or relate to that person. Remember, control is the basic need of the codependent. He or she will give up the relationship before he or she will give up control.

Needs and Boundaries

When we break the destructive codependent patterns, we must be sensitive to the needs that exist around us. At the same time, we must refuse to love on others' terms. We must look to God's definition of love. Likewise, we must establish clear boundaries. We must refuse to cross the boundaries of others. We should not do for others what they could and should do for themselves. We must allow every person to make his or her own choices and live with his or her own consequences. We must also establish our own new boundaries. We should not subject ourselves to communication and relationships that undermine our sense of confidence. These new boundaries have been the missing safeguards that would have protected us all from one another.

> PEOPLE WILL GIVE UP THE RELATIONSHIP BEFORE THEY WILL GIVE UP CONTROL.

Because the codependent is so sensitive to guilt, it could be easy for the other members of the system to manipulate him back into showing love in unscriptural ways, thereby reestablishing the codependent pattern of relationships. Guilt is the weapon of choice for all types of codependents. They often save it for their last strategy. Just when you think you are breaking free from the codependent cycle of relations, you are subjected to every ploy of the other members of the group. They may use charm. They may use conditional kindness. They will keep changing their tactic until they find the one that draws you back into the system. They will process through all the tactics: anger, rejection, pouting and maybe even violence. But when all that fails, it is straight to guilt. They try to use guilt to draw the person back into the codependent relationship, into the unscriptural ways of expressing love. After all, as corrupt as it was, the system is the only way they know how to show love and maintain some form of relationship. It takes continual vigilance to maintain our independence from the strategies of those who want to preserve things the way they were. Only a continual connection to God as your source will give you protection from the barrage of emotional strategies used to draw you back.

We must refuse to do for others what should happen between them and God. We also should be careful not to take that position in an unloving way. It is important to reaffirm love and worth, but we must only yield to biblical concepts of love. No matter how humane other methods may seem, if it is unscriptural, in the end it will be destructive! It will undermine their self-worth and derail any hope of their knowing God for themselves!

The frightening thing about breaking the cycle is that we can't predict the outcome for those around us. When we do anything in love, we are creating the most opportune environment for a good outcome, but there are no guarantees. We really don't know how others will react. We have no biblical promise that if we do the right thing, everyone else will too. Walking in true love is not an acceptable form of manipulation. It doesn't come with a guarantee of results. If it did, it would just be another form of control. Love says, "I will give you the truth if you want it. I will treat you in a way that reflects your value to God. But I will also give you the freedom to make your own choices. If the outcome is not good, I will allow you to learn from the situation rather than attempt to save and fix you!"

Though this is the most challenging part, it also is the most liberating for everyone! By our breaking out of the cycle, we are creating the only real opportunity for relationship with those around us. But they may not want it. They may view our breaking free as the ultimate betrayal. "We were happy the way things were. Why did you mess it up?" What they don't know is that they were the only ones who were happy. They don't see how bad it really was. They are not where you are and you cannot expect them to be. They must come to their own understanding in their own way!

Your Faith Is Your Response

Faith is not necessarily believing God for a specific outcome. You can't work faith for someone else. Faith is your response of trust to God and His promises to you. It is not what you can believe God to do in someone else's heart. You want the people around you to be saved and live a great life. You want to see true love and wholeness abound with those who have been in your life. But, it may never happen. Although you can't believe God for everyone else, you can believe God's Word for you. Your trust of God is not for a specific outcome, but for a specific victory.

> WE HAVE NO BIBLICAL PROMISE THAT IF WE DO THE RIGHT THING, EVERYONE ELSE WILL TOO.

Regardless of what everyone else does, you know you can have personal victory. God is the source for your happiness. He is the source of your security. Other people cannot determine your future joy. Only you and God can determine it. Only when you are who you should be, in Jesus, can you be an influence on your family and friends. They need to see someone living the life they desire. They may taunt and test you for a period of time to see if what you have is real. When you pass the test, those who want help will come to you! You will be the light in their darkness. But you can't be part of the dysfunction *and* be the light!

Personal dreams should be that...personal. We have looked to our future and we have placed the people we love into our dreams. We have determined the role they will play in our future happiness. We see ourselves being happy with a particular job, a particular friend or a specific situation. Although all of this sounds good and brings a lump to the throat of any person who longs for a life of true love, it is a part of the codependent fantasy. I don't need to see myself as being happy *with* anyone. I just need to see myself as a happy person. I have no right to assume the roles others will play in my life. To do so is an attempt to impose my will on them. It is also a form of placing my hope in them and not in God!

It's Personal

There is a way that we link people to our future happiness that can be very destructive. It is often a part of our need to control them. It is often a part of why we stay in an abusive, destructive relationship. We have linked our future happiness to someone in our life.

> FAITH IS YOUR RESPONSE OF TRUST TO GOD AND HIS PROMISES TO YOU.

I look forward to growing old with my wife. It is difficult to imagine life without her. It would be an unbelievably painful experience to lose her through death or relational conflict. I do envision us playing with our grandchildren. I see us spending our life together, but I also have personal dreams. My personal dreams are about me, my life, my ministry, the things I intend to accomplish with my life and the kind of person I choose to be. Although I allow her to visit in this internal picture, it is not about her and me. This has to do with me and God. I will fulfill my commitments to the Lord regardless of who is there and who isn't. My dreams will be fulfilled because I am the man I want to be in Jesus, because I have character, peace and joy—not because anyone specific is there with me.

There is an unhealthy way we link people to our personal goals that make us feel that if we lose those people, we cannot fulfill those goals. We never made these people our source in a deliberate way, but because we brought them into our personal goals and dreams, we linked them in such a way that it seems impossible to fulfill those goals without them.

If my picture of ministry is one that envisions my wife being there with me in ministry, I have created a conditional situation in my heart. It means that on a deep level I do not feel I can fulfill my call if she is not playing the role I have envisioned. So what if she has a deep desire for a different role? Then I will feel that her pursuit of God's will for her life is an attack on my dream. In fact, I will feel that she is sabotaging my destiny when all she is doing is pursuing what she feels to be God's plan for her life! If my destiny is linked to some role of her that I have imagined, I will feel righteous in forcing her to do what I think she should do. I will usurp the Lordship of Jesus in her life!

> EVERY PERSON SHOULD HAVE HIS OR HER OWN PERSONAL DREAMS AND GOALS.

Every person should have his or her own personal dreams and goals. We should recognize how others can share those dreams with us, but we should not be dependent on them. After all, we need to let them have their own dreams. One of the greatest excitements and reasons to grow is so we can walk together with our mate as he or she grows in his or her own destiny. There are aspects of my faith and character that I would have never developed if I had controlled my wife's destiny. By allowing her to fulfill her unique sense of destiny, she often challenged me in ways no one else could. My love for her caused me to listen and grow beyond many of my limitations and beliefs. Us being one only happens when I allow her to be who she desires to be in Jesus and when she allows me to be who I desire to be in Jesus. The new "one" that we become happens in the growth that has to occur so we can be compatible.

Coming out of codependency is not the changing of one belief or action; it is the changing of a life philosophy. Our entire life's motives are changed by the changing of our source. Because codependency involves everyone around us, our freedom will also involve everyone around us. Breaking the cycle will change the way we relate to everything and everyone because everyone is part of the cycle.

Endnote

1. Dr. James B. Richards, *Wired for Success, Programmed for Failure* (Newburg, PA: MileStones International Publishers, 2010), 73.

LIFE ON NEW TERMS

Now we have the information we need to live a full, uncomplicated, enjoyable life. For the first time, we get to find out what it really means to enjoy the adventure called life. We have the opportunity to experience God to the fullest, free from the control of others. Our relationships can be overflowing with incredible love and wonderful friendship. What were once obstacles become exciting challenges. What once threatened us becomes an adventure. With no man as our source, we are finally free to know God for ourselves. With God as our source, we can meet life on completely different terms. This thing called life can finally work!

Now we are ready to enjoy life as a journey rather than a struggle to reach a destination. There will never be a specific destination where we say, "I have arrived." The abundant life is not a destination; it is a process. It is a quality, not a quantity. Life, on earth, must be understood as a process. There is no mystical plane that we reach whereby we never have problems. Despite the manipulative promises of codependent preachers, politicians, potential partners and other idealists, there is no utopia. The very promise of utopia is now seen as a warning flag to run, run, run! Daily we go through the process of trusting and yielding to God, and for the first time we have the opportunity to enjoy this journey!

Because there is no place called "there," I will always be growing and transforming. But it will no longer be a negative process where I am vainly attempting to gain God's approval. How wonderful to know that God accepts me where I am because I am in Christ! I know I have changes that need to take place. But these changes only make me more lovable to people, not to God. They make me better able to function in this life, but they do not make me more righteous. There are still areas of my life where I want growth, but I am comfortable with me. Since I don't have a destination, I am comfortable on the ride. Since I don't have a destination, I can be contented, happy and satisfied with where I am today. My question is not, "Am I there yet?" My question is, "Am I actually making the journey?"

> LIFE, ON EARTH, MUST BE UNDERSTOOD AS A PROCESS.

I live in that paradox of "being" internally while developing externally. With one eye, I look to the future, expectant of positive changes in my life and character. On the other hand, I am satisfied with where I am today. I understand it is not my responsibility to change. It is merely my responsibility to be open to change as the Holy Spirit brings it into my life. It is not my responsibility to know the path. It is mine to know and follow the Savior who leads me on the path! Now I can really allow Jesus to be my Shepherd!

Change, Change, Change

Everything about life is continual change. Much of the stress we experience is simply the resistance to change. If we are alive, we are changing. When we stop changing, we die. Even if we found the perfect relationship, it would require change as it evolved. Every relationship changes as people and circumstances change. Therefore, we must change to stay in step with the relationship. Each day that we age, how we relate, what our needs are and even what our priorities are will change. If we have children, as they grow there will be constant change. The economy, the government and a thousand other things outside our relationship are daily changing, bringing about the need for new responses on our part! There is no avoiding change!

In this new mindset, change, as demanding as it may be, is no longer motivated from the feeling of lack, deficiency or need. Change is no longer negative or threatening. The need to change is not the red light on the dash that signals trouble. Change is the way I stay in the flow of life. Change is the process whereby I stay capable of enjoying life to its fullest. Change is really my friend. I don't change because I am wrong; I change because I am alive and I exist in a dynamic, ever-changing environment.

The believer who accepts life in Jesus has the wherewithal to relate to the world and all its pressures in a totally different manner than the average person. And we certainly have the capacity for a more productive response than those inundated with religion and legalism. Jesus gives us a personal invitation to escape the negativity of religion and the manipulation of codependency. *"Are you tired? Worn out? Burned out on religion? Come to me. Get away with me and you'll recover your life. I'll show you how to take a real rest. Walk with me and work with me—watch how I do it. Learn the unforced rhythms of grace. I won't lay anything heavy or ill-fitting on you. Keep company with me and you'll learn to live freely and lightly"* (Matthew 11:28-30 The Message). Life in Jesus is not a life of additional burdens and pressures. It is easy and light!

MY RESPONSIBILITY IS TO BE OPEN TO CHANGE AS THE HOLY SPIRIT BRINGS IT INTO MY LIFE.

In Christ we know that all growth is simply that which is within us becoming the way we express ourselves externally. We are not really becoming; we are transforming. We became all we needed to be when we came into Jesus. As we yield to Him, that is seen in our outward behavior. We are never trying to become what we are not; rather, we are putting on who we really are in Him. It doesn't get any easier than this. I am; therefore, as I yield to Him I transform into my true God-given identity. I do not become by changing. I change because I am. I am righteous, in Him. I am anointed, in Him. I am in Jesus.

I determine to be satisfied and comfortable with who I am in Jesus. I can't be who you want me to be. I can't live for your expectations. I can only be who

I am, in Jesus. If that is not good enough for those around me, then they must take that up with my Father and my Savior. This is not an excuse to be rude, inconsiderate or unloving. It is the reality that we all must live with. I am who I am today, and that's all I can be at this moment.

Free to Be

As we discover the freedom to rest in our identity in Jesus, we tend to give others more freedom to discover their own journey. I am going to let you be who you are. If you want to be who you are in Jesus, that's fine. If that's not what you want, that's your choice. No matter how much I disagree with that choice, it is still your choice, not mine. Who and what we choose to yield our lives to may mean we drift apart, or it may mean we draw closer. I will love you wherever it takes us, but I will not assume the need to make this relationship come out a certain way.

> I DO NOT BECOME BY CHANGING. I CHANGE BECAUSE I AM.

I must let Jesus be your Lord, just as you must allow Him to be mine. He is the One you must follow. If you follow Him and I follow Him, we will ultimately arrive at a compatible destination. You are His servant, not mine. I cannot violate that relationship. Likewise, while I seek to hold you in as high regard as possible, I am not your servant, I am His! You can never succeed in forcing your way into the place that belongs to my Savior and Lord! One thing for sure, if we are following Him, we will walk in love and mutual respect throughout our journey.

If I attempt to make you into the person I want you to be, you will never have your own identity. I will have committed the most subtle, yet horrible form of murder. I will have caused you to abandon your life, making it impossible for you to find your own destiny. If you're the person I want you to be, you can't be the person you want to be. If your life is revolving around me, it can never revolve around Jesus. If you are living my dreams, you will never live your dreams. Thus, any control on my part ensures that you will never be truly happy because you will look for my approval to make you happy. I can't make you happy. In fact, my need for control reflects how unhappy I really am. If I were truly happy and satisfied with my life, I would never resort to running your life. However, if I set you free to find your happiness in Jesus, you will look to Him as your source. If we are both fulfilled in Him, we can both contribute to the joy and fulfillment of others without the unrealistic demands of making one another happy!

With God at the center of your life, for the first time, your life will be secure. All that you do will flow out of the confidence that comes from being a child of God. He will be your source. He will be your confidence. Religion will have no place in you. You will only have room for the pure, undefiled love of God that you can feel…the love that makes you feel good about God, yourself and others.

With a heart full of the love of God, you will be free from the manipulation of man. Others can affect you, but they can't control you. They can wound you, but they can't destroy you. They can bend you, but they cannot break you. Trying to hurt you would be like trying to steal a cup of water from the ocean. It's no big loss.

> MY NEED FOR CONTROL REFLECTS HOW UNHAPPY I REALLY AM.

Once you have tasted the goodness of God for yourself, you are hooked for life. You've got the ultimate addiction, the real deal, the genuine craving, but you're satisfied. As the Psalmist said, *"Oh, that men would give thanks to the Lord for His goodness, and for His wonderful works to the children of men! For He satisfies the longing soul, and fills the hungry soul with goodness"* (Psalm 107:8-9). Living in the ultimate paradox of deep addiction to the love of God and of complete satisfaction from experiencing that love the rest of your life will be a journey of experiencing the goodness of God and the best life has to offer!

35

Simple Solutions

The answers to the codependent issue as well as to the majority of relational and social ills are not really that complicated. They are just not what we want to hear. We want to hear that there is a way to force everyone else to do what they should do and then the world will become a safe place for us! That erroneous solution is the problem. Trying to satisfy a need externally is always what creates the mess.

The sin principle is at work in the world. People have their own free choices. Not even God is imposing His will on others. The solutions we seek are already in ourselves, in our own heart where we meet with God. The only way God could give us the world we want without violating the will of others was to do it internally! The Kingdom of God is within! That which we long for, that which we need is only found when it happens in our own heart. The solution is not hard; it is just not what we want to hear.

God explained to the children of Israel that having a certain quality of life was simply a matter of choice. But He knew they would try to make it hard. Man complicates matters as a way to resist change! If we can make the solution hard to find, then we can justify our problems. We have a reason to stay the way we are. However, life is not that complicated. Life is a matter of choice. Listen to His warning: *"For this commandment which I command you today is not too mysterious for you, nor is it far off. It is not in heaven, that you should say, 'Who will ascend into heaven for us and bring it to us, that we may hear it and do it?' Nor is it beyond the sea, that you should say, 'Who will go over the sea for us and bring it to us, that we may hear it and do it?' But the word is very near you, in your mouth and in your heart, that you may do it"* (Deuteronomy 30:11-14). So here is the simple solution. You can make the choice to close your eyes, pretend it is hard and have more of what you have had. Or you can trust you Creator and discover life in an entirely new dimension.

Love Is Required for Normalcy

We are created in the likeness and image of God. God is love! Therefore, love is the normalizing factor in how we are wired. In order to be normal, we need to give and receive love.

We must love God, love people and love ourselves. When asked what was the greatest commandment, Jesus not only answered the question but also went on to explain how through the observation of only three principles one could be sure to fulfill all the law. *"Jesus said to him, "'You shall love the Lord your God with all your heart, with all your soul, and with all your mind." This is the first and great commandment. And the second is like it: "You shall love your neighbor as yourself""* (Matthew 22:37-40).

> NOT EVEN GOD IS IMPOSING HIS WILL ON OTHERS.

In order to love God, I must first believe and experience the reality of His love for me. *"We love Him because He first loved us"* (1 John 4:19). His love for me was demonstrated by His sending Jesus to become my sin, suffer the punishment for all my sins and deliver me from God's wrath! *"In this the love of God was manifested toward us, that God has sent His only begotten Son into the world, that we might live through Him. In this is love, not that we loved God, but that He loved us and sent His Son to be the propitiation for our sins"* (1 John 4:9-10).

I must choose to believe this love God has for me. It is the starting place of all that is to come in my relationship with Him, a healthy relationship with myself and a relationship with others. Everything about my new life will be based on God's incredible love for me. Discovering His love for me will be the starting place for all healthy relationships!

Accepting God's value for me causes me to have a healthy value for myself. It is the end of low self-worth. From this place of healthy self-worth I can now express healthy worth for others. Discovering and experiencing the love of God is the deathblow to codependency. Why would I depend on you to get what I have already found in Him?

As we have clearly established, God's love has to do with value. According to Jesus, in order to fulfill all the law, we must value

> BELIEVING THIS LOVE GOD HAS FOR ME IS THE STARTING PLACE OF ALL THAT IS TO COME IN MY RELATIONSHIP WITH HIM.

God, value people and value ourselves! By implication we understand that when we fail at any of these three, we are not operating within the true meaning of the law.

In order to show you love I must apply the same value for you that God has, but in so doing it must neither violate my value and relationship with God nor my value for myself.

In Christ I have a new identity. If I renew my mind, I will see myself the way God sees me. If I love (value) myself as Jesus commanded, I will not relate to you in any way that violates or undermines my new identity.

Guard Your Heart

The wisdom of God's Word tells me to guard my heart above all that I do. *"Keep your heart with all diligence, for out of it spring the issues of life"* (Proverbs 4:23). My heart is the seat of my identity. Failure to guard my identity in Christ will result in my having an identity based on your approval and control. I must not allow anyone to usurp the Lordship of Jesus in my life! That place belongs to Him and Him alone.

If I have love (value) for you, I cannot do anything that undermines your opportunity for dignity and worth. This means that I can never do for you what you can and should do for yourself. I can't fix you. I can't rescue you. If you want my help, I will lovingly show you the steps I know. I will share my experience. I will love you no matter how many times you fall. I will help you get up by encouragement and kindness. But I will not rob you of your opportunity to experience God for yourself! I will give you the truth in love, but I will never use the truth as a way to manipulate or judge you.

MY HEART IS THE SEAT OF MY IDENTITY.

I realize there is no possible way to do this in my own strength. Therefore I trust the grace and power of God to work in me and make me able to live in this new identity. All my hope must be in God's power and not in my own.

The one thing that qualifies me for all that God has done is the death, burial and resurrection of Jesus. In Him I am made righteous (as I should be) before God. There is nothing I can do to make myself more qualified and more acceptable to God. All I can do from this point on is seek to walk worthy of such a gift, as an expression of my value (love) for God!

36

A HEART THAT HEALS

The writer of Proverbs said, *"For as he thinks in his heart, so is he"* (23:7a). Behavior is not really the seat of a man's sense of identity. Behavior is merely an expression of what is really in a man's heart. To permanently change any behavior there must first be a change in the beliefs of our heart. The heart is the seat of our identity! It is the source of all of our beliefs, which ultimately comprise our sense of self. How we feel about life, no matter how good or bad the circumstances are, is nothing more than a reflection of how we feel about ourselves. There are not enough good things in the world to compensate for or quench the unhappiness that comes from not loving, i.e., having value for, ourselves!

This revelation brings us back to another powerful insight provided by the writer of Proverbs. *"Above all else, guard your heart, for it is the wellspring of life"* (Proverbs 4:23 NIV). People must do everything possible to guard their heart, i.e., their sense of self, their identity, their ability to have value for self! Remember, Jesus said to love our neighbor as ourselves. The implication is that I can have no more value for you than I do for me! If I look to God to understand my value, I will look to God to understand your value. A healthy heart not only keeps me in healthy relationships with others, but it also keeps me in a healthy relationship with God. Why? Because I am in a healthy, God-centered relationship with myself!

The word *wellspring* implies the source from which all of my life flows. One definition of the word used in the original language also implies boundaries.[1] My heart, or my sense of self, is the basis for all the boundaries I perceive in the world around me. We have thought the boundaries were out there. But the truth is, they are all "in here," in our own heart. The only way to move or expand the perceived boundaries in our world is to expand our sense of identity in Christ! Heart beliefs always affect our sense of self.

> A HEALTHY HEART NOT ONLY KEEPS ME IN HEALTHY RELATIONSHIPS WITH OTHERS, BUT IT ALSO KEEPS ME IN A HEALTHY RELATIONSHIP WITH GOD.

The Bible teaches, *"Christ in you, the hope of glory"* (Colossians 1:27). Among many things, the word *glory* can also be understood as God's view, opinion and reality.[2] The only hope of us becoming in this life who God says we really are is Christ in you. Christ came into you when you believed that God raised Him from the dead and acknowledged Him as your Lord. But like all things of the New Covenant, it must be believed in your heart before it can be experienced in your heart. Do everything you can to know, and you will experience Christ in you. The degree of our awareness of Christ in us is the degree we will live in the reality of our new identity. Every effort must be made to know and experience this reality.

Meditation

One of the most powerful tools I have ever developed to help people in their journey in the awareness of Christ in us is a 30-day life renewal program called Heart Physics Essentials®. The Bible teaches us to meditate. The Apostle Paul said this: *"Finally, brethren, whatever things are true, whatever things are noble, whatever things are just, whatever things are pure, whatever things are lovely, whatever things are of good report, if there is any virtue and if there is anything praiseworthy—meditate on these things"* (Philippians 4:8). *Thayer's Greek Lexicon* defines this word as "to reckon inwardly, to count up or to weigh the reasons, to deliberate."[3] These are all terms that describe meditation.

Meditation is where we internally ponder, consider, think, review and imagine something until it becomes real in our experience! All that has been given to us in Christ must be actualized through meditation, reflection and pondering that moves us to unshakable faith! Since this is a skill that is pretty much lost to our generation, it is rare that one will rediscover this biblical exercise on his or her own. Heart Physics®[4] is designed to help you acquire a skill in just 30 days that the ancients spent a lifetime developing. Whether you use Heart Physics® or not is not the issue. The issue is for you to do whatever it takes to have an unshakable, immovable awareness of Christ in you at all times!

The heart works in the continuum of sowing and reaping. What we sow is what grows in our heart. What we give is what we gain the capacity to receive. This is not a matter of legalistically earning from God. It is just the design of our own heart. This explains the importance of the golden rule: Do unto to others as you would have them do unto you. What and how you "do unto" others is the capacity you have to receive from others. Do not give to others what you do not want in your heart. Show people the value you want to feel for yourself by expressing it to them. Even if they do not show it in return, you will expand your capacity to experience it from God!

> DO WHATEVER IT TAKES TO HAVE AN UNSHAKABLE, IMMOVABLE AWARENESS OF CHRIST IN YOU AT ALL TIMES!

The Importance of Forgiveness

Be quick to forgive! The word *forgive* simply means to "send away."[5] Forgiveness is not about the person who wronged you. It is about the offense you feel. Too often the words *mercy* and *forgiveness* are used interchangeably. Mercy is what we give to the person who wrongs us. Forgiveness is what we do with the offense. You have two choices about the offense you feel. You can hold it or send it away. Offenses enter into us and create the potential to stumble. They lie in us, polluting everything good that comes in our life. The only healthy thing we can do with an offense is "send it away." The Message Bible says it like this: *"If you forgive someone's sins, they're gone for good. If you don't forgive sins, what are you going to do with them?"* (John 20:21b). It is obvious, if you don't send them away, you hold them. As long as you hold them, they affect you.

An offense is something that someone does that has the power to make us stumble. But it can only make us stumble if we hold it! Holding an offense gives us the excuse to hold hatred in our heart. It justifies revenge. In other words, it causes us to allow attitudes, feelings and behaviors that destroy us. It is probably a lifetime of holding on to pain and offense that drove us into our codependency in the beginning. It will be the sending away of all offenses that will deliver us and keep us free from this trap.

> FORGIVENESS IS ONE OF THE MOST ESSENTIAL DEFENSIVE TOOLS OF THE HEART.

Because we have made mercy and forgiveness synonymous, most people are unwilling to forgive. We have been told that forgiveness means everything is right between us and the offender. Or that we should overlook his (or her) actions toward us. We feel that if we forgive him, we let him off the hook. No! Forgiveness is not for the other person; it is for us! It the place where we send away the offense. In the absence of that pain we may be able to then show him mercy. But showing him mercy does not deliver us from the effects of the pain. Only sending it away is true forgiveness.

Sending away an offense seems like an impossibility. However, as people learn to function from their heart, they realize that in the heart they are able to do what their mind will not permit them to do. In just a few minutes a person can get into his or her heart zone, send away pain and offense, and return to this outer world refreshed, renewed and free from the power of the offense. This is what it means to forgive from the heart! Forgiveness is one of the most essential defensive tools of the heart.

As we move our focus from external to internal we find a stability we have never known. We are no longer tossed back and forth with changes that occur in the world around us. We understand what it means to stand on the Rock. We move from "out of control" to "self-control."

Proverbs 25:28 in the New Living Translation says this: *"A person without self-control is like a city with broken-down walls."* When our dependence is on Him, we feel the security of resting in a walled city! The Psalmist called it "dwelling in the secret place" and "abiding in the shadow of the Almighty." All of these are metaphors for the person who feels safe and secure in God!

Enjoy this new journey of life. Now that you have reconnected to your Source, all the feelings of being out of control are fading. There is a deep emerging of dignity and worth that belongs only to those who know and believe who they are in relation to our God and Creator.

Endnotes

1. *Biblesoft's New Exhaustive Strong's Numbers and Concordance with Expanded Greek-Hebrew Dictionary* (Biblesoft, Inc. and International Bible Translators, 1994, 2003, 2006), OT:8444.
2. *Thayer's Greek Lexicon*, electronic database (Biblesoft, Inc., 20002, 2003, 2006), NT:1391.
3. *Thayer's Greek Lexicon.*
4. See www.heartphysics.com.
5. *Thayer's Greek Lexicon*, NT:863.

About the Author

James Richards is a pioneer in the field of faith-based human development. He has combined spirituality, energy medicine, scientific concepts and human intuition into a philosophical approach that brings about congruence in spirit, soul and body, resulting in incredible breakthroughs in health, emotional management, financial abundance and intimate connection with God. He is a life coach, consultant, teacher and motivational trainer. He holds doctorates in Theology, Alternative Medicine and Human Behavior. He was awarded an honorary doctorate in World Evangelism for years of service in the Philippines. His many certifications include: substance abuse counselor, detox specialist, herbalist, handwriting analysis, EFT, energy medicine and an impressive number of additional certifications and training certificates.

Dr. Richards has been successful as an entrepreneur who has built several successful businesses ranging from contracting to real estate to marketing. As a national best-selling author, Dr. Richards has written several books that have sold several million copies around the world. His most noted work is Heart Physics®, a life renewal program designed to equip people to transform any aspect of their life through changing the beliefs of their heart.

When asked why he has studied such a broad field his answer is simple: "If it helps people, I want to understand it!" The goal of all his work is to "help people experience wholeness: spirit, soul and body!"

To contact Dr. Richards, call or write:

Impact Ministries
3516 S. Broad Place
Huntsville, AL 35805

256-536-9402
256-536-4530 — Fax
www.impactministries.com

Other Publications by Dr. James B. Richards

Taking the Limits Off God

Grace: The Power to Change

Supernatural Ministry

The Gospel of Peace

The Prayer Organizer

Leadership That Builds People, Volumes 1 and 2

The Lost Art of Leadership

My Church, My Family: How to Have a
Healthy Relationship with the Church

Becoming the Person You Want to Be:
Discovering Your Dignity and Worth

Breaking the Cycle

How to Stop the Pain

We Still Kiss

Effective Small Group Ministry

Satan Unmasked: The Truth Behind the Lie

The Anatomy of a Miracle

Wired for Success, Programmed for Failure

Heart Physics®

For more information on these and
Dr. Richards' other products, please visit:

www.impactministries.com

CPSIA information can be obtained at www.ICGtesting.com
Printed in the USA
LVOW081831060412

276518LV00020B/224/P